Re-position to Unleash the Power of News Channels

N Bhaskara Rao

ADROIT

Adroit Publishers
New Delhi

ISBN : 978-81-87393-54-2

First Published in 2017

Published by
ADROIT PUBLISHERS
4675/21, Ganpati Bhawan, Ansari Road,
Daryaganj, New Delhi-110 002
Phone : 011-23266030

Exclusively Distributed by:

Akhil Book Distributors
4675/21, Ganpati Bhawan,
Ansari Road, Daryaganj
New Delhi, INDIA
Tel: 011-23266030

Typesetting—Gaurav Graphics, Delhi-110002
E-mail: gauravsingh1908@gmail.com
Printed at: Rajyoriya Prints, Delhi.

Contents

Section IV
A Way Forward

Preface

The book is about unleashing the potential of 24x7 news channels in India. It is not about news media, nor television. The book restrains from discussing larger picture except where relevant in the context of news channels. The 13 chapters under four sections argue that news channels could change the face of the country if only they are determined to pursue their power and reorder their content priorities.

The first section gives an overview of the larger scenario and the contextual background to do with growth, content models, marketing concerns and the idea of public service broadcasting for making a difference. The second section analyses the trends in the stunted spread and plateauing reach of news channels, despite proliferation. The considerations and compulsions that determine the content model as in the case of TRPs and awards are also analysed. The societal compulsions as against the market and consumer are discussed too. The third section discusses the media reforms scenario and initiatives as well compulsions of regulatory mechanism and ethical framework. The fourth section outlines with specific examples what news channels tend to miss in coverage which could shift the paradigm and rejuvenate these channels in a win-win way. Two chapters in this section briefly suggest interventions so that news channels can get out of the grip of constrained expansion of their reach and relevance of their contents. Some correctives that could help channels unleash their full potential are given more as examples.

When something is written on such issues with concerns based passion, it is bound to miss something and repeat something else. But when that concern and passion is backed or based on hands on experience and armed with primary analyses, it is bound to create dilemma. That is what this book is all about. I was fortunate in having four distinctly different backgrounds. I was a grassroots activist (like green revolution, family planning campaigns, rural development, etc) before going into academics and then became a field researcher with pioneering studies in the country and also in developing survey research methodologies. Then I had the rare opportunity of becoming part of policymaking at the highest level in the government and later advise more than a couple of central ministries. And then I became an independent (not depending on any sponsorship or doles) analyst of public policies and public opinions touching on a host of basic issues confronting the country. In most of these functions, news media and news television specifically has been a fascination of mine with a belief that they can do much more even where the governments have failed to make a difference. I am convinced of that even more now after seeing what some news channels did recently. It is with that belief that I have attempted this book.

Good News Channels capture in their coverage aspirations of people, reflect the concerns of the disadvantaged in given situations, and contribute in bringing out the better in people. That is not possible unless people themselves take interest. But what we see more often is a '*Jugalbandi*'[1] phenomenon where profit-seeking enterprises take the lead and viewers remain passive while the government is busy weighing the opportunities. In such a scenario opportunities for news channels are far more to make a mark or difference.

It is often said that 'content is king' in the case of television and India is content capital. How much of that is evident given the kind of boom particularly in the last one decade of television channels. Round the clock news channels completed a decade in 2011 in a competitive context. How do we take stock of that? Unabated proliferation of channels has been despite their un viability. Not even half of survived channels are likes to be financially viable on their own even in their tenth year! A new realisation of limitation of content model being followed appears to have set in some news channels – though it is more on account of series of scams in a short span of time. It is thanks to RTI Act and Anna Hazare that there's a new enthusiasm in channels. "It is good

1. Jugalbandhi is a terminology of music orchestra where a team of different instrumentalists coordinate their tunes and sounds for a common out come and play together to each other's echo. In the context of mass media, investors, advertisers, marketers, advertising, public relations and market research agencies work towards maximizing their interests as if in a coordinated way but give the impression that they play their role independently

enough in America to be bad news in person as long as the television sees all that as good news". That is what I used to hear 45 years ago when I was doing my Ph.D. in the USA. This appears to sum up the situation in India during the decade.

I benefitted from Centre for Media Studies (CMS) Media Lab analyses and field studies over these critical years of news channels growth story. No book on news channels can claim to be "updated" particularly because things are changing so fast, without even coming under public purview. Updated data for compatibility with earlier decades / years is difficult to come by for more than one reason. One is that the provider of the data sometimes does not want any such comparisons over time to be made. One other reason could be that database is not robust enough same way for all the years. And sometimes certain desegregated data is not given any more because of changes in the analysis plan and or methodology. That is why we do not see any analyses presented by these (TAM/ Nielsen, etc) agencies of trends over the years. In fact, that is how some trends do not come for public discussion promptly. That is why certain analysis could not be updated in the book with data for beyond 2012. We even wrote to TAM for certain data compatible with previous years and agreed to pay for such a data which is supposed to be otherwise in public purview. Even then they did not give us the data on one pre-text or other. One pretext was that CMS was "historically against TAM/ TRPs", which, of course, is true as there was no "conflict of interest" in CMS endeavours and analysing the data a lot more closely from the very outset.

Certain issues or notions are repeated perhaps more often in almost every chapter of the book as they are basic and at the core of a much needed paradigm shift. These include: More is not merrier, more of the same; what attracts viewers and what is in their interest are not necessarily same, etc. But together such concepts determine the scope of content priorities and direction of news channels. These are discussed and re-referred as they are relevant to explain the larger picture and future prospects. The examples given and the case of regional channels pertain to the ones in Andhra Pradesh. This is because I am familiar more and also have lot more analysis available for Telugu channels.

This book is a first person account of someone who was part of history of news media growth in India over a period of four decades (at policy level 1974-2004). This is not written as an academic or as a researcher; neither it is peer group centric. I tried to trace the developments with concerns and insights in the context of on-going proliferation and privatization of news media.

In fact, my engagement with news media goes much beyond. Even before 1974, when I was formally part of the Ministry of information and broadcasting at a senior level, I had noted in my assignment as part of Jan Jagran group at Bharat Sevak Samaj during Indo-China border clashes end of 1962. Later, I was part of Green Revolution with responsibility for extension work for urea fertilizer (1964-66). It was thereafter that I attended three US academic campuses and did PhD in communication (1968-70). I initiated several research studies from ORG as its chief, including introducing large scale survey research in India. That is when I shifted my focus from an advertising perspective to that of development and social change (1972-74, 1978-98).

In between, I steered family planning communication strategies at Nirman Bhavan and Ford Foundation and Union Ministry of Health and Family Welfare (1970-72). In all these roles, I had either used news media, contributed to it or was involved in shaping policies. During the last 30 years, I have been engaged in a series of analysis, research and advocacy, especially on media.

I was fortunate to stay engaged over such a long period. My involvement in all these assignments has been passionate, provocative and proactive even if not of a certain academic rigor. I was never influenced by peer group compulsions as well. And that could be seen in this book, in its style, notations, citation and lack of consistent conceptual and theoretical orientation. I believe the readers of my book will benefits from my background and vast experience as well.

N Bhaskara Rao, Ph.D.

Foreword

News channels in India have been proliferating for more than 15 years, as nowhere across the globe. However, viewership to news remains insignificant and almost stagnant. As if all the no-holds-bar competition, privatization without regulation, and newer technologies, made no difference. This book tries to explain this and is much more.

It offers a overview of news scene with specific analysis as to why news television channels have not acquired mass, as if - seeing is no longer believing! or that more is not merrier! This book raises many contentious issues and provokes a larger debate.

Written by a doyen of media and communication research in India, this book is almost encyclopaedic. Many sections in this book could be an independent book by themselves and is also the reason for many issues are left open ended. For, these are on-going issues fast unfolding. Some points are also repeated in the book as they have multiple implications...

I hope this will provoke media students, professionals and policy makers to further rethink and relook at contemporary news media scenario in our country.

P N Vasanti
Director General, CMS
www.cmsindia.org

Section I
A Backdrop

News channels in India have completed fifteen years of intense competition and the country's television media has witnessed exponential growth. Despite proliferation of news channels all across, viewership has not expanded commensurately and this has to do with content concerns and the model. Channels had taken to the concern is more on market in the chase for viability. Offers an understanding of dynamics is important for exploring the potential of news channels.

1

An Overview

During the decade ending 2017 media scene in India has witnessed u-turns in government policies of the earlier decades of Republic India. All that happened as if the successive governments were unconcerned of media is impeccable contribution to independent India during the 65 years or unaware of implications of these new policy moves for the future. For example, how come crime involving children had more than doubled between 2012 and 2014 and multiplied several times since proliferation of TV channels in the country? Including in Kerala the more literate state? And yet that phenomena was no one's concern.

The policy to open electronic media for hundred percent FDI, although it is 49 percent in the case of news channels, has potential to knockout "Indian Media" from serving the cause of India. What should be of concern is the excuse given while announcing that decision ...The country needs foreign investments to support "Make in India", "Skill India" and the like programs of the government of the day. The concern was not so much how media could help such national programs nor it was for contents of the media, including the news media. On the other, there were arguments in public that no FDI (Foreign Direct Investment) should be allowed into tobacco industry, directly or indirectly, ignoring that gripping power of channels is no different from that of tobacco consumption.

Every time there is change in political regime in a general election, as in 2014, there were efforts to tame news media in guise of a policy towards furthering political control of news media, both directly and indirectly. But news channels renewed their drive with renewed vigor in political coverage, followed by cinema centric entertainment and negative happenings. Repeat and replay has been such a way that extent of news coverage of round the clock news channels has declined without much change in the qualitative character of news being covered and viewership.

If big business corporate were having ownership stakes in 40 percent of news media prior to 2014, that must have gone beyond 60 percent in 2017. One difference is that fact was not so much in public preview as it is today in 2017.

Competition between channels did not bring out any dramatic change otherwise or much in plurality. News bulletins and discussions continue to be "shows" and also described as shows, as if no more pretensions about preferences, priorities and prejudices. So also the dramatics, noise level, clutter and confusion in the bulletins and debates of news channels was never so high earlier.

The key trends that were responsible for certain stagnation in the scope of news channels or their societal contribution have not indicated significant shifts over the years. The channels which started professing a new model no sooner joined the "rat race". Nevertheless some key indicative trends are worth putting together. For, it is these trends which sustain adopted model of news channels. These indicate that news channels continue to peddle same old model with no shift in paradigm in sight. It continues to be a chase for eye balls!

Conflict of interest and quid-pro-quo factors are no longer issues to be concerned about. Neither by lawmakers nor by any other stake holder group. With corporationalisation of media establishments becoming the order of the day, role and stature of journalists is no longer the same as when the idea of Fourth Estate was initiated or thought about. Even the provision of Wage Board for journalists under an Act was made dysfunctional.

Decline of News Television

For a couple of years now there have been indications of stagnation in the growth of viewership for news channels despite continued increase in the number of news channels across languages. This is despite that there is no improvement in the viability aspect of news channels. Now with digitalisation coming in a big way and broadband connectivity taking roots, news channels are bound to take a beating in a matter of time next five years.

With young taking to internet based new media or social media much more and in a much faster way, increase in viewership to television channels is bound to effect, news channels even more in the coming years. By 2020 eve In the case of advertising support, channels are likely to face that pressure eve more. The number of e-magazines, daily e-portals, and news platforms are getting added every few months in an interactive mold. This to some extent has opened door for alternate voice, scope for individuals to remain relevant with their view points. All this meant a dent into not only viewership, but very credibility of conventional news media, including news Channels, irrespective of who owns them.

The phenomena of "Paid News" were neither limited to election time nor a discovery of last decade. It[1] has become an issue of concern only recently. Although Press Council of India helped formalize the practice, it is because of the Election Commission of India's persistence that government is considering now to name it a cognizable offence legally. It however needs to be seen whether and how effectively paid news issue will ever be tackled.

Efforts towards Self regulation of television broadcasts somewhat independently has been a good initiative of TV channels including news channels, notwithstanding the extent of difference such efforts have made. That channels who are members of the Broadcaster's Association were made to seek viewer's views on contents regularity. This has been worthy initiative, not good enough to make a difference. Some new found sensitivity has come in producers and editors as much as viewers. Such initiatives yield better results if viewer activism also becomes obvious.

After more than a decade of crusading, including by this author consistently, against limited relevance but big influence of TV ratings, thanks to Telecom Regulator of India (TRAI) which has been assigned with responsibility of regulating issues to do with television although on an ADHOC basis, has taken a stand for certain minimal reliability and transparency aspects required for TRP system. For the first time viewing meters are being set up in few villages and states not covered earlier and are being brought under the coverage of viewership measurement. The new viewership ratings are expected to provide an opportunity to reconsider content priorities and scheduling strategies.

TRAI has also reopened debate after more than a decade on certain basic issues that most countries had considered at the very outset of making free for all scenario, including cross media controls. But the government yet to take a view of much needed propositions of TRAI.

Corporates control of news media more specifically has been a phenomena of last couple of years in India to the extent one could ask today in 2017 is there any free press or independent news media? But this has been yet another opportunity to reposition news channels for a more influencing role in the society. This has gone unheaded.

Digitalization of distribution system is expected to increase revenues of TV channels. Government has taken initiatives to make digitalization obligatory and the deadline has so far been shifted twice in less than two years. End of 2016 only around 60 percent could be said as effectively implemented. When channels dependence on only MSOs and Cable Networks is expected to be first in Andhra Pradesh where every household is expected to be connected with broadband by 2018 and facilitate better delivery of services including TV channels and internet. But the monthly subscription is expected to be within 200 rupees much lower than what households in all spend for subscribing news media, entertainment and internet use.

The year 2012 was a turning point for the news broadcast business with the opening of the Pandora's Box due to a [2]TRP (Television Rating Point) hoax by none other than NDTV (New Delhi Television). The ripples continue to push the media business for a re-look and are bound to reset the yardsticks for a more creative content model in the Indian television media, particularly the news channels, in the coming years.

The previous year, 2011, had ended with a provocative question by the then newly-appointed Chairman of Press Council of India, Justice Markandey Katju, a retired Judge of the Supreme Court. He had raised questions pertaining to media's special status as the Fourth Estate. The year before that, 2010, was that of Radia tapes;[3] it revived the idea of a *Lakshmanrekha*[4]. In 2009, paid news was formally recognised as a phenomenon; 2008 was the year of private treaties with several media organisations riddled with conflict of interests. Prior to that there was a debate on contract system of hiring journalists as a result of the decline of the wage board and reversal of the 1956 Cabinet decision pertaining to foreign direct investment (FDI) in the sector. Hundred per cent FDI was allowed (between 1994 and 2000) into "media support services" that indirectly set the priorities for the country's mass media.

All these were not unconnected or overnight developments. But they were not taken note of and we did not seriously pursue their implications. Instead, the focus was on turnover, growth rate, size of market, etc.

From 1998 onwards, to blow up the size of the sector in terms of volumes, mass media and "entertainment sector" were clubbed together by trade bodies and financial wizards. Foreign analysts helped and expedited that process with more concern about investments, takeovers and mergers rather than concerns about the content. Together, these reflected an emerging scenario that had several inherent contradictions.

Some of these trends could have been addressed or corrected early enough had there been a national media policy and transparency in various ad hoc decisions of the government that triggered boom and proliferation of the media sector in general and television channels in particular.

The last decade has seen the formulation of national policies on every conceivable service and sector, and across ministries. However, one area that has had no national policy is media, which, in fact, should have been one of the first ones to have such a policy. It wasn't as if there was no effort towards this end. For example, in the 1970s, at the suggestion of the UNESCO, the government took up the task of formulating a national media policy. [5]However, somewhere down the line, it was given up as silently as it was taken up. It was realised early enough by the political bosses that such a policy would not suit them as they wanted to retain their intervening power, as and when required. Even after the Supreme Court's directive in 1995, the government avoided having a policy, no matter which political party was in power. By then the political bosses had realised the advantage of "case by case approach". That suited the big media houses even better. My Public Interest Litigation (PIL) in the Delhi High Court in 1999, questioning the ministry's ad hoc decisions, did not help either[6].

Thus, the paradigm shift in media operations was not overnight, as in the case of boom in the number of television channels, particularly the ones dedicated to news. It happened over a decade or more, and in a reinforcing way. While the change is talked about, the basic factors that caused the shift in content priorities were neither debated nor grasped as much. The concern of the discourse, if at all, was more on symptoms – as in the case of private treaties, paid news, contract system, Radia tapes, Katju's questioning, size of sample for TRPs, etc.

To cope with frequent public complaints against content priorities of television channels and their implications, the government constituted working groups, [7]both formal and informal, to come up with initiatives more in an ad hoc manner. Despite minister after minister publicly favouring a national policy at the outset of taking charge, one saw them choosing political convenience and giving in to pressures of "media giants", who, for obvious reasons, preferred "no national policy". For them, an ad hoc approach suited their interests better. That is how more than two decades went by in government dithering about a national media policy. As a part of its makeshift approach, in 2002, the government handed over licensing issues to the Telecom Regulatory Authority of India (TRAI).

Meanwhile, the "biggies" in broadcasting came up with a "long rope" for the government by way of constituting their own "authority" – though hardly a quarter of broadcasters are members of the Indian Broadcasting Foundation (IBF) or that of the News Broadcasters Association (NBA) – roping in a couple of credible public personalities. It was instituted in 2009 for news channels and in 2011 for the non-news channels. But they acted more as "complaints cells" against individual programmes rather than regulators or proactive bodies. This step was more to enable the government to showcase the industry-initiated pre-emptive measures as a good enough arrangement (as with the Advertising Standards Council of India) to ensure responsibility among the broadcasters. The issue here is not so much about sufficiency or adequacy of this Broadcast Content Complaints Council of IBF or News Broadcasting Standards Authority of NBA, as having a national media policy involving all significant issues. The issue is whether such an arrangement is good enough to be a surrogate for a national policy. This is what Justice Katju referred to. By not having a national policy on media sector and services, the government facilitated further "exploitation of the media".

If information equity is a pre-requisite for economic equity, a market driven approach to media, even going against the spirit of the Fourth Estate, jeopardises the very potential of news media in shaping and sustaining national perspective, pursuits and priorities.

Paradigm Shift Implications

For a couple of years now, a channel has been positioning itself as a "news channel", describing itself as India's "number one news channel" with the help of Television Rating Points or TRPs, although what it deals with and doles out more often cannot be considered as "news" or current affairs of the day or week. What explains such a possibility? Is this related to a change in definition or is it due to a paradigm shift in media operations from "news" to "infotainment"? The government is as much responsible for whatever distortions have already come up and the ones in the offing in the media scene.

In this context, it is pertinent to ask: How can one appraise the media scene in India? What are the basic criteria that could be considered universal and such that they explain the present priorities and provide insights into the emerging scenario? Ownership pattern, monopolistic trends, cross-media ownership, content concerns, measuring readership and viewership, access to information, impact implications of contents, etc. are some of the basic issues that a national media policy should be concerned about.

Various changes have been taking place in the structure and scope of media for more than a decade. Economic policies and reforms have facilitated that process. The change in priorities has been one of directions; as if there has been no reluctance about such a trend; and, as if there is no other option or alternative model of media development. Interestingly, any criticism of the trends has not been given space and not even allowed to be debated. For example, a Centre for Media Studies (CMS) analysis[8] of some of the trends and an initial perspective on paradigm shifts in 1999–2001 took a couple of years to get space in the news media. The big media never appreciated these initiatives, although they were the early beneficiaries of this pioneering research.

Two reasons could be cited for news media not debating the trends related to its role and relevance. First, in India, there has been no empirical and concurrent or time series research on the subject. The NRS, IRS[9] and (later) TRP-centered surveys have sidelined a more reliable and relevant research on impact and implication aspects and alternatives for availing of the potential of the media. The concern and priority of advertising-centric research is limited to "recall" the top of the mind aspects. Between "proving" and "improving", the concern, more often, is improving visibility, not so much about consequences or making a difference. For example, NRS/IRS is being conducted for over three decades and "viewership" is being tracked for nearly two decades, but what difference have they made in terms of reach, relevance and influence at the macro and micro levels? Comparisons that are made each time through these figures and put out are, at the most, limited to the previous year or two; the long term trends over a decade are not considered. This is why such a data hardly ever contributes to policy formulation or timely proactive initiatives.

Secondly, due to preoccupation with competitive compulsions, the fundamental issues never come up for public discourse. While on the one hand, there's no public debate on issues of critical nature and pertaining to larger public interests, there has been unending debate on immediate symptoms, which are of much consequence to investors. The Broadcast Bill, for example, was deliberated across and on various fora for over a decade and given up, of course, with an excuse that a "more comprehensive Convergence Bill" was coming up. But that, too, was never pursued on some other pretext. The landmark judgment of the Supreme Court on airwaves never came up for a debate, but Conditional Access System (CAS) was debated. Similarly, the issue of "content regulation" is being deliberated across and on various fora for more than a decade now and the government in 2011 had the excuse of an industry initiative for not coming up with a national policy or an independent content regulator. In fact, the government has not even decided about the "ad hoc role" assigned to the TRAI for a decade now!

What Justice Katju said on assuming office as the Chairman of Press Council of India has already been mentioned, though in different shades of politeness, during the last decade by two Presidents, [10]two Prime Ministers and two Chief Justices; of course, without provoking and prompting a national debate the way Justice Katju did. Even the Vice-President of India had voiced his views on similar lines. I, too, have been writing since the past 13 years using facts and figures to explain the emerging phenomenon.

The government was found in a quandary twice in October 2011, indicating how weak it was and how powerful the big media establishments had become. [11]The government had to either retreat or yield on both of its initiatives. One was on modality of renewal of broadcasters' licenses and the second was withdrawal of an important provision from the Press and Registration Bill, 2010. Within 24 hours of a revised uplinking policy in October 2011, the NBA, the Broadcast Editors Association (BEA) and all those representing investor interests questioned the powers of the government to issue such a notification under the existing guidelines.

Cross-Media coverage and ownership is another vital policy issue, which should have been taken up more than a decade ago before allowing "free for all, to as many" and before it became too late to do anything, as we are witnessing today. [12]In 2007, the ministry had referred to this matter to the TRAI for advice. As the TRAI was about to submit its report, the ministry assigned the Hyderabad-based ASCI the task of preparing another report on the same in 2008. It was, perhaps, because neither of those reports was favourable (for the "growth of the market") that they remained confidential till 2012! What is curious is that there has been no public discussion, not even in the news media, after those reports were made public on the Internet in 2012. How can this be understood?

[13]In August 2010, the SEBI had ordered that all media houses in the market should disclose their stakes in corporates. They specifically asked them to disclose it on their own websites as well as newspapers or/and channels. The specific intention of market regulator was to bring on record conflict of interest in and between media houses. But till mid-2012, hardly any media house complied with it; and neither did any media outfit report it nor did any government agency follow it up. The civil society did not advocate the desirability of such disclosures either.

The provision for disclosing news media's sources of revenue has been dropped from the Press and Registration Bill, 2010. Except one financial daily, it was not reported by any news media or countered by any leader either way in spite of the Bill being in public purview for several months, awaiting introduction in Parliament. Obviously, it was avoided because it was not in the interest of media establishments. Whereas the other ministry notification that made the renewal of broadcast license conditional was all over the news, as if it was an assault on media, within 24 hours of the notification. In the next 24 hours, the government backtracked. Both the initiatives would have ensured some transparency, enhanced the credibility of news media, and saved them from embarrassing situations like the award of Rs. 100 crore by the High Court against a big media firm from an (purportedly) inadvertent error in November 2011 during the course of functioning of a channel.

On the other hand, the decision taken without any consultation process included increase of FDI to 100 percent into advertising, market research, public relations, media planning and to 26 percent in the case of newspapers, DTH, etc. and, then, the decision to increase this FDI per cent from 26 to 40 percent. [14]The TRAI was being asked to consult "stakeholders" and recommend. Since then, the demand to increase the FDI limit into news media continues – first for 20 percent and then to 26 percent and now the demand is for 49 and 64 percent, respectively. It is these quiet decisions, which made substantial difference and caused and sustained the paradigm shift in media operations.

Yielding to such pressures, the Cabinet on September 15, 2012 decided (that too within a week after Parliament session) to increase FDI into media services (DTH, Cable TV, HITS and MSOs) to 74 per cent. "Most consequential reform" was how Uday Shankar, President of IBF and CEO of Star TV, described the Cabinet decision to increase FDI into broadcast services, including digital cable networks, to 74 per cent from 49 percent[15]

The industry was jubilant. One reason for that was there would be "more investments" that "Indian economy needs". No one talked of reforms needed in the content priorities and the kind of structural initiatives needed for ensuring a decentralised, pluralistic and need-based television for the country.

It is against such a background that the content priorities of news media, particularly the news channels, need to be understood. The compulsions for the content priorities are derived from these policy trends.

Growth and Expansion

Growth and Expansion are two different concepts, particularly in the context of Indian Media. Growth of media could be without actually expanding to areas that have so far remained untouched. Growth is a larger concept; it is a macro view. Expansion, on the other hand, is a desegregated view of growth and it is more concerned with equity. Growth, in the case of media, could be a way of selling to the same people without reaching out to new section, otherwise not reached. For example, growth in the case of newspapers could happen because of a person reading two newspapers daily instead of one or reading three instead of two last year. Or, in the case of media, it could be because the ones reading newspaper previously are also viewing news channels now or vice-versa. These are cases of reaching the same people because they are the ones who could afford (have deep pockets) and are active in the markets. Targeting the same people is obvious, but it is not a big deal as it is inevitable in a development process. Expansion is reaching areas which haven't been ventured into and it goes a long way. Going into "mature markets" adds to growth, not expansion. Growth has more to do with economic aspects, while expansion has more to do with development and equity that requires going beyond market view and deliberate initiatives.

"Reach" is something that took roots in media vocabulary in 1972. I remember the kind of efforts that were made to push this concept of "Reach" in place of "circulation". "Reach" outlook was promoted as a part of promoting NRS as the basis for media planning. I did not realise then (1972-77) that editors, advertising agencies and advertisers would take to that concept as a criteria and that too, so fast. Even government agencies, including those concerned with rural development and family planning, had taken to that as the basis for their advertising plans. However, despite that "Reach" in those years was primarily an urban phenomenon.

When I first made presentation on highlights of the first NRS in PIB conference hall at Shastri Bhavan in 1974 for the then I&B ministers and the media heads, I pointed out the context of "Reach" concept used initially based on that first NRS. But that caution was conveniently ignored, particularly by the advertising fraternity.

In 2003, I brought out a monograph, "Miles to go.....The Indian Media Scene: Newspapers 2002-2003", [16]on unexplored opportunities to expand the reach and, hence the, growth of newspapers. That process, I described, required a "media development" approach. The increased "growth with expansion" in the later years in the "Hindi belt" happened after that analysis. My contention was that in expansion lies the growth opportunity and sustaining that growth rate across India without limiting it to one or two regions.

The only source for knowing the reach (with whatever limitation of methodology) and from one survey to another for newspaper and TV was NRS/IRS. TRPs are not indicative of overall reach of Television, much less growth or expansion from one year to another. TRPs are only surrogate indicators.

Such an overwhelming preoccupation with reach, cycled and recycled by NRS/IRS, has overshadowed the larger concern for the entire country, comprising all sections and regions. [17]An analysis of the trend of newspaper and television reach over the years brings out that readership surveys have not stirred or stimulated anything "beyond-reach" concerns. The orientation of these media with regard to their contents or their marketing strategies did not adjust or gear up (with the increase in literacy levels, for example) to explore (new) opportunities.

Such an outlook and approach has deprived media sector of the "Growth with Expansion" approach to explore opportunities. The concern for "unreached" came after 1995 with new competitive scenario. But even that was more to do with or as a part of marketing strategies rather than a concern for the unreached or their content concerns and priorities. That is how "Growth" and "Reach" have become the criteria and benchmark for industry and for competitive positioning.

Between 2000 and 2010, the reach of newspapers and television increased much more – in urban areas from 78 to 82 per cent in the case of TV and in rural areas from 35 to 45 per cent after a period of stagnation between 1980 and 2000, both in the case of Newspapers and Television. Some spurt in growth and expansion between 2005 and 2010 was not commensurate anywhere to the proliferation and boom in the media sector, particularly news channels.

Newspaper readership vis-à-vis TV viewing: Urban

(Per cent of adults)

Year	Newspaper readers	TV viewers
1972 – NRS	37	No TV
1978- NRS	53	9
1983- NRS	47	18
1986- NRS	56	-
1990- NRS	44	71
1995- NRS	46	76
1997- NRS	45	78
2000 – IRS	45	78
2002- IRS	54	-
2005	58	75
2010	57	82

Source: CMS Analysis of NRS & IRS

Newspaper readership vis-à-vis TV viewing: Rural

(Per cent of adults)

Year	Newspaper Readers	TV Viewers
1972-NRS	7	No TV
1986-NRS	8	5
1989-NRS	9	27
1995-NRS	10	30
2000-IRS	15	35
2002-IRS	24	-
2005	24	33
2010	30	45

Source: CMS Analysis of NRS & IRS

Per copy readership, a concept derived from NRS data, was not availed for developing marketing strategies or for content priorities, as it was intended when I first insisted that this analysis should be included in the NRS reports (first and second NRS). In the beginning, the myth in the industry was that the higher the per copy readership the better the newspaper, when, in fact, it should have been the other way. In any case, content (editorial) priorities (and marketing strategy as to the cost of copy) were not to promote readership so much as sales and circulation.

The NRS/IRS data was initially used more to position the newspaper in a competitive scene rather than to distinguish itself and expand instead of merely catching up with the growth rate. The same thing happened with television channels in 1990-2000 and continued even after sensitivity about the limitation of that model became obvious in the industry. Nevertheless, certain stagnation in the growth trend was obvious. The doyen of media entrepreneurship and champion of prolifcration of channels in India, Subhash Chandra Goel of Zee TV had referred to such a trend in 2010. [18]In 2011 October, Uday Shankar of Star TV, too, referred to that phenomenon

This trend coincided with economic reforms and interest of foreign investors in the Indian media during the late 1990s and thereafter. By the time industry leaders realised the trend, the TRP driven "content model" had already taken roots. It may help sustain growth, but for expansion locally relevant content concerns and priorities are more important. It was a global and greed-based) strategy rather than an Indian need-based strategy that pushed the TRP norms.

The government, on the other hand, was trying to expand (more to reach opinion making voters) during the 1980–90 by decentralising terrestrial networks (hardware). It wasn't done with a view to promote local programme origination or encourage local participation. For, they did not go for programming staff beyond state capitals. I wrote in praise of this decentralised approach of one transmitter a day in *The Economic Times*, but advocated that with so much creative talent everywhere, Doordarshan should go for programme staff at each of the district transmitters and that only would make actual difference.

As some studies on economic reforms have indicated, the divides and disparities continued in the country despite higher economic growth levels. And it was the better off who benefitted more from that growth. In the same way, in the media context, the ones who were reading one newspaper earlier were reading more than one and also watching more channels than before. The ones who did not have access to either media continued to be outside the reach of all conventional media. In fact, even those who had some access to television had not gone into the domain of news channels to become more empowered whereas those who had access to one news channel had access to many more now.

[19]In the wake of the boom of news channels between 2005 and 2012 (more than 200 news channels were permitted during this period), one would have expected a higher spurt in the overall reach of media and expansion in the reach of television, more specifically. But the NRS/IRS for these years did not indicate any such expansion. Even going by TRPs, no such difference was evident of the boom in news channels. In fact, the signal was that increase in the number of news channels did not commensurately increase viewership to news bulletins or even to TV as such.

It was, of course, the new regional channels, which brought expansion based growth in 2005-11 and, of course, more competition within the language regions helped that process. In a matter of less than a decade, the number of news channels in Telugu, for example, had gone up to 15.

Growth of News Channels

The number of "news channels" in the country increased from less than 10 in 2000 to 39 in 2005 and to more than 240 permitted ones in 2012. Between 2005 and 2012, the number of news channels increased by more than 200. This growth was unprecedented, as nowhere else in the world so many news channels were added in such a short span of time. One would expect that with the proliferation of news channels, expansion will receive a boost, if not a big jump, and, in turn, a big transformation will take place in terms of equity in access and empowerment because of contents. Was that the case? Since news channels multiplied after 2005, has there been any spurt in the share of news channels in the overall television viewership in the country? Whatever change was there was because of expansion; growth in viewership was marginal. Between 2006 and 2010, the share of news channels in viewership increased marginally – from 6.7 to 7.3 per cent. The initial euphoria was soon over. It had gone up to 8.1 in 2008 and declined thereafter as the model of news channels did not evoke the kind of interest that was expected.

Share of News Channels in the Total Viewership

Year	Share of news channels in per cent of viewership
2006	6.7
2007	7.9
2008	8.1
2009	7.6
2010	7.3

Source: TAM CMS analysis

The expansion in regional languages led to some decline or stagnation in the share of viewership of English and Hindi news channels.

Media entrepreneurs, as [20]Uday Shankar summed up the scenario, have seen through the opportunities for consolidation and expansion much more smartly than what our political masters in the Planning Commission had realised in the context of the larger national scenario. In its concern for growth, it had neglected the concern/priority for equity and empowerment, and these objectives had become secondary. The growth had been at the cost of social inclusion and equity. In the context of media, reach beyond "market confines" to social system or societal concerns was not a priority for whatever reason. In the case of media, there were no such empirical studies as in the case of economy to bring out the outcomes and inconsistencies in the trends. With TRP becoming the pre-occupation, no longitudinal studies were conducted. It was competitiveness and entrepreneurship that led to some isolated efforts, not so much a concern at the receiving end.

Has Regulation Stifled Growth?

The Cable and Satellite Broadcasting Association of Asia (CASBAA) is a Hong Kong-based advocacy forum of the television industry. From time to time, it reflects and lobbies on behalf of the industry. In September 2011, it came up with a[21] "comparative study" covered prominently in the Indian news media. Its "finding" was that "over–regulation is stifling growth in the Indian television sector". It noted that "in spite of the vast size of the market and its creative capabilities, India's TV sector remains stifled". The study sounded an alarm that the "cash flow needed to invest in new talent and content is depleting". It further observed,

"Content has been largely commoditised. This limits returns while eroding any sense of quality for the consumer."[22]

This was perhaps the first time that an industry body had acknowledged that there was certain stagnation or stifling despite "boom", "proliferation", or "growth" in the number of TV channels in India and in the volume of turnover in the previous one decade, more specifically. But what is intriguing is CASBAA's diagnosis of such a trend. A close reading of that report, however, indicates that though it highlighted regulatory aspects as responsible for the stifling, it stopped short of going into the "real reasons" – that is the relevance of contents and lack of a win-win outlook in the priorities of channels. The pursuit of TV channels in India has been a "growth model" rather than an "impact model". In this process, the growth model is driven more by TRP-based programming rather than allowing the channels to unleash their complete potential. The way channels of all genres have "mushroomed" and are beaming their contents reveals that lack of an appropriate and India specific regulating environment has contributed to the stifling of TV as a potential medium. An independent analysis of television scenario in different countries is more likely to bring out that the Indian story is more about "under regulation" than "over regulation" as the industry lobbies try to put it. The growth model of television in India has been ad hoc, lacking policy, and yielding to the interests of individual investors rather than the interests of "the sector" or that of viewers or readers. This has been so even when it was clear that there cannot be an effective backtracking or reversing the direction of the growth path. A "win-win model" would have helped and paved the way for a better environment. In that model, growth is related to role and relevance of channels to national objectives. That is, instead of "maximisation" of Return on Investment (RoI), it should have included the interests of viewers, "we the people" of the country and national goals.

The model of growth without impact is somewhat like democracy without people's participation. The impact of channels expected otherwise is in terms of making a difference to the lives of their people; i.e., in their quality of life, not merely in their lifestyles; and in facilitating harmony, not prompting divides and inequalities. With continued support to inequalities and injustice, how can television expect to have a continued growth? The "size" of viewers and "market" would expand more from such a growth outlook. The television should have growth with impact and the impact has to be in terms of "moving minds and touching hearts," not capturing eycs only.

The extent and the kind of government regulation obviously depend on the kind of role an enterprise plays. And it is well established that television makes a difference to the agenda setting process by grabbing public attention. When channels work for private interests and business results, certain regulations are bound to be there in the larger public interest. One could argue that the concerns of TV channels have not been so much the Fourth Estate's priorities to deserve special exemptions from any regulations. [23]The CASBAA report has mentioned that content has been largely commoditised and that has eroded TV's orientation. Why and what contributed to that process is what Indian TV, particularly the news channels, should be discussing about and finding ways to correct the fault lines in exploring greater opportunities.

It was perhaps a coincidence that the September 2011 week CASBAA released its report, the News Broadcasters Standards Authority, set up by the News Broadcasters Association (NBA), also came out with a startling initiative about reporting viewership ratings or TRPs, which was to become somewhat like a Bible for channels. But what is pertinent to take note in this context is the logic of NBA for such an initiative. It concluded that "news channels, being distinct from other genres, have a responsibility to inform and empower its viewers with quality programming... rather than providing content merely for garnering viewership". The NBA further argued that "news programme cannot always be linked to popularity or audience measurement" as content standards could "only improve with time spent on strategic planning and research, rather than knee jerk reactions taken on a weekly basis"[24]

NDTV's senior managing editor Sonia Singh deplored the way news channel marketing often includes ads claiming the "No.1 position" on the basis of fragmented weekly rating. A senior editor (name not mentioned in this news report) at a leading Hindi news channel agreed: "Weekly TRPs are one of the reasons for the dumbing down of news channels," and "the sword is always hanging over your head that the scenario might change by Wednesday when viewership ratings are released[25]. Senior journalists Ashutosh and Rajdeep Sardesai (both working for of IBN network then), too, maintained that indulging in mindless race of ratings has led to poor content of news channels; and "sensation is replacing the news". Channels concede that ratings are having "detrimental effect on content".

The Mint's report on NBA's decision sums up the situation very well. That story, prominently positioned in the *Mint* said that, "The country's television news channels are blaming the rating system for driving them towards headlines that are sensational; reporting that is breathless; bulletins that are loaded with celebrity gossip; and programming that is aimed at the lowest common denominator." [26]

Television was introduced in India with certain objectives in mind. It was allowed to expand to pursue those goals in the context and relation to the country's developmental endeavours. It was tried on a limited scale first on an experimental basis for the cause of agriculture and farm communities; it was extended then into a regular channel, but, again, limited to one city and limited to a couple of hours of programmes only. TV has expanded not exactly in response to "market demand", but it was developed and promoted by the government with certain objectives facilitative of ongoing processes, including ASIAD. And it was with the same objectives and outcome expectations that TV was expanded into a national channel and then into a network of regional channels.

How well television had served the objectives for which it was promoted in the country is a different matter to dwell upon. But what is pertinent here is that television was never promoted nor allowed initially to expand as a [27]"business enterprise". The explanation has always been that such an expansion and growth facilitates "national endeavors". All that happened until a decade ago, when airwaves opened up to private investors and foreign broadcasters, by even going against the ruling of the Supreme Court to go for an independent regulator.

The growth of TV in India has become "market driven" only after private TV was allowed to enter the field with no new regulations. In fact, the government facilitated that process by not coming in the way of television viewership rating. Against this background, CASBAA coming up with a finding that "over regulation" is stifling growth" should be viewed more as a "bullying tactics" or strategy of "investors" for maximising profits and for retaining market domination.

For almost two decades TRP influence and domination was not questioned and the government did nothing about it until 2011. All that the government did was to appoint a committee after consulting the industry and with their consent. It was more because of increased public anger and frequent questioning in Parliament. Earlier, between

1999 and 2006, twice I brought the perils of TRPs to the attention of the minister and secretary of Information and Broadcasting. But there was never any intervention; as if the government was unconcerned of its implications.

It is against such a background that content priorities of news channels need to be understood. The compulsions for the content priorities are derived from these policy trends.

This chapter gives an overview of the book. It refers to issues, dilemma, and presents the setting for the chapters that follow. Also, certain background which is relevant for that discussion is offered in this chapter.

Endnotes

1 Andhra Pradesh Union of Working Journalists Union reported first in 2004 based on its field inquiry in Nalgonda district that during the assembly elections local news papers were collecting a tariff from contesting candidates for giving favorable coverage about them for period of the poll campaign. On bringing the matter to the Press Council of India by one of its member, Mr. Srinivasa Reddy who was also a functionary in Andhra Pradesh, the Council appointed a subcommittee to further enquire in to the phenomena. The subcommittee of Mr. Guha Takurta went about inquiring the matter outside Andhra Pradesh and specified and in detail as phenomena of "paid news". This author in an edit page article in The Hindu daily "paid news, a deep seated malaise", 10 January 2010, elaborated the practice as a much deeper, beyond election times and as spread across news coverage far more widely and contests.

2 Television Rating points (TRP), supplied by audience measurement agencies, continue to be viewed by channels and even more by advertising agencies as reliable yardstick for viewership not withstanding limitations of different kind. Because of big city bias of sample, English channels benefited more from TRPs. The channels which were shown relatively lower ratings tend to point out one or more errors in TRP methodology. Initially, New Delhi Television (NDTV) too benefited. But with more English channels entrenching, NDTV's rating was indicated as lower than some other English channels, which NDTV called as "TRP hoax" by bringing out some of the lacuna In Sample selection and the claims of the agency which conducted the rating exercise. in a press meet as well as by issuing a note to media accusing the agency by show casing clippings of interviews with some alleged sample households including some retail shops with meter. The timing of the accusation being what it was, NDTV tried to explain its potential to generate much higher revenue than what was indicated in its balance sheet. This expose caused flutter in the market about credibility of TRPs.

3 Radia tapes. At the height of 2G controversy 2010 in India during UPA govt. on allocation of air waves, CBI traced tapes of conversation by public relations agent, Mrs. Nina Radia with many high level political ministers trying to influence on behalf of certain big corporates. These tapes lead to accusation of misconduct of some political leaders of the time and big corporates.

4 Lakshman Rekha is a proverb from epic Ramayana. Lines were drawn by Lakshman, Rama's brother, advising Sita the danger of crossing those lines, which Sita was made to cross by Ramanasura in imposter form and abducts Sita. Lakshmanrekha indicates that it is in no one interest to go beyond lines. Honor is when one is within limits...lakshmanrekha. The author organised a national round table discussion in Hyderabad on 1 June 2005 in colloboration with the Press Academy of Andhra Pradesh And also brought out a publication "Should there be a Lakshman Rekha", National Round Table, CMS, New Delhi, and Press Academy of Andhra Pradesh Hyderabad, June 2005.

5 Mr. I k Gujral Minister for Information and Broadcasting was Informed by UNESCO in 1974 to come up with a national policy on information media which they asked other countries as well. This was a few months before I was assigned as head of evaluation in the ministry (official designation was Visiting Professor at Indian Institute of Mass Communication with an Office in the ministry also). But before getting into, the government referred the exercise to the Ministry of Education as the present ministry of HRD was known then. This was because UNESCO was coordinated at that time by that Ministry and also because film censor section was part of that ministry at that time. Later I learned that the Government had decided not to take that advice of UNESCO seriously. Idea of a national policy was never pursued there after seriously although some Ministers referred to later years.

6 This author filed a Public Interest Litigation (PIL) in Delhi High Court in 2004 questioning the Ministry's decision to open up the channels for Australian based media baron, Murdoch. The Delhi court rejected the argument but advised probe into. See for details of the case in Indiatelevision.com breaking news on "PIL in Delhi high court seeks" on 4 August, 2004.

7 Mr. Jaipal Reddy then Minister for Information and Broadcasting (1996-98) took to this idea of having working groups as he was under pressure from women's groups of left parties for some pro active initiatives against films and TV serials depicting women and children adversely. This writer was one of the member of the over view group. Mr. Arora, secretary of the Ministry, prepared the minutes of the groups. No sooner, thereafter, both the Minister and secretary were either shifted or retired. The only policy decision was that television channels would come under TRAI and ASCI (Administrative Staff College of India) will be asked to study the social effects of channels.

8 N. Bhaskara Rao, "Of contents and controls". In Frontline, 14 September 2001

9 NRS is National Readership Survey and IRS is Indian Readership Survey. The NRS the first of large scale sample survey based enquiry into readership, listener ship and viewership came out in 1974 in finalising that report and making its presentations initially this writer was the key functionary at Operations Research Group (ORG). The IRS started by Indian Market Research Bureau (IMRB) in 1982

10 Reports of Press Council of India annual souvenirs http://presscouncil.nic.in

11 Under an Act of Parliament any printed periodical has to register with the Registrar of News papers of India (RNI) and that registration reference should be visible every time it is published. Further, every such registered periodicals should declare by publishing in the same periodical certain basic information as to who the investors are, who is responsible for the contents, etc. Such obligation

is not there for the television channels. The government referred regulatory concerns of channels to Telecom regulatory Authority of India (TRAI) which had come in to being for telecom regulatory issues as an obligation.

12 Administrative Staff College of India (ASCI) In Hyderabad is a government funded having started as a training institute took to consultancy services. It was commissioned in 2008 for a report by the Ministry of Information and Broadcasting on media ownership pattern and cross media aspects . The researchers came to this writer to share highlights of its report.

13 SEBI (Securities and Exchange Board of India) issued an advise in 2010 http://sebiupdates.blogspot.in/2010/08/media-companies-to-disclosedetails-of.html.

14 As a follow up to the consultations of the ministry, TRAI was advised by the ministry to consult stakeholders on a su motto basis. TRAI in turn wanted to take other initiatives as well and sent a list of initiatives to the Ministry which the ministry kept with out indicating its advise. At this point TRAI chairman, Mr. Bizal who could not even see the minister to personally explain, talked to this writer to bring the matter to the attention of the Minister. It was on his suggestion that the Minister Jaipal Reddy agreed to meet the chairman at his home. There after TRAI proceeded with its stake holder consultations.

15 Mint 20 September 2012

16 "Miles to go, the Indian media scene; News Papers 2002-2003",CMS publication 2005 in the foreword for this publication, methodology was explained. This publication offers baseline analysis of the state of media, including television at that time point.

17 CMS Media Lab, set up at the instance of this writer and under his direction, has been monitoring in New Delhi selected news channels in Hindi and English (six to nine) and analysing the trend in the contents of news bulletins every day since 2000. CMS Media lab In Hyderabad also monitoring and analysing Telugu Television Channels (nine to sixteen)initially for a few years both news and entertainment channels for select months. Since 2010 only entertainment channels are being covered with specific contents like girl child, environment, road accidents, women etc . This analysis earlier also included viewership data of NRS and IRS and on and off TRP data in public purview . Additionally once a year a couple of Hindi and English daily news papers are being content analysed for a few days to enable comparative trend. This data from CMS Media Lab is being published periodically in CMS websites and its various reports and periodicals which include Transparency, Review and Green Voice.

18 Udaya Shankar, CEO of Star TV and chair of TV Broadcastors Association. In various interviews in News Media see the Financial Express Brand Equity 18 October 2011. Also see Mint, 20 September 2012 "Broadcast Industry has reached a plateau: Uday Shankar", Exchange Media 16 February, 2015.

19 Boom in News Channels in the last fifteen years is so obvious, year to year figures on the number of channels in operation are put out by various agencies including government ones like TRAI from time to time. CMS reports and reviews used these sources as the web site of TRAI, The Ministry's annual report, and by FICCI and CII and others like KPMG .see http.//www.trai.gov.in, and http://www.cii.in

20 Udaya Shankar, CEO of Star TV and chair of TV Broadcastors Association. In various interviews in News Media see the Financial Express Brand Equity 18 October 2011. Also see Mint, 20 September 2012 "Broadcast Industry has reached a plateau: Uday Shankar", Exchange Media 16 February, 2015.

21 There were hardly any field studies with primary data on media reach and effects and trends on their development over the years despite that NRS, the first large scale survey based field study was conducted 1971-74, this writer was the foremost to analyse trends earlier from ORG (1972-73 and 1977-89) and later from CMS.

22 (*Newsline, 30.09.2011, Television Sector Over-regulated: Report, Bureau Report; The Hindu, 29 September 2011) http://www.thehindubusinessline.com/industry-and-economy/marketing/article2497288.ece,*

23 Fourth Estate notion implies certain priorities in the concern and coverage of media. As fourth estate, media are expected to reflect voice of people, reflect their concerns including basic issues of people at large. Certain societal concern has to be an under current of mass media as in the case of other pillars of the state, i.e: judiciary, legislative and the executive.

24 (*The Hindu, 10 September 2011,* Monthly format for news channel rating opposed, Priscilla Jebarai, *http://www.thehindu.com/news/national/article2440031.ece., 9* September, 2011).

25 (*The Hindu, 10 September 2011)* (Monthly format for news channel rating opposed, Priscilla Jebarai, *http://www.thehindu.com/news/national/article2440031.ece.,* 9 September , 2011).

26 *(News channels blame weekly ratings for quality decay; it's the relentless weekly pressure to perform that's bringing out the worst in them, according to the channels; Abhilasha Ojha and Anushree Chandran; http://www.livemint.com/2011/09/07002631/News-channels-blame-weekly-rat.html; Posted: Wed, Sep 7, 2011. 12:26 AM IST)*

27 News media in particular are being criticised for their being business enterprises and market driven in their priorities. When news media enterprise are driven more by business interest than journalistic concerns it becomes more a profit maximisation enterprise far more than any service motto worthy of a fourth estate description. When media reflects more market interests than societal, it is viewed as market driven. One of this writer's publication, "Mass Media and Marketing Communication. Perspectives into 2020" explained that phenomena as early as in 1995. TRPs or viewership ratings based on instant and sample surveys dictate content priorities. In that pursuit Concern for effects aspect of channel contents at any given point or over time will not be there and it was not evident in any of the discourses. What matters, instead , is what instantly interests viewers, not what is in their interest. In that channels get oriented to consumer elements and prompts and promotes consumerism as main stay as channels get viability more from such interests.

2

Content Priorities Shifts in the Paradigm

One oft repeated point of **A P J Abdul Kalam**, when he was the President of India (2004–2009), was that "the urban oriented Indian media" should become "media for one billion people" instead of concentrating on the 300 million urban people.[1]

This is evident from the fact that despite boom in media, their overall reach in the country has not expanded much. Similarly, former Chief Justice of India Dr. Anand had said, "While commercialism has a legitimate place in the business office of the newspaper, it becomes a danger when it invades the editorial room."[2] Stating that "today, there are some genuine concerns about the way in which some sections of the media function," he said, "the liberty of the press cannot be confused with its licentiousness". They were both commenting on the dramatic changes in the media concerns. That was a decade ago. Have those observations made any difference? What is happening in the media is known to many of us; but why is it happening is not. In fact, it is hardly discussed. I raised this issue more than a decade ago and my analysis on the trend was not accepted by mainline dailies, until the *Frontline* featured the article in its issue dated September 14, 2001.[3]

Despite the boom in 24-hour news channels, their overall credibility has not increased, nor has their reach and coverage expanded anywhere commensurately. In terms of contents, it is more of the same or the same from more. No wonder newspapers continue to enjoy relatively higher credibility and are often used to confirm what is seen or heard on TV news bulletins, as if reading is more believable! CMS research described the phenomena as "appetizer effect" of TV news bulletins. Seeing is no more believing as was the case in the previous decades. How did that happen?

The role and relevance of news media are related to their concerns and contents. Until a few years ago, these were connected with the Fourth Estate notions and "watchdog" features. That is how news media enjoyed certain privileges and societal status. The news media organisations are expected to have larger and long range concerns, not just market compulsions or competitive concerns or business interests. Today, news media have become the corporate's voice rather than that of communities. New definitions, news values and priorities dictate the news media today. It is in this context that the question of a *Lakshmanrekha* arises.

What does this paradigm shift mean for the dilemma involved in the media operations and to the very credibility and accountability of news media? Is media for public service or for private interest? The dilemma includes societal concerns versus market priorities, stakeholders versus shareholders, short-term versus long-term implications, image versus impact, etc. Then, of course, there are controversies related to blurred distinctions between news and views, news and advertisements. How much do we understand these priorities, pre-occupations and shifts? It is only recently that these shifts are being discussed within the media and by anyone concerned about its policies and future. There is no independent and objective analysis of these changes in the media operations and their implications. How else could it be explained that even very provocative analysis by the President or Prime Minister or Chief Justice in this regard over the years were never followed up. But when it concerns the interests of individual media houses or competitive compulsions between two media houses, such issues figure all over, as if they are of national concerns.

Not so Much Reader/Viewer Lead!

Today, advertising and market research, in many ways, determine the scope of mass media, including that of journalistic trends. With allowing 100 per cent FDI in both these fields in the last more than 15 years, both these functions have become corporations, controlled mostly from abroad. Advertising, market research and media planning set the pace of media, including that of ownership pattern and journalistic trends. By and large, the major stakes and control of these "determining factors" have changed with no one raising an issue on its long term implications and no debate taking place at any level.

In 2002, a minister of Information and Broadcasting expressed his ignorance about the fact that 100 per cent FDI had been allowed a few years earlier. [4]He was reacting to a presentation I had made on the implications and trends unfolding after that decision in the absence of a national media policy. In a way, this amounts to corporates disciplining media as much of what the public media covers or carries and the priorities in that process. Corporates do this in five different ways.

Power Shift

[5] First, the share of advertising in total revenue of media has been on the increase from that of a "supplementary" (25-30 per cent) nature some decades back to that of a "supportive" one (45–55 per cent) now. In fact, in the case of television channels, advertising has been the "primary source" (70-85 per cent) of revenue to the extent of "determining" the priorities and preoccupations. Even in the case of big newspapers, revenue from advertising constitutes to be as high as 60 per cent of the total revenue. That is how the recent boom in media is being attributed to the increased availability of advertising. That is, advertising today sustains media, even more so news channels.

Secondly, advertising through newspapers and TV is today significantly high among multinationals and big corporates. Top 20 advertisers account for three-fourth of advertising revenue of newspapers and television channels.

Thirdly, the ad agency business in the country has been getting concentrated in fewer hands in the last couple of years. Top 10 ad agencies are either foreign owned or with major holding from outside the country. They account for significant share of ad business in the country and this has been on the rise. Entry of foreign ad agencies has been going on parallel to the entry of foreign brands and increase in the share of foreign corporates in the total advertising in India. In fact, lifting the limits of foreign capital in ad agency business has opened the floodgates. Well over half of Indian advertising now is accounted by overseas agencies operating in the country.

Fourthly, market research is the basis for proliferation of brands and consumerism, for preoccupation and priorities of media and the very scope and character of advertising. Until 1990, we had about nine-ten market research agencies owned mostly by Indians. Today, top eight market research agencies, accounting for more than three-fourth of research, have either been taken over by foreign corporates or such a corporate has acquired significant interest in the research firm. In fact, with recent mergers and acquisitions certain monopolistic trend is evident in this function with an annual turnover of well over Rs. 1,500 crore (2011).

More specifically, market research agencies are the ones that also conduct "readership" surveys and "rating" of TV viewership, thereby directly influencing ad agencies as well as the news media in terms of priorities and preoccupations. The methodology being followed for readership surveys and viewership rating is not without bias in favour of sponsors and subscribers and in their interests.

As someone involved in launching India specific readership and viewership studies 30 years ago (1972–88), I feel guilty for what is happening today, particularly the way the findings of these surveys are being (mis)used by newspapers and TV channels; it is as if national agenda has been hijacked. The "TRP trap", as we call the phenomena of assessing "popularity" of TV programmes, has larger and long-range implications. It took more than a decade (1995–2005) of CMS efforts to warn and sensitise about this phenomenon of superficial quantification of top of the mind impressions as surrogates for setting priorities of the Indian television.

Fifth, with media becoming complex and specialised, two "new" mediating functionaries have emerged since 2000 with serious consequences for the very character of journalist-centered Fourth Estate. Both these functionaries of "media planning" and corporate "public relations", in a way, erode into core prerogatives of journalists and their editorial jurisdiction. The media planners are the ones involved these days in buying wholesale space and time of media for advertising and selling the same in retail on their terms. In the process, they have acquired a role in doing away with media contents by virtue of setting priorities for placing commercials. In case of public relations, functioning of these "experts" implies certain undermining or interference in the functioning, particularly of reporters and editors, and their marginalisation. The function of PR is to ensure coverage for a particular viewpoint or otherwise. "Disinformation" being talked about recently is a part of these new phenomena. Today, major control of these PR corporates – some seven-eight leading ones operating nationally – is in the hands of foreign firms.

Based on CMS studies, I have written and warned about the impending implications of "paid news" and PR phenomenon more than a decade ago. Radia tapes-based expose effectively brought out this phenomenon to centre stage in 2011[6].

Adding to these trends leading to a paradigm shift have been ad hoc decisions of the government sans a national media policy. In fact, through such temporal outlook of the government, evident in reacting issue by issue and going by push and pulls, issues were further complicated. The landmark judgment of the Supreme Court in 1995 on airwaves is now forgotten. Minister after minister has violated the spirit of the judgment and gone about taking decisions without reflecting the concern to face the challenges before the nation and in the context of the news media. In that process and as a consequence, the "wage board" has become irrelevant. It has resulted in the emergence of the trend to hire journalists on "contract". Wage board was devised by Pandit Jawaharlal Nehru to ensure that journalists work beyond the pressures of commercial interests. That is how today in the context of some major media, journalists and content creators do not operate as per their full capabilities and potential, in the process denting a basic feature of the Fourth Estate.

The Content Model

What is the content model that could help reap the potential of television as the most potent mass medium, particularly for motivating people, individually and as communities, raise newer heights of living standards, human relationships, productivity and active citizenry?

Such a content model should enable creative ideas to flourish on the merit of their own strength, not because of external motivations or compulsions, including advertising and TRPs. And channel should be able to chalk out the course on its own as it visualises its opportunities. Any dependence on external resources for the survival and viability of the channel should not be less than 50 per cent of total capital and not depend on any one source for support. Contents of a channel should not get momentum from other news channel(s), rather each should set its own agenda and go about with its own contents pro-actively. At the same time, certain elements of competition between channels should also be evident.

Such a content model will be based on certain concerns to cater and broadcast with an intention of serving the interests of a larger public. For that the channel should avail quantitative and qualitative field research, based on experimentation in production, presentation and schedules. Such a content model should make a difference in the life and living standards of people and in the functioning of public institutions.

The content model followed so far has been for maximisation of viewership. There are no holds on the process of maximisation of revenue primarily from advertising. About that model there is hardly any debate and questioning. There is no regulatory provision nor is there any consideration or national policy. Also, there is no transparency in this regard. That is what this model is all about. Broadcasters can beam into India anything rather easily or with least conditions or obligations to the State and responsibility to viewers. And whatever conditions are there, they hardly matter as they are more of a procedural nature. In any case the "embedded support services' (the new gatekeepers), who are already allowed hundred per cent foreign equity and are in control of priorities, are there to facilitate the process of free for all and a content model that sustains such a framework of "no holds barred".

Maximisation of viewership being the prime goal, people need to be lured with whatever content it takes to do so. How much research is there for broadcasters to understand the logic of expediting that process of adding and holding on to viewers? Do we have any? It is a chicken and egg syndrome, supported and sustained by TRP.

To sustain such a content model, the *Navarasa*[7] view of human emotions comes handy for TRPs. The content model is based on unleashing these elements, which the viewers are made to take and seek out. All this is unconcerned of potential impact of such viewing on various sections of viewers, particularly vulnerable sections, specifically the children.

A finding of August 2012 national survey by NDTV[8] was that between mobile phone and TV, a much higher per cent of people prefer to possess a mobile phone. In fact, in Uttar Pradesh, Bihar and Jharkhand over 80 per cent of respondents preferred a mobile phone. In these three states the number of local originating Hindi TV news channels at that time was more than a couple in addition to more than six Hindi news channels beamed from outside the state. The voters in these states find programmes of TV channels in their respective state are not of much significance as compared to the mobile phone. This is because the content priorities of the channels in these states are of hardly any relevance and consequence to them.

The research model avoids considering impact on any section of society other than markets, investors and consumer. That is why TRP is based on mere presence before a TV set and that is how temporal exposure is viewed as "viewership".

Advertising Model

Media should serve markets and consumer too, but by making consumer more sensitive, discriminative and with concern for tomorrow, not by luring for indiscriminate consumption and unconcern of a "rainy day". I am not arguing against advertising as a function. I am only saying that news media should not function at its mercy or courtesy. Advertising would like to avail television as much for demand creation function, for motivating individuals and pursuing ideas even if they are in the interest of a few at the cost of many.

News channels in particular could explore the idea of limiting to sponsorship advertising instead of brands promotion advertising. And, the time devoted for advertising should be limited (12 minutes per hour) and it should be left to individual channels to evolve their own model of placing and scheduling ads. They should reduce dependence on advertising to flatten dependence on a few advertisers. The model we have gone for is what is in vogue in the US. Unless we realise the pros and cons of that model, we cannot benefit and evolve a better one. We are capable of evolving a better model – because we have the advantage of knowing the experience of others, including the US. The US model is based on the principle of more and more. It puts more confidence in markets.

Let us take the radio listenership "measurement" as an example. [9]In 2011, the IRS which uses a questionnaire administered through a face to face interview method, had registered a decline in listenership by more than eight per cent over the previous year. In the earlier round, an increase was reported by the same agency. However, Television Audience Measurement's (TAM) Radio Audience Measurement (RAM) system – that follows the diary method to capture listenership data requiring listeners to write down the details of programmes listened to – showed considerable increase in listenership during the same period. Both the findings were released in 2011. Both claimed robust sample base. This aspect reminds what I advocated at the outset of meter-based viewership after 1989-91 that the TAM should use three different approaches for an "inclusive methodology" instead of limiting to a "meter measurement" – (1) recall method by face to face interview, (2) diary method of recording by viewers and (3) meter measurement. That suggestion was brushed aside as that combination approach would have meant bringing out impact rather than mere exposure or presence before a TV set, which is being described as "reach".

What is interesting is that the "decline" finding of IRS was questioned by the industry and government, because the government was preparing to auction new FM frequencies as the third phase of its efforts to privatise the "business" (to raise foreign investments). The doubt of the industry about those figures rested on the fact they were the same media companies that operated TV channels and were trying to acquire hold on radio licenses by demanding lower basic price in that auction. Media planners, who buy time, were worried too as that finding of decline in listenership affected their bargaining power. It means that the purpose of the ratings is not as much related to contents as to the business interests of advertisers and broadcasters.

Endnotes

1 Dr. Abdul Kalam, as president of India, believed that if some of the urban facilities and services like electricity, media availability, communication connectivity are made available to villages, the face of India could be changed. With such a belief, he advocated in his writings, public engagement and appealed to Govt. to take to PURA (Providing Urban amenities in Rural Areas). In this regard he called up on media to development of India. He suggested media to reach out billion people rather than limiting to hundred million. The Hindu, 7, December 2006

2 Justice Anand, Former Chief Justice of India and chairman of National Human Rights Commission. The Hindu, 7 December, 2006. Speaking in a function to felicitate Pronay Roy of NDTV for receiving award for Excellence in Journalism for 2004. Refer for more Http://www.ndtv.com

3 N Bhaskara Rao, " of content and control" In Frontline, volume 18,issue 18, 1-14,September 2001 www.frontlineconnect.com/18180950.htm.

4 As a minister for information and broadcasting in July 2000, Arun Jetley was chief gust at a Delhi Union of Working Journalists in New Delhi Punjab Bhavan when I was the key note speaker on trends in policies to do with media. When I showed a slide depicting how hundred per cent foreign direct investment were allowed into advertising, market research and public relations , Arun Jetley intervened and said that he was not aware of such decisions by the previous Govt. The point being made here is that such critical decisions were made without a public debate and even without awareness and knowledge of people even in Delhi and in the Parliament.

5 "Content and Control" article in the Frontline in 2001, referred earlier, is summed up here by way of five mega trends. These trends in each case were arrived based on primary reseach and analysis in the previous more than a decade at ORG (Operations Research Group) and later from CMS. This included advertising expenditure trends, contents of news media, trends in media and advertising sector and one to one discussions with many personalities of the time in Mumbai and New Delhi.

6 The Hindu edit page article of this writer with 12 specific suggestions to deal with paid news syndrome. This writer was one of the professional to be invited by the Press Council to discuss Paranjoy Guha Takurta's Report on paid news..Dr N Bhaskara Rao, "paid news, a deep-seated malaise". The Hindu, 20 January 2010.

7 Content model is the kind of priorities with which channels go by over time. "Navarasa" view of contents is an expression to indicate different and multiple combination of whatever a channel packages its transmission time with Navarasa is a conventional way of offering multiple variety of food or music or tunes etc

8 NDTV survey, http://www.ndtv.com

9 IRS (The Indian Readership Survey) 2011 is conducted by MRUC (Media Research Users Council) and RSCI (Readership Studies Council of India) http://www.mruc.net

3

Media Concerns or Market Concerns?

Should there be a *Lakshmanrekha* for media?

Legislative

In 2011, the Public Accounts Committee of Parliament on spectrum allocation quoted in its report a senior journalist who figured in the Radia tapes controversy, conceding "utterly unprofessional and transgressing the line of propriety – the *Lakshmanrekha*"[1]. Former Lok Sabha Speaker Somnath Chatterjee reminded that institutions in a democracy have to operate within a *"Lakshmanrekha"*. He talked in the context of the need on the part of the pillars of democracy to maintain "constitutional balance", so that harmonious relationships are maintained between them in such a way that each one does its job in a better way and more competitively[2].

What senior journalist [3]Surya Prakash of *The Pioneer* wrote in 2010 summed up the essence as – (the) "Irresponsibility and lawlessness that has crept into the working of media organisations in recent years... has completely stripped the profession of ethics, social responsibility and pursuit of truth". Similar view was expressed by some other senior journalists, too, in the wake of the Radia tape revelation.

Former Prime Minister **Atal Bihari Vajpyaee**,[4] while inaugurating celebrations some years ago, had called upon the news media not to cross the *"Lakshmanrekha"* in their coverage. Since then, many other leaders, too, have reminded the news media of violating the *"Lakshmanrekha"*. In fact, cautioning the media against "unwarranted criticism", the Supreme Court on April 25, 2005, felt that the "freedom enjoyed by the media was no license to indulge in sensationalism and a mechanism should be devised to check the criticism for crossing the limits". The motivation for such observations was adverse of excessive media coverage of one or other institution or individual leader or political party or the government. Since 2005, the CMS has organised several national-level meets on the concept of *Lakshmanrekha*.

The concept of *Lakshmanrekha* implies that there is a need for certain equilibrium between relationships and responsibilities of various pillars of democracy and each of them should restrain itself from going overboard and not lose track of boundaries separating their functioning within the provisions of the Constitution, written and unwritten. *Lakshmanrekha* implies operating not only with certain responsibility and accountability but also with certain concern for the consequences of what is being done or not done today with regard to the larger values related to freedom, objectivity, equity and ethics. *Lakshmanrekha* involves both legal and ethical dimensions. Nevertheless, most elected democracies in the world have one or other restraint on the operations of media, even when they are relatively free from government's interference. In India, a free and independent media is inherent in the Freedom of Speech that is guaranteed by the Constitution under Article 19(1)(a), but "subject to restrictions operating in a very narrow sphere". It assumes that media is fair, free, responsible and operates under certain checks and balances, a hallmark of the Constitution. It is expected that media observes certain standards of objectivity and responsibilities and responsiveness inherent in the concept of the Fourth Estate.

Media is expected to maintain its own code of conduct and credo of self-restraint in such a way that the dignity of other democratic institutions and the privacy of individuals are, in no way, adversely affected. [5]That is why a two judge bench of the Supreme Court in 2005 called for a mechanism "to check the publication which transgresses the limits of fair and bonafide criticism". Freedom and democracy require responsibility to the larger public and observance of certain standards of behaviour and self-discipline. That is how, in the context of broadcasting, the Supreme Court's landmark judgment of 1995 observed that "airwaves belong to public" and cannot be used for personal profit; it also called for an independent regulator. Going beyond, a former Chief Justice of a High Court, M.N. Rao, observed: "Freedom without responsibility denigrates into license. The very role that the media plays as a disseminator of news, educator of the public and creator of public opinion imposes onerous duties of a high order. High ethical standards the media must adhere to. Truthfulness in reporting of news, objectivity in presentation of facts without any bias, avoidance of giving undue prominence to persons and events to promote the business or political interest of the media owners are some of the minimum ethical standards expected of the media." He further observed, "When media is run as a business enterprise with the primary object of earning profit without any commitment to ethical values, often, objectivity in the presentation of news is brushed aside. Facts are edited to promote the unstated objectives of the media operators. The right of the public to have correct information comes into conflict with the private interests of the media operators. [5]The working journalist often finds himself in a helpless position."

Another former Chief Justice of India, Dr. A. S. Anand observed, "While commercialism has a legitimate place in the business office of the newspaper, it becomes a danger when it invades the editorial room." Stating that "today, there are some genuine concerns about the way in which some sections of the media function," he said, "the liberty of the press cannot be confused with its licentiousness"[6]

With the proliferation of TV, radio and newspapers, the overall role, reach and relevance of media should have expanded much beyond (two-thirds of people). Also, the range of contents in the coverage of the news media should have expanded much beyond urban India. But those changes have been marginal. It's because the competition within and across media has been for the same sections of people – the ones having deeper pockets. That is why rural reach and coverage of basic issues of concern to common people have a long way to go. Some increase in circulation and viewership, nevertheless, was achieved because of factors related to demography and aggressive marketing. Multiplicity in channels and newspapers, too, has contributed to it, but more by way of adding to duplication. Despite the boom in 24-hour news channels, the extent and range of their coverage has not increased. Then there is the contradiction associated with blurred distinctions between news and views, news and advertisements, etc. There is no independent and objective analysis of these changes in media operations and their implications for the larger developmental endeavors of the country.

Contents and Carriage Aspects of Media

While journalism is a profession, media is an enterprise. The former is related to contents, the latter is a carrier. Often, we mix up the two in our public discourses. Media does not always include or is based on, journalistic inputs. Journalism, as any other profession, has certain core characteristics. The first and foremost is accuracy, followed by public service, fairness and ethical concerns. Whereas media as a carrier is concerned about reach, viability and profitability. While codes, guidelines, self-regulation, privacy, ethics are issues related to contents, ownership, license, cross-media holding, etc. are related to carrier. The ethical concern in media operations is nothing but a kind of self-regulatory culture. While most media have some kind of self imposed guidelines and codes, a few always try to "outsmart" or do a "Jack and Jill" to such standards. The number of such (rogue!) media increases, as they perceive threat of competition of whatever kind – individual or together. Globalisation and corporatisation has brought about new compulsions, new priorities and new values in this sphere. The proliferation of media from all across the globe and the resulting competition have put self imposed standards and codes to test today. This phenomenon is too obvious and blatant in broadcasting in the absence of consistent national policies. A content analysis of television brings out that perhaps self-regulatory initiatives work better with some outside regulatory mechanisms, supported by legislative provisions. A regulatory mechanism could be both from within and from outside and works parallel. The outside one could be government-prompted through initiatives by civil society watch groups, parents and teachers. Codes and guidelines from within could be by channel operators (together and individually), programme producers and journalists. Regulation should not be viewed always as constraining or limiting freedom. These self regulation initiatives also distinguish one media from the other in terms of market stature and professionalism.

The laws of the land are applicable in the functioning of both content and carrier. There have been no new initiatives to regulate contents in the last decade. Thus, it could be said that there is nothing like absolute free media or unfettered freedom anywhere, including in countries having democratic systems. It is in this context that the Supreme Court's landmark judgment of 1995 stated that "airwaves belong to public" and cannot be used for personal profit when it called for an independent regulator. This is even more pertinent now compared to the judgment more than ten years ago. The broadcast scenario in the country has undergone dramatic changes with mushrooming of broadcasters and channels with all kinds of contents. If an independent body could help promote responsibility, standards and self-discipline in broadcasting operations, it should be welcomed.

Keeping the experience of the Press Council of India over the last 45 years, it could be restructured and repositioned with responsibility for the broadcast contents as well. In that case, the TRAI could be fully entrusted with the responsibility related to the carriage issues. When PCI was conceived and constituted, there was neither TV nor any satellite broadcasting. PCI recognises that content issues call for some standards and there should be a provision for redressal of complaints from the public and also from within the media itself. The PCI comes into picture after an individual publication violates basic tenets or when there is a complaint against a newspaper. Pro-active responsibility and affirmative action against blatant violations or excesses are needed more in the case of TV. So, the capability to act and correct in such situations is critical for news broadcasting. Indian newspapers by and large are world class and stand out for quality and self restraints. The same, perhaps, cannot be said about broadcasting as yet. The broadcast regulator should be an empowered and independent body that can help unleash potential and harnesses creative powers of many in the interest of many.

Reforms and Market: No Guarantee

[7]In the wake of economic reforms since 1991 and as a part of that the country has been witnessing globalisation, liberalisation and privatisation in most sectors, including the media. At the outset, certain big media houses formed an informal group and lobbied against "globalisation" involving FDI into media enterprises. However, within a couple of years, they not only welcomed FDI, but also have been since then arguing for higher levels of FDI – from 20 to over 40 per cent and more. As a part of liberalisation, the government has been going along with such demands, like entry of foreign media and higher percentage of FDI. The telecom sector, which has been witnessing globalisation, liberalisation and privatisation, has become an example for media, including the news media. However, while there is a regulator body (TRAI) for the telecom sector, there is no such regulator for media, except that the carriage aspects are "temporarily" entrusted to TRAI. Ever since, the debate has continued for and against an independent regulator for media. However, big media houses have been opposing the move of content being brought under a regulator with an argument that the "market" takes care of such needs. The argument is that TRPs and similar quantitative indicators take care of content adjustments, supplemented by industry sponsored mechanisms like the News Broadcasting Standards Authority.

There are equally forcible arguments from women groups and social activists that such assumptions or mechanisms (of industry) are not good enough and, in fact, have failed to be concerned about societal sensitivities. Their argument has been that "market forces" view will not hold as much in the case of media, particularly in the case of electronic media, where "reversibility" (or undoing of undesirable content) is not possible.

In a landmark observation, a two Judge bench (Justice B Sudershan Reddy and Justice S. S. Nijjar) of the Supreme Court of India noted in May 2011 that "free market" is no solution and guarantee for a welfare State. The Supreme Court noted that "market forces" tend to be useful to a few and, as a consequence, add to inequalities and amount to leaving things of larger public consequence in the control of a few hands. The judgment of the apex court was that "market factors and operations" should be regulated independently, (Army Medical Colleges vs. Delhi Government).

Although the Supreme Court's observations (which were made in the context of reservation in Army Medical College) were not made in the specific context of media, they are relevant here. [8]Former Chief Justice of Supreme Court, Ranganath Misra, had said at a CMS roundtable on Children Television in 1998 that the way the satellite television operates, it implies "undeclared war on unprepared people". Since a broadcast once put out cannot be reversed or its impact undone, the need for an independent regulator is all the more felt (more than one dependent on "market forces"). Even better is a "checks and balance" regime, where different stakeholders try to do better of what is expected of them. This, of course, includes viewers, citizens, entrepreneurs and the market. A national policy enables a holistic growth of the media and also allows it to function as the Fourth Estate.

Endnotes

1 Lakshman Rekha: Discussed earlier. Also see "scribe admits doing unprofessional work" by J Balaji in the Hindu 29 April 2011 http://www.hindu.com/2011/04/29/stories/2011042961940400.htm).

2 "judiciary should not legislate: Somnath Chatterjee", T Ramavarma , 8 August 2005 Www.hindu.com/2005/08/08/stories/20050804161300.htm.

3 Suryaprakash: a senior journalist and editor Pioneer in 2010, http://www.asuryapraksh.com, "India and the media boom" in Think India. Quarterly, January- march 2003

4 Atal Bihari Vajpayee: (**The Hindu at 125,** T.S.SUBRAMANIAN, www.hindu.com/thehindu/thscrip/print.pl?file=20031010005512800.htm&date=fl2020/&prd=fline-14Sept 2003 http://www.hindu.com/2003/09/14/stories/2003091406220100.htm).

5 Two judge bench of Supreme Court in 2005. Justice M. N. Rao refer to Press Council of India annual souvenirs and their site http://www.presscouncil.nic.in

6 Justice A S Anand address at "IPI India Award Function for outstanding work in journalism, 2004" on 6 December, 2004, Delivered at Vigyan Bhawan, New Delhi http://nhrc.nic.in/speeches.htm;

7 Big media bosses formed an informal group to lobby against govt. allowing foreign media into India. This writer was in the loop of these parallays. This informal group Includes Times of India, Hindustan Times, India Today, interestingly in a matter of five years once these media groups had proposals for investment, they took uturn and become advocates of increase In the extent of foreign investment in media establishments. See "private broadcasters decry concessions to DD" in the Hindustan Times. 3 September 2007

8 "CMS round table on children and television", CMS, New Delhi, 21 November 1998.

4

Public Service Broadcasting

Public Service or Public Interest Service

As there is no "National Media Policy", we neither have any thrust nor a holistic view about the growth of the media sector. Because of that, India could not channelise the potential of media to highlight and solve its peculiar basic problems such as social development, poverty and inequalities. All that we could claim and contend with is that as a democratic country we have a "free media". Free media is popularly understood as the one where government interference and legal restrictions on its operations are the least or relatively few. It was not realised that while being free media could play a proactive role in the larger cause of the country or at least with least exploitation or few benefits at the expense of many.

Surprisingly, the role for media was assumed to be that of a "public service" media. The idea of Prasar Bharati, conceived in 1979, envisaged a particular model of broadcasting. That Act came into operation only in 1997; 18 years after Parliament had passed the Act. During this period, the country had gone through dramatic changes related to its economic policies resulting in the beginning of the "market economy". This notion of public service had changed during that period. But the push and pull factors against the concept of "larger good" had come to stay.

The Prasar Bharati[1] Act indicated its primary objective as "organising and conducting public broadcasting service to inform, educate and entertain the public" apart from "safeguarding citizen's right to be informed freely, truthfully and objectively on all matters of public interest". Clearly, more than 30 years ago, the Act envisaged a certain activist role and agenda for broadcasting – All India Radio (AIR) and Doordarshan (DD).

To what extent are DD and AIR operating as autonomous bodies by differentiating themselves from those of government enrolled media requires to be publicly discussed and debated. But based on developments in the broadcasting sector over the years, it is clear that what ultimately matters for any media is content relevance, proactive programme implications, credibility of broadcasters, and transparency in operations.

The question that should have been debated and considered is that such objectives should have to be the concerns of all media and broadcasting as well – as a win-win proposition. The difference could be in the degree or proportion of those elements that are expected of Prasar Bharati outlets. The other feature that should be a concern for all broadcasting (irrespective of origin: public or private or public-private partnership) is the impact or difference that contents or broadcasts make, considering the all pervasive nature of broadcasting, cutting across all socio-economic divides and demographics. Of course, all broadcasters assume and expect that their broadcasts make a difference to their viewers/listeners. But the larger concern is - what kind of difference do broadcasts make, to whom, to whose advantage and what kind of ripples is it causing in the market and society. All broadcast will have ripple effects – immediate and deferred or over time, and directly limited to viewers/listeners and, indirectly on the larger social, economic and education systems. This concern can only be ensured by having a national policy and longitudinal field studies. TRPs are not an indicator of impact. Even as a surrogate, they are misleading.

In India, we had no other type of broadcasting other than as a public service, until the idea of Prasar Bharati was initiated. There was no concept or practice of "other kind" of broadcasting as in the Western countries, where broadcasting concerns included "private", "markets" and "certain interests" as against the interests of the "larger public". Having realised that certain interests or concerns of the "larger public" or long term concerns, were not getting reflected, those countries thought of "public service broadcasting" and certain public trusts went out to support such services. [2]The governments, too, came along to support such initiatives in some cases. Pandit Nehru and Indira Gandhi were both impressed by what public service broadcasting did for children in the US. India went for privatisation of broadcasting much later, after experiencing a single track State controlled broadcasting, (that was how Prasar Bharati objectives were spelled out). We should have had a national policy at the point of opening up the sector for private actors and allowing global satellite broadcasts from all directions. During these periods, there was never any effort for "media literacy" (except in the case of film/cinema, for a while) to enable citizens and civil society to take a serious view of broadcasting contents and be critically discriminative in availing broadcast services. Notwithstanding all those "missing opportunities" to get better broadcasting for the country, it is perhaps not irrelevant to better understand the scenario so that corrective measures could be undertaken at various levels, and realise the nature of government's contradictory decisions.

The Dilemma of Public Service Broadcasting

[3]India has been celebrating November 12th as the Public Service Broadcasting (PSB) Day for some years now. How much concerned are we today about public service broadcasting? PSB cannot be appraised in isolation of the larger broadcast scene in India. There is a misnomer that "public interest" contents cannot maximise viewership and that "commercial viability" is not possible without going for "popular" programmes - irrespective of their public interest. That being a general assumption, there could be three options for content strategy and priorities: (a) Maximise viewership for public interest broadcasts, unconcerned of commercial viability, (b) Maximise viewership so that commercial interests can be served better; unconcerned of public interest, (c) Balance between commercial interest and public interest where popular programming could subsidise public interest programmes or/and make "public interest" programmes in such a way that they, too, become "popular". Or is it that there is nothing like "public interest" separate from "commercial interests"? The intervening factor that dictates the course is the government policy towards broadcasting. For example, if the government is serious about PSB, community radio scheme should not have remained dormant.[4]

At the end of 10 years of a policy, hardly two hundred community radio stations are in operation out of several times more applications from across India. Even their license is not regularized. The priority has been "commercial broadcasting". More than hundred FM broadcasts have come into operation during the same period, as if generating funds from auction was the main motto of the government.

AIR Model!

[5]AIR has set good benchmark about what PSB should be all about. AIR has been offering information, entertainment, culture and motivation and targeting different sections of the society. It has adapted to changing

times with commercial broadcasting service (CBS) and opening up its channels for advertising. The difference then and now is that AIR service was not looked upon as a source of revenue. If "airwaves belong to public", as advised by the Supreme Court in 1995, their use cannot be "primarily" for the "private gain" for a few. Going by that norm, broadcasters have to cater to public service as a responsibility and obligation. The government could prescribe a minimum level for such concerns and contents.

The role of PSB becomes even more important where socio-economic inequalities within the country are glaring. It means that the concern should be not only reaching out but also special concern for the poor and disadvantaged. The trend of privatisation of government funded bodies should not be extended to Prasar Bharati as Yojana Bhawan and North Block have been mooting in the recent years – from a limited perspective.

Public Interest and Popularity Concern – Are They Same?

What is "public interest"? Is it the same as what interests the larger public at a particular point of time and also "in their interest"? Not necessarily. More often, in a competitive scenario, as broadcasters have to "attract" viewers/listeners, they go more for what interests the public. In fact, channels do so constantly. "Popularity" should not be mixed up with "public interest"; even more so in the context of visual media. All broadcasters should have public service concern and programmes even in a competitive situation, but it is the degree of concern for public service or the extent of such contents that matters. Otherwise, every broadcaster would claim that he is serving the public. Some may describe the extent of coverage of "public interest" by the time devoted and others by the importance or significance of certain programmes.

The TRP system is the villain of in PSB scene. Measuring viewership programme-wise and region–wise day in and day out has become the criteria for popularity, not impact. Since this has become the sole yardstick for advertising outlays, all broadcasters/channels have succumbed to such a benchmark. It's so because going beyond the original objective for which TRP was evolved, it has become the basis for content priorities.

The concern should be about implications and impact of broadcasting. This also means recognising the fact that broadcasting could influence people, and change their attitudes, motivations, values and lifestyles.

That is why advertisers do so much research and spend so much for TRPs and that is how TRP system ended up being advertising centric, because the advertising agencies were sponsoring it.

Can something become "popular, without being liked"? Yes, a programme could be instantly popular in terms of TRP because of sex or some such scenes (or lures), for example, without being liked in retrospective or in a serious view (after viewing some such contents!).

Policy Contradictions – Denunciating PSB!

Expecting Doordarshan to be a "Public Service Broadcaster" in isolation of the broadcast scene and without any restraints on the part of government's *laissez faire* policy for channels is an unworkable and unfair proposition. The Public Service Broadcaster cannot be left at the mercy of market forces or expected to fight an unequal competition and with irrelevant and pro-market benchmarks. Adding to this basic contradiction in the government policy on broadcasting is the issue of not assuring Prasar Bharati budgetary requirement as a long term commitment. Any such budgetary commitment for PSB has to be assured irrespective of which political party is in power.

All broadcast channels should be obligated for certain "minimum public service" standards in their programme contents. Such obligations could be in terms of time devoted to community interests (as determined by channel), in the interests of children and vulnerable sections by way of ensuring pluralism in debates and discussions, response to public grievances, and having an internal mechanism for transparency and public disclosure of minimum information about the channel.

At least three conditions are expected to ensure that a PSB remains so. But does the government want a PSB today? If so, is it ensuring these conditions? The first and foremost condition is guaranteed funding (as an obligation, not as a dole/allowance) that is adequate to meet its objectives in a competitive market. The second is independence in terms of organisational structure, operation and programme priorities. The third is the accountability to larger "public" (Parliament and other such bodies) and certain transparency in that process. A set of public service concerns related to "national issues" (not necessarily of the government's) like communicable diseases, literacy, vocational education, Right to Information, minimum wage, etc. should be identified for all broadcasters (not just for PSB). Also, certain sections of people like children, farmers should be identified for special programmes. The idea of a "Universal Service Obligation" (USO) as a policy need not be limited to telecom services. It is more relevant in mass media, more specifically television and satellite broadcasting. If the government could think of using the funds available under USO for free cell phones to BPL households, why not some such funding could be ensured for public service concerns of channels, particularly news channels.

Prasar Bharati or whoever is making such ad hoc decisions on its behalf does not bother to learn from past mistakes. Most of the satellite channels had initially reached television households riding on DD channels. [6]These private broadcasters are now trying to create another revenue stream for themselves by using DD's infrastructure and software. For the private satellite channels acquiring time slots on DD could be very beneficial. A few years ago, I lamented Prasar Bharati's decision to auction its prime time slots to private broadcasters and content producers. Doordarshan announced its plans to auction not only evening prime time slots but also slots in the morning segment. Given that the growth of the satellite channels was at the cost of DD's viewership, CMS claimed that these moves by Prasar Bharati not only conflict with its role as a public broadcaster but also a sure way of demolishing the public broadcaster. The idea of auctioning channels amounts to hijacking Doordarshan. It was a very short sighted approach that further demoralised its staff. It was a conspiracy to demolish DD and wind up whatever was left of PSB in India.

Prasar Bharati – Who holds it?

In India, none of the three basic criteria necessary for PSB have been met, not even the easiest one, i.e., constituting a functional board for Prasar Bharati. Having formed Prasar Bharati as a public corporation, the government has never reconciled to the fact that it is supposed to operate with some independence and financial commitment. In both respects, the government has let down Prasar Bharati. On the issue of finance, the government has shown its neglect of public service by amending Prasar Bharati to "earn from the market", in competition with other broadcasters but operating without any government control and obligations. There has been much indecisiveness and inconsistencies in the government's decisions on broadcasting. When the problem is with broadcaster or content supplier, the government will be after the cable operators. The government should view budgetary allocation for Prasar Bharati from consolidated fund in the same way as in the case of allocations for education, drinking water or irrigation. The government should fund research, especially for reaching the unreached, as a part of the universal obligation principle. As we have for telecom sector, there should be "Universal Service Obligation" on the part of all broadcasters and compliance should be monitored and reported to the public.

The Tasks

As Sevanti Ninan[7] a veteran columnist on media matters wrote in *The Mint* on September 20, 2012, "India desperately needs a quality public service broadcaster". Commenting on a Cabinet approval for financial restructuring for Prasar Bharati (writing off of Rs.1300 crore debt and agree to meet hundred percent of salary costs for the next five years), she further wrote "what has been done for Prasar Bharati... is no more than applying an adhesive bandage to stop bleeding". If it took almost two decades for the government to come to an understanding for a public broadcaster, what more can we expect in support of the idea of a public broadcaster in the changed scenario?

The concern for PSB should not be limited to Prasar Bharati. The government should ease the procedures for setting up community radio and make that a viable proposition. Every broadcaster should do some extent of PSB as an obligation. The extent of dependence on ads needs to be moderated, both in the case of Prasar Bharati and other broadcasters. All broadcasters should observe certain accountability discipline and transparency obligations. An independent commission or regulator should be entrusted with the responsibility of a nodal agency to regulate broadcasting services – both within and outside. Decentralised broadcasting is better for PSB and yet Prasar Bharati went for DTH, which is supportive of centralised broadcasting. Prasar Bharati should be assured of funding as annual budgetary provision; it cannot be expected to be viable otherwise. There should be specific monitoring and time series research studies and series of independent research studies should be annually assigned to professional groups. Sources for funding PSB should not be limited to the government, and the public and industry should also be mobilised. A more proactive Board for Prasar Bharati is even more urgent and it should have professional HRD policies.

In its study,[8] "Vision and Mission for Prasar Bharati", the CMS has advocated a long-term view rather than a short sighted one for Doordarshan and pleaded for maximisation of the potential that it could do for larger public as well as specific public. "Revenue at any cost cannot be DD's model. It is funded by the public and, thus, it should necessarily make decisions keeping the interests of the larger public." DD's strength lies in its unrivaled reach and extensive infrastructure built over the years. The fact that DD could not showcase it is a different matter.

In 2001, Doordarshan dropped from its schedules, the school specific educational programs including the UGC (University Grants Commission) and IGNOU (Indira Gandhi National Open University) classes, as if the country had accomplished the goals.

Endnotes

1 The Prasar Bharati, although was set up by an act of Parliament in 1990 as an autonomous body, its employees continued on govt. pay roll and since it had to depend on govt. for most or significant part of its budget, It continued to function sometimes under direct control of the ministry or mostly by remote control. Both Doordarshan and All India Radio under Prasar Bharati continued to be viewed as of "govt. Media". With unleash of private channels operating under liberal conditions, Prasar Bharati arrangement was more a restraint on Doordarshan and AIR to compete in the market. Besides, the govt. pushing Prasar Bharati to earn from market and curtail budgetary grants restrained its potential as a public service broadcaster. In fact, the big Indian private media lobbied for govt. with drawing support of all kind to Doordarshan. See the Hindustan Times, 3 September 2007.

2 Public service broadcasting in United States (started with an experiment in Boston in 1960). Operating as an independent nonprofit broadcaster with support from corporate outfits like Ford foundation, its program structure and priorities impressed with In and outside USA all those who loved democracy. It could become a bench mark for objectivity and credibility among people. Its children's programs like **Sesame Street** were acclaimed world over and continued for decades. Impressed by this model **Pandit Jawahar Lal Nehru** took to experiment television in India with Krishidarshan, taking cue from rural radio forums experiment a few years earlier around Pune, has further convinced Nehru that public service broadcasting should become a policy. "Krishidarshan" continued with Doordarshan for years and lead to many regional channels taking to similar such program catering to farm community. A daily feature of ETV Telugu, Jaikisan, too has in turn become good example for public service broadcasting and a model for many other news channels.

3 November 12, on this day in 1947 Mahatma Gandhi visited Akashi Vani Bhavan or Broadcast House, headquarters of All India Radio, and addressed the nation over radio first time. Since Gandhi's life is a message for public it was decided to commemorate the day as public service broadcast day. That was how it was declared in 1997. For some reason television was not viewed at par with radio

at that time. Since television was no where around when Gandhi visited Akashi vani Bhavan, it was perhaps not clubbed with radio in viewing it as public service broadcaster.

4 Community radio are operated by local communities or by nonprofit organisations for development support. They are not allowed to broadcast news, other than relay of All India Radio News. Even after almost a decade of debate govt. could not decide about allowing news broadcasts. India has 196 community radio operating as of July 2016. They are permitted under a five year agreement after a lengthy process of approval by more than a couple of ministries. Although TRAI in 2014 came up with guidelines for renewal, govt. has been giving temporary extension of the permission putting community stations in uncertainty.

5 AIR model. Unlike the content model of news television channels which is copied or adopted from USA model of broadcasting, All India Radio model is something evolved with in the country keeping unique national needs, strengths and aspirations. This is based on clear understanding that state has responsibility to inform larger public and nurture cultural heritage and promote creative talents of people. Initially news were broadcast thrice a day and later hourly headlines were added. AIR news bulletins enjoyed highest credibility for decades. Commercial service was introduced years later more on request of advertisers. This writer opposed the idea of television going for American model of advertising by proposing an alternative of not allowing brand based advertising of consumer goods and services. This writer and Nandlal Chawla committee of the ministry (1975-7) submitted a dissent note In this regard, supported by then deputy minister Dharma Vir Sinha. Succumbing to pressures of Mumbai then minister V. C. Shukla opened flood gates of television for advertising of all kind initially even without time ceiling.

6 Private broadcasting In India had took off out of state run AIR and Doordarshan in many respects, it was people who ventured into private television and later private radio were initially from AIR and DD. They even continued with programs with which they were associated earlier and built up their identities. Aaj Tak, and NDTV are only two examples.

7 Sevanti Ninan. Mint,.20 September 2012

8 "Vision and mission for India's public broadcasting.: Prasar Bharati Corporation", by Dr N Bhaskara Rao, Aditi Chatterjee, and P N Vasanti, CMS, New Delhi, 2000.

Section II
The Idea of 24x7 "News Channels"

This section Tracking of trend in the growth of news channels and the content preoccupation of round-the-clock news channels during the decade brings out how they could not put together a original content model. Can news channels get out of the TRP psyche and explore an alternative? Not able to achieve headway, news channels recruits are now on the lookout for new content initiatives and repositioning options. In an anxiety to refurbish, channels tend to take to new instruments such as awards, though in a constrained way. Awards, of course, have a role. They should be for differentiating and promoting good (from not-so-good) practices and initiatives. Basic criteria for appraising news channels are looked into in the context of society as against markets, ways of going about in the competitive context and in search of viability of channels.

5

The Scene of News Channels

Introduction

The years between 1995 and 2010 witnessed unprecedented growth and changes in the Indian media scene – both qualitatively and quantitatively.[1] The media scene went through structural changes as a result of this growth and proliferation. The larger socio-economic-political scenario too added to these changes. This change happened due to the gearing up of news channels to reach out and cover happenings competitively, faster and with field footage. The competition with which news channels started covering certain curiosity or interest generating content also helped this process.

This proliferation has been within each and across mass media. There is no parallel in the world for this kind of dramatic spurt and change in the media scene. And one of the significant structural changes has been the emergence of television as a news media from being primarily an entertainment media until around 2000.

Licensed Channels of Various Genre (2011)

Channels (categories)	No. of Channels	N %
Entertainment	172	37.55
Education/knowledge	10	2.18
Lifestyle	4	0.87
Music	39	8.52
Movies	41	8.95
News	134	29.26
Sports	12	2.62
Kids	19	4.15
Health	3	0.66
Religious	22	4.80
Others	2	0.44
Total	**458**	**100.00**

Source : CMS Media Lab

Against one TV channel (Doordarshan) with one or two news bulletins a day 25 years ago, there were 39 news channels in the country in December 2005. By March 2011, this number rose to 137 (excluding BBC, CNN and other foreign channels), each with round-the-clock news in one form or the other and half-an-hour "news bulletins". Also, some non-news channels (general entertainment) too have two-three news bulletins per day.

While the news scenario earlier was dominated by English language newspapers, it is the Indian language ones that continue to proliferate now (including in the case of television). News channels are there in every major Indian language (in 14 different languages). In fact, the growth and proliferation in TV, particularly news channels, has come from regional languages particularly in South Indian Languages. There are certain regional languages where the number of news channels is as high as the number of general entertainment channels. There are more than 15 news channels and 18 GECs in Telugu. Kerala, with 33 million population, has more than 10 news channels and nearly twice as many entertainment channels, some of them with two or three news bulletins daily.

News channels have received further boost with their active role in covering party politics, elections, political controversies and corruption. The kind of political uncertainty the country is experiencing in the last decade has contributed to TV emerging as the "primary source" of news. Overall, news channels were one-third of all channels by the end of 2012. The model being followed by 24-hour news channels has been going through shifts in priorities and changes in structure. The national news scene in the case of TV is dominated by Delhi-based Hindi channels. With over 135 million TV homes and well over 500 million weekly viewers, the potential of 24-hour news channels is mind boggling in many contexts – political, social, markets. But the share of news channels in the total viewing of channels of all genres is much below expectations – less than two per cent in 2000 when there were only nine news channels. Increase in news channels has added to the overall viewership. But why so many news channels have not changed the course of TV in India?

Year	Number of news channels	Share of news channels viewing in the total TV viewing
2000	9	1.19
2003	23	-
2004	-	6.38
2005	39	
2008	67	8.70
2010	122	7.69
2011	137	-

Source: TAM, 4+years, all India

One reason for the spurt in the number of news channels permitted during 2010-11 was increase in net worth requirement for registration with I&B Ministry from Rs. 3 crore to Rs. 20 crore. All kinds of people applied for permission before that. Although there are more than 400 permitted or registered news channels as on January 2012, the ones TAM included for its analysis are only those in operation, which is less than 150. There are some who took permission from the ministry as a news channel more for "hoarding" and waiting for an "opportunity". One-third or more of those who got permission but are not operating are those who are already in the news business; many of them are running newspapers, channels, radio and new media ventures. [2]According to the TRAI, 825 applications for operating all kind of channels were approved by the ministry as of March 2012 but only around 670 are actually operating.

Emergence of Television as a News Media

Language-wise Total Channels Permitted in 2011

Channels (categories)	Number of total channels permitted	Number of news channels permitted
English	77	24
Hindi	79	108
Bengali	28	22
Gujarati	9	5
Kannada	30	16
Malayalam	40	16
Marathi	11	15
Oriya	14	9
Punjabi	37	5
Tamil	38	31
Telugu	35	39
Urdu	17	3
Assamese	8	5
Bhojpuri	5	3

**Some news channels permitted by the government are in multi languages; Not all these are in operation.*

Because of round-the-lock news channels nationally and regionally and their live coverage potential, television today has emerged as a primary source of news. Nevertheless, newspapers remain a serious and more credible source of news, as tracking studies by CMS have brought out. Interestingly, these studies have brought out the "appetizer effect" of news channels. That is, the one who watches news bulletins on TV is more likely to read newspapers. It implies, contrary to general perception, that proliferation of news channels has helped newspapers to consolidate and grow both vertically and horizontally. This trend in the growth of newspapers was corroborated first in 2005 by two national surveys, NRS and IRS. Some increase in the circulation of newspapers and viewership of channels is more because of multiplicity, and not so much because of expansion of their reach. The ones watching TV are watching more channels or programmes, and the ones reading are reading more newspapers. No wonder then that multiplicity of news channels has not led to increased viewing of TV news nor has it led to any decline in reading newspapers though there is a decline in the time spent on reading. Also, the duration of viewing TV news on an average day has declined in metros. This trend was indicated in viewership surveys. Thus, "growth" does not necessarily imply "expansion" by way of reaching (new) unreached ones.

CMS studies are the years indicate that television is the most potential media is known. But that it can change the very mindset of people and their priorities has been realised too. News channels not only set an agenda for the nation but also change the very course and direction of the State and public discourse. Television can change the face of the country in so many ways for better or worse, depending on the specific efforts made to moderate such a potential.

When round-the-clock news channels started proliferating after 2000, there was a hope that India would soon enter information age and become a knowledge society much faster, cutting across the divides in the country. There was a hope that these news channels would help bring people closer; citizens would become more sensitive to their neighborhoods; and level playing opportunities would be more. It is now more than a decade since the boom of news channels. To what extent have they helped that process? They did, but with ifs and buts and not commensurately in many respects. On the contrary, a feeling is gaining ground that more news channels are perhaps not necessarily merrier. More news channels could mean more problems, more conflicts and more deviant behavior, because concerns and priorities of news channels, by and large, are not sensitive enough and channels themselves have not fully realised their own potential and opportunities until the arrival of Anna Hazare at Delhi's Jantar Mantar in July 2011 and [3]Amir Khan's *Satyamev Jayate* in 2012. Until then, there were not many instances of news channels unleashing their potential at macro level. Even then, it could be said that not all news channels were seen distinguishing themselves from entertainment ones as well as from each other.

Competition between media (newspapers and TV) and within each media (between channels) has given boost to numbers, expanded the scope of media, opened new vistas and potential for further growth of mass media. However, the same thing cannot be said about the overall credibility of news media. Thanks to 24-hour news channels, credibility of newspapers has gone up, though marginally. News channels, on the other hand, have not improved their credibility or commensurately increased overall reach or expanded as one had expected. The increase was more sporadic in nature and not conducive to realise full potential. This is perhaps because of their pre-occupation with the subject matter of coverage, orientation, practices such as scrolling, structure of programmes, repeat and restricted sphere of coverage. Nevertheless, channels have emerged as the primary source for news and current affairs, without eroding the importance of newspapers as it is happening in some countries. In the initial period, TV news bulletins were guided more by the contents of newspapers, but of late the trend has turned the other way round. Together, newspapers and news channels set the public agenda – regionally and nationally – for politics, Parliament, government and the market. The contents of news media in some respects influence market and reflect the mood of the nation, concerns of policymakers, and priorities of government.

News channels are expected to be concerned about expanding the scope of coverage and viewership of news bulletins, increase pro-activeness and make a distinct difference. The four parameters in this regard are: origin of news, concern as evident from the subject matter of content covered, extent of certain news reports, scope of coverage as news or features and participation or inclusiveness in reflecting the viewpoints or engaging people. To understand these trends, since the past seven years the [4]CMS Media Lab has been tracking news media every day for its content and doing analysis of the same. In case of TV news, bulletins of major "national" channels are recorded every day and contents are analysed by news analysts. While contents of DD News, NDTV 24x7, Aaj Tak, Zee News, Star News (ABP News) and CNN-IBN are being analysed for the past seven years, some four to 16 Telugu news channels are also being analysed for the past five years. Besides, some other news channels/ news bulletins are also being analysed for shorter period.

October 2004

DD NEWS CHANNEL IS ONE-YEAR-OLD, LONG WAY TO GO AS A NATIONAL CHANNEL SO ALSO OTHER NEWS CHANNELS

Doordarshan News channel in its present avatar completes one year this month. As a 24-hour national news channel, it stands out for its overall performance. But bulletins of none of the news channels, including DD News, distinguish themselves as representative of India. An analysis of seven news channels for their contents brings out this fact. The extent of coverage of rural India, even in the case of DD, is limited. This has been much below two per cent of items in a week across news channels. In fact, about half of the items of news bulletins, including DD News, are from Delhi and Mumbai. DD News lags in terms of fineness in production quality and transmission at the receiving end in case of cable TV households.

The 24-hour news channel of DD came up in November 2003 rather abruptly in place of its then popular Metro channel. The earlier DD News channel was closed in January 2002, 18 months after it came into being without a convincing explanation. NDTV/STAR (April 2003), Sahara News (March 2003), Aaj Tak (December 2000) and Zee News (1995) had been there for longer period than DD News. Last couple of years has witnessed hectic activities on political and economic front to enable news media to catch up and prove its mettle. Despite uncertain support and ambiguous policies, DD News channel did better than what many critics expected at the outset. DD News channel witnessed certain "revamps" in terms of people manning the channel. But operations remained at the mercy of the ministry. DD was thrown into a competitive mode in the "market place". That is how I supported the amendment to Cable TV Regulation Act, making it obligatory for cable TV operators to show DD News. It could not have withstood competitive compulsions in the case of cable TV households without such an intervention. Aaj Tak, NDTV and Star News channels came into being as brand names riding initially on DD's shoulders. In fact, these news channels owe their origin to DD. Also, the best of names associated with TV news in India were DD's discoveries.

Coverage of the Prime Minister's initial formal press conference corrects a general impression that DD News has a bias in favour of the party in power. An analysis of PM's press conference by different news channels brings out that DD News did nothing. On the contrary,

Star and NDTV did better coverage of PM's press conference by way of follow up discussions. DD, on the other, did relatively less coverage in the subsequent half an hour bulletins and it hardly had any follow up analysis. If DD News could maintain such a restraint, it should be able to get rid of certain "hangover of the past". Also, more recently, DD has come out of a trap of "spin gaming" that every time the country goes to polls as an opportunity for TRPs, commercial revenue and filling time chunks. Instead, it rightly chose "simple analysis" as a common denominator approach. Display of prices of basic commodities should have been done long ago. Initiatives like that are never too late to take on. More such initiatives are needed on the part of DD as a public service broadcaster.

News channels are expected to be concerned in their coverage about at least four parameters. Such a concern is expected to expand the scope of news coverage and viewership of news bulletins much beyond the present levels. The four parameters are: origin of news, concern as evident from subject matter of contents, extent of repeat of certain news, and scope of coverage as news or features. Contrary to general impression and claims by some channels, DD News fared relatively better. Although 40 per cent of news items of DD News bulletins are Delhi-originated, against 37 per cent of other news channels, in terms of spread of news coverage across India DD does better. For example, little over 10 per cent of news items in DD originate from Kolkata and Chennai, as against hardly a couple of per cent in the case of other news channels. Half or more of news bulletins of national channels cannot be from Delhi and Mumbai month after month. Coverage of rural India by all news channels, including DD, has been a casual affair, as if to remind viewers that they are "national channel". Hardly one per cent of news items in the bulletins of various channels are from rural areas. 90 per cent of Budget coverage by channels in July-August, 2004 was limited to Delhi. Even at times like elections (national and state), the coverage from rural areas does not cross three per cent against seven per cent crime related news. In the case of DD News, however, only two per cent of news items are on crime. The extent of items in the news bulletins from abroad has been far higher, next only to Delhi. About one-fifth of items in the bulletins are from abroad, one-fifth of them are India related. Certain shift in news coverage in favour of business and sports is striking.

Even as to the subject matter of news items covered by round-the-clock news bulletins, the range has been limited, which explains why the "penetration of TV" in general and news channels in particular have remained stagnant in the last one year. The preoccupation with politics of news channels is more than that of the newspapers as is evident from [5]CMS Media Lab analysis. DD News, however, devotes only a quarter of items of its bulletins for politics, against about 33 per cent by other TV news channels. Despite proliferation of channels and intense competition, their overall coverage of India has not expanded beyond what it was earlier in terms of news origination or subject focus. On the contrary, certain hype and trivialisation in the coverage has been too obvious and in the process, the very definition of news has changed. But technical quality and designing elements have come a long way, so also in terms of anchoring and interactivity.

News channels have of late been under hype in their coverage of certain items much beyond their relevance or significance as if it is a misperception that such coverage earns TRPs. These channels seem to have not realised that their very credibility over the time is getting eroded as an analysis of CMS study has recently brought out. Despite so many news channels and round-the-clock bulletins, TV news is being viewed as an "appetizer" for prompting newspaper readership. That is, the more one sees news channels, the more likely they are to read newspapers. That is how newspapers have recently proliferated and improved readership more where TV viewership has been higher.

There is an urgent need to revisit the basic tenets of public service broadcasting. DD must cater to larger majority of the Indian audience. This means going much beyond cities. DD and AIR, put together, have far more field reporters across the country to ensure such a balance. Doordarshan and AIR are facing challenges on several fronts. These include financial sustainability, human resource development and deployment, marketing and positioning of the news channel. To be able to meet these challenges and make the most of new opportunities that technology brings in, it is far more important for Prasar Bharati to operate as a corporate entity and professonalise the organisation. For this the government should ensure financial support as annual "budgetary grant". Some serious efforts have been made in this direction recently.

What is lacking with AIR or DD to become global players, except perhaps a vision and mission and sustained support? An ad hoc view of broadcasting by successive regime during the past 30 years has let down these national institutes despite their unique role and immense potential. In fact, sometimes one gets the feeling that DD is being sabotaged, wittingly or unwittingly. Unless we have a vision first about broadcasting in its various forms and an understanding of changing global scene in this regard, right kind of initiatives cannot be expected. Towards this end, CMS had brought out a publication "Vision and Mission for Prasar Bharati" a couple of years ago.

Also, DD needs to get out of the trap that "TRP culture" implies for a public service broadcaster. In that process DD has converted itself from being a "pro-active" institute into a "reactive" one. An irrelevant TRP system has misled the priorities of not only DD but also other news channels. Unlike other channels, DD has remained passive until recently. The TRP system has suppressed the real viewership to DD using an inadequate and faulty research methodology and tools. "Readership Surveys" have done similarly in the case of AIR over the years.

Subject Categories of News Bulletins

Politics, sports, crime, law and order and markets - these five categories together account for nearly two-thirds of bulletin items of 24-hour news channels. Coverage of rural India by news channels has been a casual affair, as if just to remind viewers that they are "national". Even in terms of subject matter of news items covered by round-the-clock news bulletins, the range has been limited, which perhaps explains why viewership of news channels has not increased much in the last couple of years. Despite proliferation of channels and intense competition, their overall coverage of India during these years has not changed much with increase in channels and competition in terms of concerns, news origination and subject focus.

[6]In its analysis in 2007, based on a three years trend, CMS announced "Trivia eclipses political dominance in TV news" because political preoccupation of news bulletins had came down from 23 per cent in 2005 to 11 per cent in 2007. But with proliferation of news channels, content on political parties/ leaders went up to nearly 30 per cent in 2012. Same thing could be said about the extent of coverage of crime after a decline to about 5 per cent in 2008 it was 7 per cent in 2012. Between 2005 and 2012, the extent of coverage of basic needs and

development put together never crossed 5 per cent; in fact, it came down from 3 per cent in 2005 to 2 per cent in 2012.

Hardly 2 per cent (2012) of "prime time" news bulletins' content is about health, education, agriculture, development, welfare and environment. One-third or more of the news items of national channels continue to focus on politicians and party politics. News channels' preoccupation with politics is even more than the newspapers. This trend is at the root of news channels pampering politicians and vice-a-versa. Such a trend cannot be said to be consistent with democratic practices. No wonder the "Fourth Estate" stature of news media is being increasingly questioned of late. "More of the same" phenomenon in the contents of news media, particularly in the case of news channels is too obvious more recently, as if plurality and diversity features of democracy are under threat.

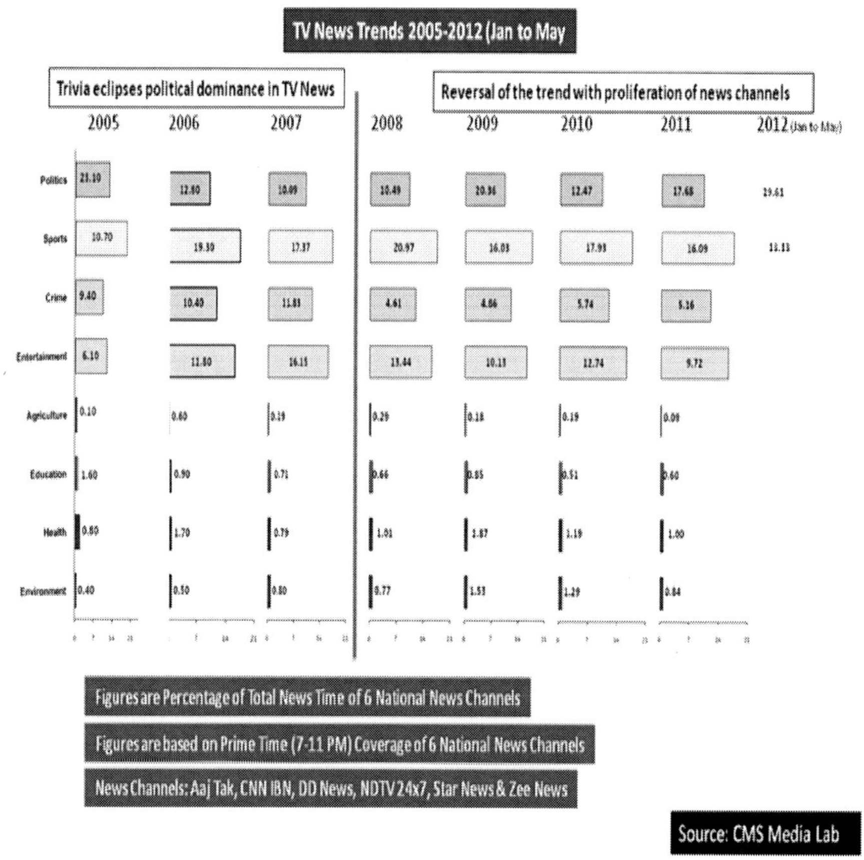

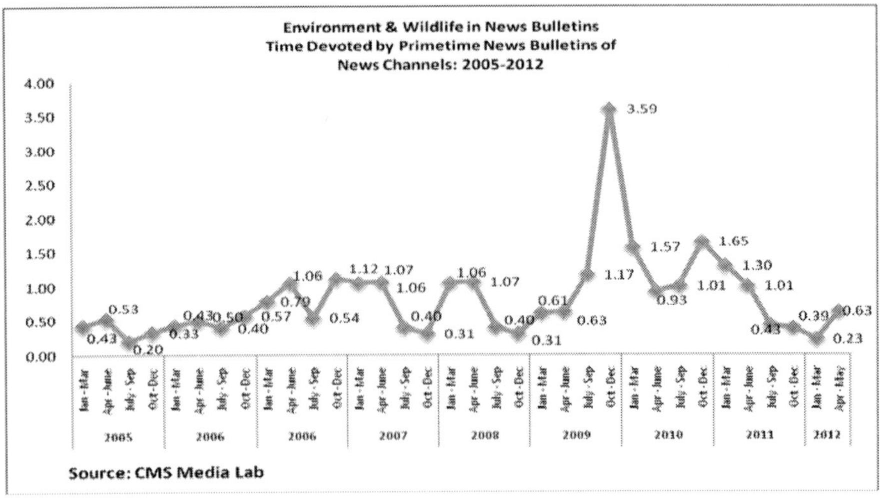

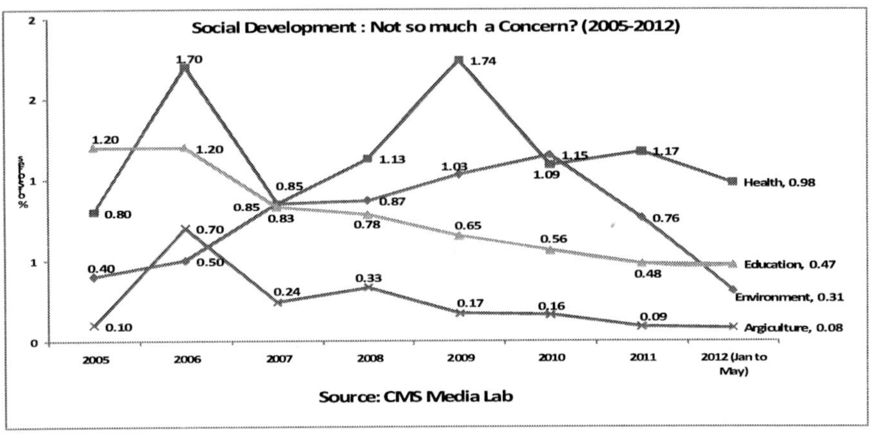

Regional language channels, however, have somewhat saved the situation. For, their news bulletins reflect concerns of grassroots far more and far better, but nowhere near the extent of what is expected of them. More than half of TV news originates from the four metros and the state capitals. In fact, more than one-third of stories of "national" channels are from Delhi, which happens to be the headquarters of these channels. This is because laws of economics dominate or determine priorities of news media. It is more economical to dole out more of the same and cater to the same viewers, where the ones already informed get informed more.

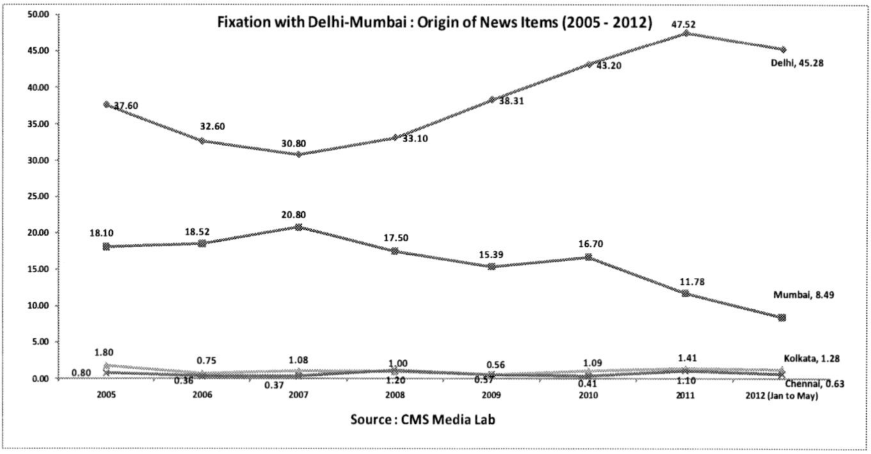

Fixation with Delhi-Mumbai : Origin of News Items (2005 - 2012)

Source : CMS Media Lab

Interestingly, international news in the last couple of years was never below five per cent, but could be as high as 16 per cent. But rural coverage in the bulletins, on the other hand, was mostly around one per cent as if it was a fixed quota and nothing more or beyond happens in rural India. In fact, most of that covered is politics, elections, crime, tragedies/ accidents and crime or deviant behaviors - even in the case of Doordarshan news bulletins. Similarly, the extent of coverage originating from the four metro cities and state capital was also almost same - around 55 per cent of total news bulletin stories and it could be more some days.

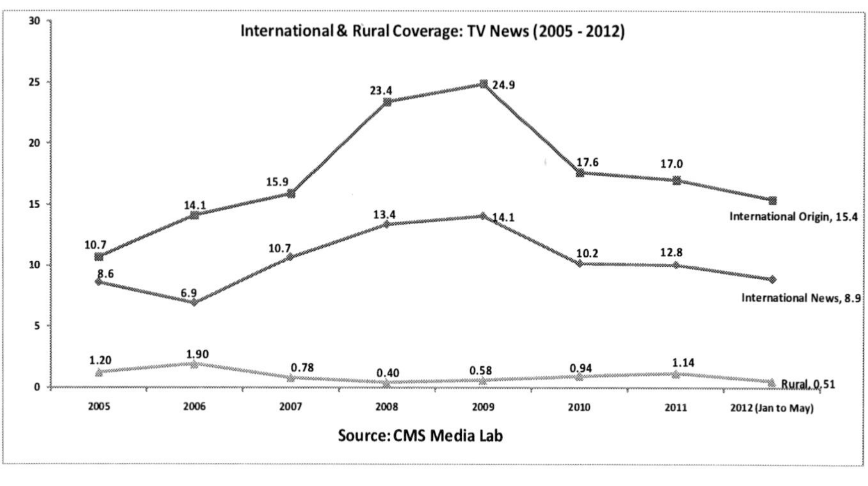

International & Rural Coverage: TV News (2005 - 2012)

Source: CMS Media Lab

Repeats/Fresh Stories

Theoretically, the extent of repeats of items in news bulletins of round-the-clock news channels should have come down with the increase in the number of news channels and increased competition between these channels. But that has not been the case so far. On the contrary, the share of actual news items of "24 hour news channels" has been on decline with their taking to "other programmes" in an effort to expand viewership and sustain interest in news channels. As a result, hardly 10 hours of 24-hour news channels are devoted to news and out of this hardly four hours cover "fresh news" of the day – not counting the extent of repeat of visuals within the same bulletin and of the same story and "file" or "library" footage (with or without acknowledging). Then, bulletins no longer have news only, but the extent of views, features and lifestyle stories has increased. That is the overall picture on an average day with "hard news" constituting hardly 90 minutes in a 24-hour news channel spread across the day. It is the bottom line scrolling constantly or the tickers with "flash" or "update", or "Breaking News" and "live coverage", which distinguish them as "news channels". (The graph is given only for 2003-05 more to indicate the extent of repeats).

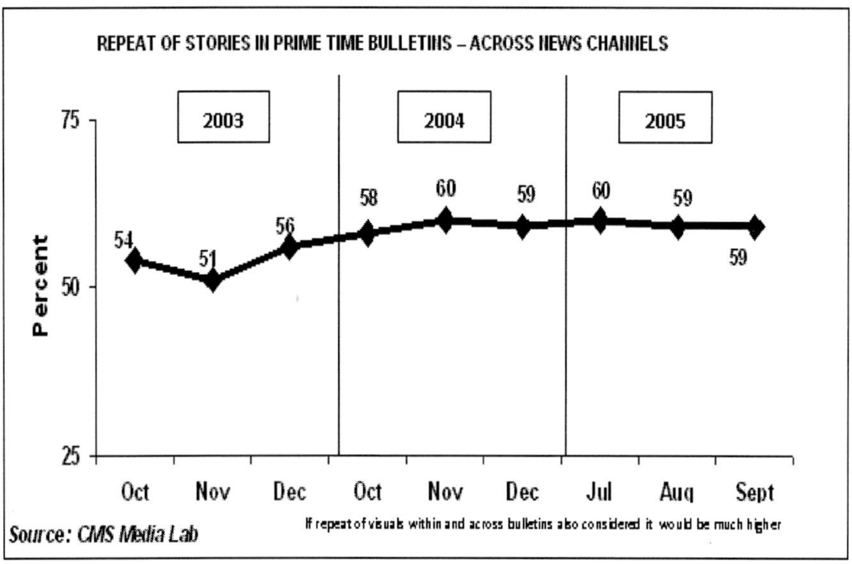

Yet, extensive repeat of the same news in the news bulletins of round-the-clock news channels gives the impression that nothing important is happening in the countryside and across. Limitations of TV (cost, logistics, time, technology) as a news medium are setting the criteria for what is news of the day and their priorities in the presentation of news bulletins are often misleading. Now, newspapers are trying to emulate and compete with TV news channels. When is India going to have a more reflective, more democratic, more representative and inclusive news agenda, catering to the "needs" of the socio-economic features of the country? As one expert commented recently, some news channels are converting themselves into crime (promoting) channels during late nights. In the process, news values and priorities are becoming more and more contentious, without any restraint on hyping and repeating gory visuals, even though they have nothing to do with the news of the day. There are also calls for specific regulations, both from within and outside, including the government.

Content Model of News Channels

Overall, with the onset of 24x7 news channels more than a decade ago, the "news" content has come down to less than half of the telecast time. The remaining telecast time in this model is being used for non-news content, some of them in the garb of news and current affairs, and others having little to do with hard news of the day or week. This trend is significant, as it indicates that 24x7 channel idea may not be viable with a couple of news channels as an exception, unless there are agitations led by Anna Hazare or Ramdev or a political crisis saga is on. This is somewhat the chicken and egg syndrome, where the kind of 'news' provided and the way in which it is provided is not attracting more viewers (despite being the primary source), and in a sustained way. As a result, commercial revenue of news channels is not increasing proportionately, and whatever allocations are there now have to be distributed between increasing number of news channels. This trend is already being realised, though it has not stopped more news channels to open shop.

Viewership Issues

The proliferation of channels did not significantly increase viewership between 2006 and 2010 though during this period the number of news channels tripled; rather, viewership declined in some instances. The year 2008 saw a marked decline in news channel viewership when regional news channels saved the situation. Viewership pertaining to English news channels declined even more, whereas increase in viewership for regional news channels was more during the same period. Even Hindi news channels did not gain viewership, as Hindi general entertainment channels (GEC) did during the period. Various rounds of national and international cricket were supposed to have increased the sale of TV sets in the country. But that did not increase and sustain the overall viewership. In fact, the share of viewership pertaining to news channels declined between 2006 and 2010 in the overall TV viewership even going by TAM.

Viewership share of news channels in the total viewership to all channels All India Market – 2006-2010

	2006	2007	2008	2009	2010
English News	0.5	0.7	0.6	0.4	0.3
Hindi News	4.5	4.8	4.8	3.6	3.4
Regional News	1.7	2.4	2.7	3.6	3.6
Business News	0.5	0.5	0.5	0.3	0.3
Sports	3.8	3.2	3.3	2.8	2.9
Hindi Movies	10.5	10.5	11.6	11.7	11.4
Hindi GEC	23.0	22.6	23.2	26.9	29.6
Regional Movies	5.2	4.7	4.6	3.9	3.4
Regional GEC	26.6	25.6	24.8	24.3	22.9
Kids	5.8	5.9	5.4	5.8	6.3

Source: TAM 4 Years- All India Market

Government Policies

There are no specific new (or old) regulations that have been made in the wake of proliferation of public and private news channel, except what has been provided in the Cable TV Regulation Act of 1995-1997, which are only broad guidelines that make no difference to actual operations or priorities of news bulletins. One of the guidelines is that there should be no derogatory coverage of countries friendly to India (as if there are permanent friends). Down-linking policy (November 2005) made it obligatory for channels to register, declare revenue and pay a one-time fee to the government. The FDI into news channels has been pegged at 26 per cent as against 46 per cent in case of other TV channels, and

26 per cent for newspapers. Nevertheless, there have been periodic demands from political leaders when the coverage has not been suitable for them to call for restraint on the news media. Reflecting on such demands, minister after minister has hinted at intentions of the government to come up with regulatory provision. This demand reached a new height in the wake of the Mumbai attack in 2009, when the coverage of news channels came under severe attack, thereby prompting the then I&B minister to reiterate the government's resolve to bring news channels under some kind of regulations. Rising to the occasion, the big news channels took the initiative of forming an association, the News Broadcasters Association (NBA), as a self regulatory initiative appointing a retired Supreme Court Judge, and seeking complaints from public. That was a good move. The complaint to this authority, irrespective of how many news channels it represented, was to be accompanied initially with a fee of Rs. 1,000. Hardly a couple of complaints were received in the first year. However, Justice J S Verma, who headed that authority, took proactive initiatives of calling TV channels to explain certain objectionable ads, coverage of news and programmes and even imposing a fine and asking them to prominently mention the advice in their news bulletins.

The eventual and ultimate interest of TRP-driven content model is to support, sustain, promote and perpetuate consumerism as subtly (even without realising it) which in this context means FNCC brands. [7]That is how 60-85 per cent of total advertising revenue is from consumer durables, automobile, food, beverage and personal care brands. These advertisers account for 65 per cent of revenue of channels and top 20 advertising agencies in India are foreign owned or controlled. It all boils down to "the business of TV news". In that process they are no longer "hidden persuaders".

Since September 2008 till early 2012, the NBA decided on only 13 complaints and issued 30 advisories to news channels. It issued 16 guidelines to news channels - on periodicity of TRP reporting, sting operations, covering court proceedings, emergency, and tourist incidents. The "advisories" issued included those on editorial responsibility, use of distress footage, "file" and "live" coverage, religious statements, coverage of terrorist activities. Five Telugu news channels violated rules in 2011-12 as per the ministry-monitored (Electronic Media Monitoring Centre) analysis for their coverage of obscenity, biased reporting, maligning. But none of these made a difference on the overall trend in news coverage or their priorities, notwithstanding what is being claimed by the NBA executive.

Catering to the Interests of Advertisers

Mindshare is a leading advertising space buyer and it sponsors high budget special programmes on TV channels. In an interview to *Business Standard* reporter (September 18, 2012) Anita Kotwani, Principal Partner of Mindshare, said that "if the channel is guaranteeing eyeballs for the committed outlays, advertisers will not shy away from it (the programme). And, if the brand is interweaved into the content, with a perfect fit, as part of the outlay committed, it adds as a sweetener to explore the property" (sponsored programme). What is the message that contention sends out to channels, to content producers not only for the content priorities but even the structure of the programmes? The intrusion into channel's prerogatives is direct by ad agencies and the implementation of their plan by way of TRPs. This is what the CEO of a Telugu news channel (innocently) told (reading out the prescription from a TAM advise) at a CMS workshop in 2005 on paradigm shift. News channels are more interested in catering to the needs of advertisers and convenience of ad agencies as viewers are not seen as direct cause of revenue. Channels are interested in figuring favourably in TRPs so that they could get the support of ad agencies. But if TRPs, the way they are designed, are analysed and remain same as now, I am afraid, it is not going to change the dependence on advertising as the primary source of revenue.

In 2005, the revenue of news channels from advertising was about Rs. 500 crore out of the total advertising outlays of TV channels of about Rs 1,500 crore. Yet, only a couple of news channels had become viable financially. The trend since has not changed much except that in 2011-12 there may be a couple of news channels that could claim the "break even". Regional news channels command 45 per cent of total advertising in news channels, which is likely to grow to Rs. 1,800 crore by 2015.[8]

Three aspects of ads in the context of news channels determine the scope and standing of news channels. First, news channels being free-to-air (as of now) depend primarily on advertising support for their survival and viability. A second consideration is the extent (number and frequency of breaks) of ads in news bulletins and their distraction. Third, with digitalisation of channels will news channels become pay for view or remain as pay channels? What are the pros and cons of that? What would be the government's policy to ensure access to news to every one?

Percentage of advertisement time in news channels (2008 – 2011)	
Year	%
2008	34.0
2009	35.4
2010	35.6
2011	35.4

TRAI issued a consultation paper (No.7/2012) on 16 March 2012 on "issues related to advertisements in channels", including news channels. For that analysis TRAI extensively used CMS Media Lab data. It issued its draft regulations on 28 August 2012. [9]That analysis of advertising time in the news bulletins of (six English and Hindi) news channels, brought out that the extent of advertisement has been on increase over the last few years. On an average 35 per cent of prime time of the news bulletins are commercials against 20 per cent limit prescribed in the existing regulation. In fact, the maximum yearly average according to TRAI's paper is as high 47.4 per cent. Even the minimum has been going up from 14 to 23 per cent.

Percentage of ad time of six news channels (2011)	
Channel	%
1	23.3
2	30.4
3	34.5
4	40.4
5	42.0
6	42.1

Apart from the duration of ads, the other concern of TRAI from the perspective of the viewers' experience was the frequency of ads, their number. The frequency and timing of the ad breaks to a large extent determine the extent to which they contribute to irritation at the viewer's end, (Page 18 of TRAI Consultation Paper). The other point of TRAI was audio level of advertisement in news bulletins were so high that it added to the irritation. Clutter of screen with ads even to the extent of missing the news or making it difficult to differentiate and comprehend news was indicated. The CMS field studies in Andhra Pradesh indicated that news bulletins without any commercial breaks and screen clutter were better recalled and their credibility and retention value was better as "news source". In fact, such news bulletins were preferred even in the case of non-news channels as against the news bulletins in news channel with commercial breaks and cluttered screens. TRAI recommendations based on this consultation paper included limiting commercials to 12 minute in a clock hour in free-to-air channels and to limit them on a clock hour basis (rather than across the day). This meant that 30 minutes news bulletins could not have more than six minutes of commercials (with two breaks?). The broadcasters were unhappy about such limits and termed the recommendations arbitrary. In the case of pay channels the limit was six minutes for clock hour. It stated that "the picture and audible matter of ads should not be excessively loud". TRAI has not made special limits in the case of news channels except about cluttering of the screen. The TRAI notifications remind that a rethink is perhaps needed on the structure, nature of commercials and the extent news channels depend on them as revenue source. What happens, for example, if prime bulletins go beyond and limit to "public service" commercials or/and only to "sponsored" ads (no brand or sales pitch ads)? Will their ad revenue go down by 40 per cent as some channels argued? Even better of course is not to have any ad anywhere in prime news bulletins, as in the case of ETV.

It is a challenge for channels to see that they take such initiatives without a decline in revenues. [10]To gain somewhere (credibility and expansion), channels have to lose somewhere else (ad revenue)! But in the last couple of years, only a couple of news channel have closed news service although a couple of others have changed their name or managements. Star TV news which was foremost satellite news channels had given up in 2012 news business as it wanted to focus on entertainment. Zee News announced its exit from 24-hour Telugu news in September 2012. CNEB (Hindi) converted into a music channel, Jain TV became defunct voice of India and S-1 (Hindi channel) closed down. MAA TV (Telugu) stopped two-three news bulletins having come to an understanding with another news channel. But some news channels are in an expansion mode. NDTV has added four channels, one in Hindi and one for business (and two for general entertainment) despite nowhere on the road for a break even business. Zee TV has added a channel for business news and has gone into regional channels. Aaj Tak came up with "Headlines Today" and Tej in 2005. Sahara added a couple of state specific news channels. TV-18 added a business channel in Hindi; TV-9 and NTV added two-three channels. TV-9 expanded to four-five other languages. Most of them have been exploring and sounding market for further one or other "add-on" news channels. With three more DTH platforms getting added and digitalisation deadlines drawing close, the trend is to add more channel irrespective of the extent of ad support available. What kind of qualitative change such a proliferation would bring needs to be seen in the coming years. But news channels appear to be rediscovering themselves and trying to come up with new initiatives. Marginal changes in the last few years in the coverage of party politics has not led to any increase in the coverage of social development or other such serious basic issues. Instead, the increase has been more in the coverage of lifestyle, amusement and "human interest" features and, of course, financial and corporate affairs. Efforts among news channels has been to expand into other "business" including starting new niche channels like business, health, sports, "views" or "new media", etc. None of the news channels has come up with a channel for children or for rural or agriculture, for example. NTV (Telugu) news channel is the only channel which is operating a separate channel "for women" (at least it claims).

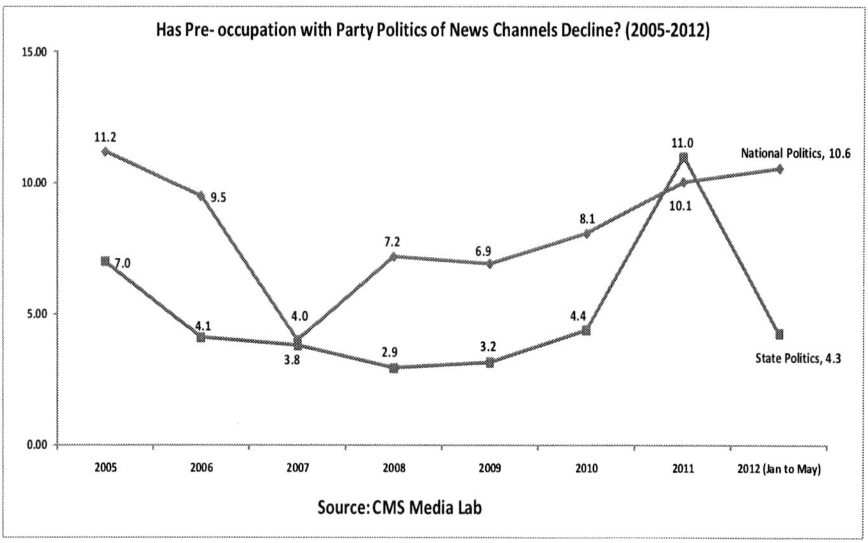

Increased competition between news channels is expected to increase news coverage from newer locations, away from capital cities and commercial centres. In the case of regional language news channels the coverage from new and far off places is on the increase significantly. The speed in coverage of spot events like accidents and the frequency of live coverage has increased even at the cost of criticism of "hyping" some events, situations and personalities. Also, increase in "interactive programming", irrespective of relevance of topics, is all over news channels including by way of "reality shows".

Not Very Distinct from Each Other

Despite proliferation of news media and competitiveness between news channels, the choice in the content package of news bulletins is not distinct from one another. This is true in case of both national and regional channels.

Notwithstanding the limitations of TAM as a reliable indicator, its time series data reflect the broad trend in viewership. One such trend is that news channels, the way they started as "24-hour news" source, have not made a big difference in adding to the overall expansion or reach of TV. But they have made a difference in chasing "news" and the way they are prioritised and presented. Then, the question arises - why are more and more news channels getting added. And, what difference news channels have made to socio-economic–political-governance systems of the country.

Going by [11]whatever information is available on the ownership pattern of news channels, one may observe that new news channels are being started either under a "political clout" of reaching out or/and because a general entertainment channel or a newspaper group seeks to expand by adding a news channel, because it costs them relatively less as a business proposition (than what it costs to a newcomer). There is a third category of entrepreneurs with "surplus money", who are taking to news channels as it would provide them "societal standing" or "marketing clout" or allow entry into "power circles" and they could "afford" to spend for three or more years irrespective of viability. A number of these new entrepreneurs are from the "real estate" or chit fund companies or capitation colleges or financial business or other such unorganised businesses with high liquidity. There are instances where politically motivated investors put money into a news channel for potential advantage it implies to their public standing. In this process, instances are not isolated where news contents get planted, tainted or excluded or moderated. Then, there is also talk of news channel managers entering into an arrangement with a commercial house or demanding money or getting into blackmailing for one or other kind of advantage or hush-hush arrangement. One or two such instances, however isolated may be, are enough to recycle such an impression locally and erode the very credibility of news channels.

Analysing about "When politicians own the media", Vanita Kohli Khandekar a veteran in analysing "media business" in *Business Standard* (3 July 2012),[12] wrote: "More than a third of news channels are owned by politicians or politico-affiliated builders. An estimated 60 per cent of cable distribution systems are owned by local politicians. These have influenced and funded several local elections. There are dozen small and big newspapers owned by politicians or their family members that influence the course of local elections. Many newspaper chains with political affiliations also own broadcast networks. Most now have Internet portals."

A second trend in the news channels and news bulletins is "repeat", which refers to the repeat of "news" stories, sequences, visuals, etc. In fact, the extent of repeats is so high in certain cases and on certain days that it is more inhibitive and repulsive than informative or interesting and often giving irritating moments at the viewing end.

Third, hoping to expand viewership and thereby increase commercial revenue, the extent of non-news contents has been going up in the last couple of years. The new type of non-news content includes crime, humour, cinema-based episodes, "reality shows" (with hardly any reality actually experienced by people), sex, fantasy, technology and a few news channels have adopted exceptional examples of real real-time issues, including in a campaign mode.

The fourth trend is the cluttering of the screen with too many points of attention, including some ads of high pitch audio levels. This is as if channels are in confusion or in a hurry or in an over zealous mode to give an impression that they are giving much more than other channels; whereas a common sense understanding reveals that the cluttering hardly enables viewers to grasp fully or comprehend either of the aspects on the screen at any one point of time. On the top of it all, certain words are constantly and repeatedly shown as "breaking news" even when the information involved is incomplete, irrelevant, incoherent or inconsequential. Further, the remote that enables one to change channels frequently has shortened the duration that a viewer, on an average, tends to spend on a channel at any time on any one bulletin/ programme. It is more glancing at the screen that is being chased. This is more in the case of news channels. This is irrespective of any "loyalty" aspect of a channel.

A fifth trend that news channels suffer from is a "competitive syndrome", where the focus and priority of coverage is determined more by the way coverage of the "other channel" is perceived. In the process, the tendency is to exaggerate, hype, and give out some time, even before an event is unfolded. There are instances of news channels going off the mark or wrong altogether or, in a few cases blatantly biased – any such coverage even once in a while erodes the very standing of the channel or/and of the source of such coverage. This tendency prompts "reactive coverage" more.

A sixth trend is the way certain issues, which require citizens to act (voting, etc) are connected or commented and covered in a news bulletin or a discussion programme in a "punditry mode" in such a way that it pampers viewer citizen passivism (than provoking citizen activism). Yet another observation (hopefully it is not true) is that there is hardly any example of news channels going for specific and original field research on their own or by an independent professional and the dependence on TAM in this regard is total (perhaps because of linkage to commercial revenue generation).

These are the general trends, with marginal to significant variation from one news channel to another or from one time to another and in covering one subject or the other. But thanks to competitive compulsions, news channels have taken initiatives to involve more and more people in interactive programmes by way of debates and discussion on contentious issues of the day. That is how news channels rallied around the "crusades" of Anna Hazare or Ramdev with "carpet coverage". However, because of some of the content model being pursued, some good initiatives have not yielded sustained viewership because of the structure of programme or redundancy in participation. Nevertheless, a couple of channels have demonstrated how experimentation and research-based initiatives can differentiate one channel from another. Some news channels have gone beyond with sponsored campaigns in support of self initiated advocacy programmes, including on voting, caste, corruption, plastic bags, dowry, ecology and transformed the same into community mobilisation movements, as in the case of environment, school enrolment, etc. Amir Khan's *Satyamave Jayate* (2012) was a unique experiment. In fact, it could be a turning point in unleashing the power of news television in formula.

On the other hand, the trend of "paid news" or "paid ratings", has come to the fore because of increased involvement of political leaders and business class in the ownership or/and management of channels and more mediapersons getting active in electoral politics, directly and indirectly.

Overall, what is missing with large number of news channels is transparency. For many channels, for example, their real ownership is not known, and it is not easy to know as if it is deliberate. In the case of newspapers, they have to declare publicly once a year (to Registrar of Newspapers for India and also print) certain basic details as to who is the editor, who is responsible for the contents and printing and declare the identity of stakeholders. There is no such requirement or practice in the case of TV channels. Newspapers are made by an Act to indicate who is "responsible" for the contents of the publication only a few years ago. But, even then, hardly 20 per cent of registered news papers comply with RNI.

Because of live coverage potential of news channels and their round-the clock transmission, they will remain a primary source of news. However, newspapers are viewed as more serious and more credible source of news. Why should the ones watching news bulletins go for validation or further information to newspapers? [13]CMS studies have indicated that contrary to general feeling and experience in many other countries, proliferation of news channels in India has helped newspapers to expand and consolidate their market. They have retained their relative credibility despite shift in priorities of content and operations, as in the case of news television. That trend in the growth of newspaper readership was corroborated in 2005 by the two national surveys (NRS and IRS). Some increase in the case of both viewership and readership was because of multiplicity, not so much by way of adding new ones to the reach. (That is, the ones watching TV are watching more channels or programmes and the ones reading are reading more newspapers). That is why manifold increase in news channels has not led to an increase in viewing time of news on TV. In fact, on the other hand, the time spent on viewing news on TV has declined in the normal days. This has been indicated by the national surveys too. That is why news channels are chasing to discover new "content slots" or "stories" or "controversies" and for new content models.

[14]In 2015, more than a dozen main news channels in the country are owned or/and operated by political parties and some others are backed by or controlled by political leaders. A few are managed directly by party. This trend is on the increase, not on decline. In fact, at this rate more than half of news channels in the country would be "politically oriented". There are also nearly as many religious/spiritual channels operated mostly or partly by Hindu, Christian and Muslim leaders. In Kerala, for

example, one channel (India Vision) is backed by a Muslim political party. Two more Muslim political groups (Jamaat-e-Islami and Muslim League) are expected to get clearance to start news channel. In other states, too, more news channels backed by political parties/leaders are expected. Can we expect a political party-backed channel to operate in the spirit of Fourth Estate? If news channels acquire newspapers and newspapers start news channels in a given state, as in the case of Kerala, Andhra Pradesh and Tamil Nadu, what are the implications to the democratic culture, public policies, law and order and national goals as envisaged in the Constitution?

This scenario is what perhaps Subhash Chandra, pioneer of Satellite TV in India, meant when he said, "Yes, there have been a few drawbacks in terms of regressive and commercialised programming, especially in the news and information space. However, in the final analysis, the benefits by far outweigh the drawbacks." [15]Chandra reiterated in July 5, 2011 that "there is no innovation in programming, technology or delivery vehicles, no newness; we are copying foreign formats."

Share of news channels in the total viewership – by age group						
	2007		2008		2009	
	4+years	25+ years	4+years	25+years	4+years	25+years
English news	0.7	0.75	0.6	0.62	0.4	0.42
Hindi news	4.8	5.29	4.8	5.36	3.6	4.18
Regional news	2.4	2.92	2.7	3.66	3.6	4.26

Source : TAM

[16]Since 2008, the viewership of news channels declined by one per cent. Except four-five news channels, most others have hardly recovered their operational costs. Advertisers, being the first ones to be sensitive of market dynamics, no longer prefer (2011) TV news channels as in the earlier years, as if they knew that news channels are slowly losing their viewership and also perhaps because they knew that editorial context for commercials is under question increasingly. With decline in viewership for news channels, contrary to initial expectations, advertising support to news channels has not gone up during the last couple of years. With the number of news channels increasing advertising support to news channels further declined. Only a few retained the ad support. Yet, even between 2008 – 2011, new news channels mushroomed in regional languages in particular.

Of well over 120 news channels, TAM did a special analysis of the kind of viewership for different genre of news channel contents – for four English and six Hindi channels. Such a data for January-December 2010 is presented here, it offers an insight for an emerging trend.

Per cent share of news genre viewed (January – December 2010)		
Content genre viewed	**English (4 channels)**	**Hindi (6 channels)**
Crime/Law & Order news	28.1	26.0
Sports news	23.9	16.0
Political/governance news	19.1	13.0
Entertainment news	12.6	14.0
Social	5.1	9.0
Other	4.8	9.0
Weather/environment	2.1	4.0
Mishaps/failure	3.2	5.0
Business news	1.2	-
Astrology	-	4.0

Source: News content pack of TAM as reported in Business Standard, 25 March 2011

An argument often given for the content priorities of news channels is that what viewer prefers going by TRPs, TAM puts out support data for that argument. According to that 28 per cent of English news channel viewers and 26 per cent of Hindi news channel audience view crime/ law & order news - that is higher than for any other genre news items. Does this argument make any sense? A content analysis of English and Hindi news for the same period brings out that crime / law & order news constitute hardly six per cent (it was 9-12 per cent during 2005-07). TAM apparently is trying to put back viewership to news to pre boom period!

What this TAM data makes us believe is that a relatively higher per cent of news channel viewers watch crime/law and order content genre in the new contents. This means that "crime shows" have become a priority followed by sports and political/government and entertainment, irrespective of the language of the channel. This has been the content model that is being promoted by TRPs and prescribed by TAM by way its "advisory service".

According to this, 26-28 per cent of news channel viewers watch "mishaps", crime and law and order stories in the bulletins. This is what TAM suggests, directly and indirectly, to news channels as part of its "formula for rating points". Political and governance related news in the bulletins has less than 15 per cent viewers in the case of Hindi news channels. And much less than 10 per cent of Hindi news channel viewers watch "social news" (assuming all that is positive and/or on basic needs of people). In fact, that is only 5.1 per cent in the case of English news channels.

Going by such findings (as supplied by TAM) how any channel can venture into anything different than what such analysis indicates? No wonder most news channels tend to go by more or less the same formula as this TAM package implies. Why are viewers "all are alike" or more of the same type! Should we continue this content model that the TAM formula implies? Is it desirable to perpetuate such an analysis? How can a channel distinguish itself by taking to different content priorities in such a way that it becomes an instrument of change and does good for more people?

Vanita Kohli Khandekar, who has been analysing business aspects of TV channels, including news channels, concluded that one-third of news channels are owned by companies or individuals not interested in building a news brand. Many of the regional channels are just political vehicles or/and "non serious players". (*Business Standard, 3 July 2012).*

An argument often made in support of TRPs is that there is no other way or basis available for channels/advertisers to go about. There is a fallacy in this argument. You do not allow and encourage an alternative to come up, and then say that there is no other basis. Despite knowing the limitations or inadequacies of TRPs, channels continue to use the same because commercial/advertising support comes on the basis of TRPs and advertising professionals support and sustain TRP system, as it is easy, simple and fits into a larger model that advertisers pursue in their business. Falling into this fallacy of taking to inadequate TRPs, they are missing a larger opportunity to distinguish themselves and take a more proactive role.

Government and politics matter relatively more to new news channels (as if they are more for a "clout") than to the long standing channels for whom crime and politics stand higher priority. As they move on news channels tend to take "safe course" after having tried to differentiate initially from the already existing news channels. One would expect that as the years pass by they can afford experimentation, new initiatives and risk taking provisions. But in case of new news channels, they are more anxious to "influence" government affairs or/and politics of the day than to influence the social order and push a larger agenda. This means going for "more of the same" kind of contents, which is what TRP formula tends to promote and perpetuate.

Channel genre-wise share (2009 versus 2010)						
	All India		Hindi market		South	
	2009	2010	2009	2010	2009	2010
Regional News	3.7	3.7	2.3	2.2	6.3	6.9
Hindi news	3.6	3.4	5.3	5.0	0.3	0.2
English news	0.4	0.3	0.3	0.3	0.5	0.4

Source : TAM

In the overall viewership of television and viewership of news has declined marginally between 2009 and 2010, according to TAM's analysis. Viewership of regional news channels, however, remained at 3.7 both in 2009 and 2010. In the South, share of regional news channels in the overall viewership had gone up from 6.3 to 6.9 between 2009 and 2010. But the share of Hindi news in "Hindi market" declined from 5.3 to 5.0 during the same period. Less than 50 out of nearly 150 news channels belonging to nearly 20 media establishments are members of the NBA. Only a few of them are regional channels. The non-member channels are not expected to follow the standards and advice.

How Different are Regional News Channels?

Scope and structure of news channels in Tamil, Telugu, Malayalam and Kannada has been distinct from the very outset. Over the years, the numbers have multiplied much faster and the key movers mostly are political leaders, real estate giants and businessmen. Their affiliation to political parties is not indirect. Yet, none of them have closed down or are even on the verge of doing so. On the contrary, more political leaders and parties have lined up to start new news channels directly or as "proxy channels". Perhaps, the competitive coverage and political compulsions and opportunities have kept those channels on the go. As polls approach, more news channels are being announced in different parts of the country. Lotus TV, for example, in Tamil, which "promises neutral, but pro-BJP", is the most recent addition to already cluttered news channel in Tamil Nadu, when, in fact, the BJP hardly exists in Tamil Nadu. With a Dalit news channel being announced there, political warfare on air is now on caste lines. Corporates, too, would come out in open instead of "proxy" as they are sometimes alleged.

In Karnataka, there are as many news channels as the GECs. Three of the seven Kannada news channels, all based in Bangalore, have come up in last few years. The first one to start a news channel in Kannada was TV-9 which within a couple of years of its success in Telugu entered Karnataka with a round-the-clock news channel. Its early in-roads and political coverage stirred local interest and prompted local political leaders (one by Janata Dal and one by BJP) and two businessmen interested in power politics to start news channels. All these news channels by and large are of the same kind in terms of content priorities, structure, orientation, schedule of presentation. Zee Karnataka, the GEC which had two-three daily news bulletins in Kannada had given up news bulletins two years ago as more local 24x7 news channels had come up. However, ETV (GEC) Kannada continues to have two-three news bulletins daily, similar to their Telugu channel.

In none of these states (Kerala, Tamil Nadu or Andhra Pradesh), news channel - old or new – have dared to evolve or even experiment with different approach of news. In no other language or state in the last 10 years has anyone taken to a different model, though most of them entered the scene with a claim of being different from the other news channels. It is against this background that Public TV, a Kannada news channel from Bangalore was started in February 2012. It is on a different footing and is in contrast to most other news channels. In less than six months, Public TV has become much talked about channel and a major news source as much as three-year older news channels.

A New Model for India

Why is this channel unique? First, it was launched by a local journalist (Mr. Ranganath) with two decades of experience in media and of heading a Kannada news channel for some time, promoted by an industrialist. He walked out of that news channel with determination to demonstrate that an "independent" channel could be put together with no conflict of interest. Second, from the very outset, a realisation that dictated the channel was that investment required for starting a news channel should be modest and much less than what news channels so far claimed to have invested. Only then reliance on revenue from commercials could be kept under a limit. For that Ranganath went about differently – no middlemen to get government permissions, no consultants to set up studio. He himself attended to all that (with the help of a few friends and old associates). He rented a much bigger place (than other channels) by going for a place lying vacant and acquired office and studio equipment at one-third cost, believing that news is not a "show business". He did not go for OB vans (against two dozen OBs, for example, by Saakshi news channel). He took to shoulder units. Going by the content ouput of this channel, such a low cost approach cannot be made out in the channel's content quality, presentation and coverage of the state.

Third, significance of transparency in the operations was recognized at the outset. On the first day of the launch, Mr. Ranganath presented live his assets and bank balances with details and challenged anyone to disprove. On my first visit he told me that two of his old friends had put in capital for the channel - one a producer of feature films and the other distributor of music, both in his view had no interest in the operations of the channel.

Fourth, Mr. Ranganath understood at the outset that existing professionals in news channels are "irrationally valued", as demand for "professionals" came much faster than imagined and no one had taken initiatives to develop skills or talent appropriately. He went across the state in search of talent. Out about some 3,000 aspirants, he interviewed 120 and ended up having a team of 30, 10 of them as his core team. He is setting example for each of them to feel ownership, motivating them and demonstrating that content output can distinguish the channel. That is how he chose the tagline of "it is nobody's business, as it is yours". He recognises that TV has ample scope for experimentation. All through Ranganath's concern has been more with contents as to what he is giving to his viewers. Public TV stands out as distinct due to its model. The key features of this model are: (1) transparency in operations; (2) low cost - almost one-third of what any other news channel in Karnataka or anywhere would have invested; (3) shortest time to launch – six months including the time of getting permission, and without middlemen or consultants, (4) select and prepare locally a new team to man the operations; (5) resisting political investment with equal distance from every party.

The branding with the name Public TV – amply indicates this approach to launch and operate a regional news channel as a potential model for India. However, we have to wait and see what shape this model takes in the coming years.

Within six months, Public TV was able to mobilise 35-45 per cent of operational costs from commercials. It needs to be seen how long Ranganath would be able to operate the channel and in the increasingly competitive scenario. He is willing to take the challenge of not having commercials altogether, the moment he gets 10 lakh subscribers with Rs.10 monthly subscription. Whether digitalisation is going to facilitate him or make it even more tough needs to be seen. He seems to be preparing for newer challenges.

Regional News Channels: The Case of Telugu Channels

Regional news channels, unlike Hindi and English news channels, which position themselves as "national", devote far more time in originating news in a competitive spirit and have far better range in the subjects covered. Relatively, regional language news channels are far more focussed, far more reflective and inclusive in their coverage than the bulletins of national news channels. This is how it has been in the case of Telugu news channels, whose number is more than other regional language news channels. There were 17 news channels in Telugu in 2012. Telugu news channels tend to have two or three distinct category of news bulletins in the course of the day: one being a "news bulletin" with a mix of national and state news and the other bulletin being a mix of state and local news. The third news bulletin is "primarily local" with extensive and reflective field coverage of the districts across the state, however briefly it may be, but always footage-based. This, apparently, is a lesson that Telugu news channels have picked up from Telugu news dailies, which have expanded their relevance as well as reach by having "district editions" for most districts of the state.

Going by an analysis of CMS Media Lab reports, it could be said that Telugu news channels' coverage is almost live with news from across the state from different regions and far off places. They are far better in covering real "issues of concern" and reflecting voice of many more than the national channels. They do so with more regularity than the national channels. Telugu news channels cover rural areas extensively and regularly, not only with special news programmes but also in the normal course of news bulletins. Such an extensive coverage of rural areas, farmers and grassroots is perhaps because television set ownership ratio in Andhra Pradesh is far more than in the case of the rural Hindi belt. It is also because of competition with Telugu newspapers and political-business interests of news channels. The analysis of news channel coverage in Hindi, English and Telugu brings out that the Hindi news channel bulletins are more TRP-driven than the Telugu news bulletins.

An analysis of their content and programme structure gives an idea about their content priorities and concerns. There is however not much evidence to validate the belief that competition increases choice and enhances the scope of news. Even in the case of Telugu news channels, it has been "more of the same" phenomenon, becoming copy cats in the name of competition. This is happening, because the subtle difference is missing between "what could be in the interest of people" and "what interests people" momentarily.

Trends in priorities of news bulletins of Telugu news channels – May 2010					
ETV2	**TV9**	**NTV**	**Mahaa**	**Zee 24**	**Saakshi**
Crime Politics Accidents/ Disasters Govern- -ance Sports	Crime Politics Social issues Human Interest Art/Culture	Politics Crime Govern- -ance Sports Art/Cult ure	Politics Crime Weather Govern- -ance Accidents/ Disasters	Politics Crime Weather Governance Human Interest	Governance Politics Accidents/Disast ers Crime Social issues

Source: CMS Media Lab

Active viewer is the best bet for a better television anywhere. But there is no evidence of that despite increase in "field based and interactive" coverage of news channels. Civil society, too, showed limited concern about what is being dished out by news channels, except for occasional outbursts here and there by some teachers or social activists. Political leaders blaming news channels whenever it is not favourable to them has become a too frequent of late; of course across the country. Occasional blaming of TRPs for such a "down-hill race" of channels of their contents made no difference towards a relook of the model by the new news channels.

TAM report for 2011 indicated that time spent on TV viewing increased only marginally between 2010 and 2011 (by one per cent) though the number of channels increased during the period by about 20 per cent. In Kerala, where news channels proliferated and multiplied, TAM reported fall in viewership in 2011. It improved however, in the last few weeks of 2011 - because of local political happenings.

Trends in priorities of news bulletins (Telugu news channels) 2007-2010 *Proliferation of news channels has hardly made any difference!*					
ETV2			TV9		
2007	**2008**	**2010**	**2007**	**2008**	**2010**
Crime Politics Governance Art/Culture Social issues Accidents/Disasters	Politics Crime Governance Civic Art/Culture Sports	Crime Politics Accidents/Disasters Governance Sports Art/Culture	Crime Politics Governance Social issues Accidents/Disasters Sports	Politics Crime Governance Civic Art/Culture Sports	Crime Politics Social issues Human interest Art/Culture Governance

Source : CMS Media Lab

Regional news channels have consolidated by increasing State specific coverage, including the coverage of districts and beyond urban areas. For example, news channels in Telugu (particularly ETV-2 and TV-9 older news) increased such content from one-third before 2000 to more than half in 2010. And, simultaneously, Delhi originated news declined significantly during the period. This certainly helped regional channels to expand their reach and facilitated competition in covering grassroots with a wide range of topics.

But nearly half of Telugu news channels' news bulletins are from the capital of the State. During the days, when the State Assembly is in session, it may be all right, but that certainly indicates an opportunity for further restructuring of coverage in the bulletins and expand the reach further.

The question is one of the concerns and contents of news channels and the kind of priorities they have. CMS studies over the years have indicated that the content priorities of channels (even in the case of Telugu news channels) are a inhibiting factor in the growth in the viewership, innovation in programming and for making a difference. For many news channels, crime matters more than governance in their coverage; and the structure of the coverage is such that it contributes for "copy-cat" phenomena more and party politics matters a lot more than social development issues, and the extent and kind of participation in such programme hardly makes a difference. Such an analysis hints at the scope that exists for news channels to differentiate and distinguish themselves, individually and together.

Conflict resolution of any situation is not considered a concern of news media. Rather reporting conflicts is what media prefers the most. Reporting about solution and way forward or resolving an issue requires some efforts, skills and sensitivity to such an approach. Conflicts in the country anytime are galore, all around and almost on every issue. In every conflict there are different versions and differently interested parties or groups – whether political, social, economic or cultural or even sports. One, reason for this lacuna in news channel's performance is, first, lack of sensitivity as to what it all means for the functioning, resources and references. Instances of deliberate one sided reporting or even biased reportage (unintended or otherwise) are on the increase as if that is to do with resource availability, viability of channel and the pattern of investments. A second reason for such an approach becoming a formula is lack of skills or training for taking a holistic view and alternative options. The third one is that (conflict) resolution reporting requires more effort and resources than reporting a conflict situation. There are, of course, some exceptions, where the solution for an issue or problem had come out of media reporting. Some channels, in fact, have taken to this approach deliberately, including on social and political conflicts. (Times of India's [17]*Aaman ki Aasha* approach to Indo-Pak). Maa TV's (2010) Batuku Jatka Bandi (life is like a bullock cart) or TV-9's Chetana (change) and HMTV's *Disa-Dasa* programmes are only three examples. They were unique when they started. The one started by MAA TV was to resolve marital disputes between two individuals (wife and husband) with their families. The other, *Chetana* started by TV-9, showcases how a systemic problem could be resolved. Jhansi, the anchor of this weekly field based, interactive specific real issue, has become a symbol for the power of TV. Chetana continue to be serious and sought after even after years. *Disa-Dosa* was a courageous experiment to make regions in conflict understand each other better and find a way forward or way out from an ongoing agitational approach.

There are many other examples of channels taking up such initiatives, but they have remained isolated and short lived examples. One does not hear of such initiatives being encouraged. They hardly figure in TRP charts, the earliest example was Rajini (1987) on consumer activism and

Nukkad (1992) on DD channel. *Hum Log* serial was the first ever in that category.

At the very outset of proliferation of 24x7 news channel, CMS had indicated the trends that need to be corrected for harnessing television as a credible news source. The first field study was on the credibility of TV news bulletins in 2001. It was only in Tamil and Telugu languages that regional news channels multiplied faster. CMS came out with the first emerging trends in news media scene in 2004. At that time, there were two news channels (ETV-2 and TV-9) and two general entertainment channels (GEC) in Telugu with two or three news bulletins a day (Doordarshan and ETV). The study was repeated in 2005, when one more news channel and one more GEC channel with two or three news bulletins came up. Those were the first field level systematic studies, which hinted at what news channels could avoid and how those, who read news dailies, view TV news bulletins and how TV emerged as a news source, as it reached many corners before a newspaper reached.

From three Telugu news channels in 2005, their number has increased to 14 in 2011 (apart from the same two GEC channels in Telugu, which continue, to date, with two or three news bulletins daily). There are 3 to 5 licensed ones are awaiting next few months. Perhaps, there is no parallel in any other State where a GEC channel (MAA) discontinued giving two or three news bulletins a day (despite the group not having any other channel devoted to 24x7 news). Despite that, CMS study (2007-2009) and CMS Academy Awards to news channels in Telugu had brought out that news bulletins telecast twice or thrice a day had better chances of being viewed more seriously; even better than the hourly news bulletins of round the clock news channels.

It is not known outside the channel offices that TAM works both by left hand and right hand such a way they support each other and ensure the particular content model is pursued. It offers parallel "advisory" and "consultancy" services to channels (old and new ones and on an ad hoc basis as well as regularly). Such a way that a particular content model get preferred and supported as if "conflict of interest" aspect is no ones concern.

The entry of new news channels has been a continuing phenomenon in the last couple of years. Each new entrant starts as if it is determined to stand out as different from the ones already there. But, it too soon fully in line with same content formula as if that is a reality. In fact, it even goes all out in giving more politics, crime, sex and entertainment. Telugu news channels reflect this trend. Because they all seek same TRPs for the same compulsive reason. The difference is who works more on TAM (!) for better understanding.

Older vs. New news channels –their approach to contents		
Content strategies	**New News channel (<2 years)**	**Old News channel (4 years +)**
"Non News" category	25%	35 – 40%
Programme schedule	Flexible to take on as and when	Rigid pattern/fixed charts more
Range of News/Current Affairs	Wider coverage	Similar/same type
Field/studio based	More field and interactive content	Studio discussions more
Crime	Less, relatively	More, relatively

This summing up approach to contents was compiled based on content analysis and also discussions with respective channel managers.

Pattern in the content priorities of news bulletins of Telugu News channels – 2010					
Long standing news channels (4+ years)		**Old news channels (2 – 4 years)**		**New entrants (<2 years)**	
ETV-2	**TV-9**	**NTV**	**Mahaa**	**Saakshi**	**HMTV**
Crime	Crime	Politics	Politics	Govt.	Govt.
Politics	Politics	Crime	Crime	Politics	Politics
Accidents/Disaster	Social	Govt.	Weather	Accident/ Disaster	Social
Government	Human Int.	Sports	Government	Crime	Human int
Sports	Art/culture	Art/Culture	Accident/Disaster	Social issues	Cinema

The differences in content priorities are marginal between news channels of different longevity. In fact, trend analysis for 2007 to 2010 of contents of Telugu news channels bring out how they tend to take same route.

What Triggered the News Channel Boom in Andhra Pradesh

In Andhra Pradesh the number of news channels in Telugu has gone up from two ten years ago to 14 in 2011. All originate from Hyderabad. Similarly in Tamil Nadu their number multiplied. There is no parallel to Telugu and Tamil for such a growth of news channels. What triggered such a proliferation? Several factors in a reinforcing way contributed for such a boom both the two States. Are they different from each other in their content? The case of Andhra Pradesh is discussed here.

With TV-9 becoming a success as a standalone news channel, TV news business has taken off in Andhra Pradesh more than ten years ago. ETV by then (2000) was already a success as a GEC channel. ETV-2 thereafter was also a success as a news channel. They belong to the Telugu news media, Eenadu of Ramoji Rao. He was viewed as a pioneer and Eenadu as a successful media house. By then this group was also in feature film production and also in advertising business with innovative ideas in their operations – language used, production discipline and content standards, delivery schedules, etc. This group discovered new talent and trained them both in print and television broadcast and even more, in news collection, analysis and dissemination. That was when TV-9 started armed with network technologies and infrastructure specially journalists who had worked as field reporters mostly in ETV group itself. TV-9 quickly become a match and even excelled the ETV-2. TV-9 enthused many entrepreneurs and journalists themselves. Ravi Prakash, the journalist behind the success of TV-9, was credited for the "new formula". He made a difference in a short time. For many journalists in Hyderabad who had gone through the discipline and rigor of Ramoji Rao but fallen out of him, Ravi Prakash showed news business as a new found field for entrepreneurship as Prannoy Roy did in New Delhi. They showed that with innovations a breakthrough is possible in news business. Senior journalists in turn motivated businessmen and politicians to take to "news business".

Simultaneously, at that time Andhra Pradesh was going through (and continue ever since) certain political uncertainty and vacuum. NT Rama Rao, a novice in politics but a much admired film hero, formed the Government within 9 months after forming a new party. He had ushered in a crop of new leaders all over the State. [18]Many of them (irrespective of the party have realized with too frequent elections (as in no other state) the need to reach out. Some of them felt they could afford (backed by one or other business) a news channel to survive in politics.

With political realignment, the State experienced nine years Chief Ministership of Chandra Babu Naidu, when the state had unprecedented boom in infrastructure development. The result of which was a boom in real estate particularly in Hyderabad and neighbourhood. During the period chit fund, civil and liquor contractors mushroomed (two-third of large infrastructure contractors in India are in Andhra Pradesh even now). The money pumped into state during that decade, including into irrigation and power projects, was unprecedented in the country. Then of course large scale quid pro corruption sourced to Government was also as never before. Some of them with new found riches too found news business as a good proposition both for consolidating business and influencing politics.

Together all these have directly contributed to the boom in the number of news channels. It was people from these categories individually or in partnership who had gone for news channels. The fact that newspaper business in Telugu had long history and film entrepreneurship too took roots in the state had helped news channel boom. Continued political rivalries and uncertainty too contributed for the proliferation of news channels.

At least half of Telugu news channels are either owned directly or indirectly by political leaders – more individually than by parties as in Kerala and Tamil Nadu. And their affiliations are talked about. For example, a PCC President (2012) negotiated to take over an ongoing Telugu news channel on his own having its own GEC and news channels in a few other languages. CPI in Andhra Pradesh is trying to have its own channel. TRS already has a news channel for a couple of years now. With emerge of *Saakshi* news channel a more blatantly "supportive coverage" and contents has acquired wheels and prompted others too as if there is no need to be hidden persuader.

In Tamil Nadu too experienced similar boom in news channels. Six political parties have news channels, some in fact have two news channels. Two more parties are considering starting news channels in 2012. Ignoring coverage of opposing party or leader has also provoked few contenders to go for their own channel. At this rate of ignoring and boycotting of channels or one sided coverage of parties and leaders, some leaders will now even formally identify with channels. In Gujarat TV-9 is being boycotted by Congress party, PT News channel in Tamil Nadu is being boycotted by DMK and so on in other states too from time to time. In Kerala too there are 10 news channels some belonging to political parties. Some 3 or 4 more news channels are expected in 2012.

Is More Merrier?

In a true sense a particular "news" cannot be presented in so many different ways however contentious that may be. Even comments or opinions cannot be so many as it is assumed. But in the context of India multiple angles are expected. Despite availability of so many channels, TV households hardly watch ten channels with any regularity (even going by TRPs).

By having four different channels in the same city, for example, in the case of FM radio, do we see any difference in the content model? With merger and acquisition or cartel, the number of players / broadcasters eventually will come down to fewer than the number of permissions being issued. Such licenses are issued by the Government more to make money and as if airwaves are unlimited! The conditions for eligibility and processing perhaps need to be more rigorous to be in the "news" category, in particular. It may even be better to limit the number of licenses in each market / language and genre segment. Only then they could be distinct from each other and chances of viability could be better. That is why I argued more than a decade ago that India do not need more than 3 or 4 DTH platforms and that DD should rather strengthen its own decentralized territorial networks (instead of going for DTH now languishing and looking ways for exit) and that the same infrastructure could also be used by other local channels in a shared way. Those who had seen the feature film [19]*Piplilive (2011)* will understand this point better. It showed how OB vans and reporters of different channels rush to a small village for chasing an innocuous rumor (and yet miss a more important local story). If all those who are already permitted to operate a news channel (400+) actually get into operation, think of the scenario – what a colossal waste and confusion the news scene is going to be. They could choke and stifle creativity and imaginations of people.

I know it sounds wearied to argue against the current "liberal" or "popular" thinking in favor of a lassiz fair where more is merrier. I am not arguing for only two or three players; but in a pluralistic society multiple broadcasters should be available anywhere anytime for each category of subject / section of people. I am also not in favor of a ceiling on any such number. But there should be entry, opportunity and exit provisions too with checks and balance mechanisms. Level playing opportunities is what has to be ensured.

This notion that "market will take care" may be good in some cases, not so in the case of broadcasting and news channels in particular.

Midnight Masala, Even News Channels!

To cope up with increasing competition and compulsions of TRPs, some news channels are taking to coverage of sex related, increasing crime, negative and promoting controversies.

Initially in the earlier years there were instances of some GEC channels taking to 'prono shows" "for TRPs". But some news channels too have taken to such "shows" earlier after 11 pm, and now even during prime time, such content is being relied to catch up with TRPs, particularly the newer channels and the ones on the downhill in their viewership (as in the case of some Telugu channels). But even the older ones, already established channels, too have taken to sex based coverage in the news to hold on to their lead in viewership and lure newer viewers. In fact they have evolved sophisticated ways of featuring "sex" or "covering and creating sexy stories" in the name of "exposing". Sometimes feature them even during prime time "shows" or as a part of news bulletins as well as stand alone features. Special interviews are being mounted and create controversies – causing more of such behavior?

[20]That some such coverage was "staged' was even talked about in the media circles. Although the claim was "exposing" deviant behaviors, sometimes in collaboration knowledge of the police, sociologist will tell that the way these are structured, featured and scheduled and repeated tend to such behavior rather than discourage. In October 2012 at least two Telugu news channels were having "prono programmes" most of week days and one news channel is having "sex exposing" coverage at least one day a week at prime time and as part of news bulletins.

A few years ago I telephoned to the chief of this group of channels about such shows on one of his channel after 11 pm. He indicated his ignorance but promised to come back within a day or two. He kept his word and informed me the next day and also thanked me. He said that an engineer (?) was switching to some Russian sources and promised to change which of course he did promptly. That is how I have been reiterating that viewer activism by "talking back" to channels could do much good.

Are News Channels on Exit Route?

While on the one hand news channels continue to proliferate as if unconcerned of viability, there are some winding up or on exit or on shift out from round the clock news channel business. How come?

What can be made out if the ones which played special role as news channels also are on that route?

Star TV group could be credited for pioneering initiatives in kick starting news channels boom in India initially together with NDTV and later with its own Star News (Hindi) in the last decade or more. With Star news channel becoming viable it too triggered news channels at national and regional levels. In 2012 Star decided to shift out of news channel business, (pass it on to ABP altogether). And there was hardly any discussion as to how Star TV walked out of news channel business but continue with its 30 or more channels in other genre. How come? Was that exit of Star from news not because it realized that round the clock news channel business had reached a plateau or heading for "hard times", including because of "conflict of interest?.

Despite being fairly in a comfortable position as a market leader, TV-9, perhaps is the only channel among Telugu news channels to be in such an enviable situation. But it is now (September 2012), likely to become part of a national media group having its own news channel in English claiming Number One position (going by TRPs that is) and looking for expansion into regional markets. How come? Once this merger (should it materialise?) "Deal" but off and on it gives message that profitability alone is perhaps no guarantee for survival or continuation of round the clock news channels.[21]

Having set an example for other channels, in the last ten years, promoter of TV-9 is exploring exit options (for whatever reason?). But that could also revive hopes of other news channels to look for similar deals or exit route? On the other, another Telugu news channel (Zee – 24 hours News) of a national media group, Zee TV, having several other channels – news, GEC and reach all over the country – and operating in Andhra Pradesh for three years is running a scroller (in September 2012) that "this channel will not be available w.e.f. September 20" because of continued losses(?!). [22]Zee is closing down, unlike in the case of TV-9, for reasons of "heavy loses". (However by end of September 2012, Zee rather preferred to strike a deal with a senior office bearer of ruling party and pass on the news channel to the new entrepreneur). And yet at least another 4 – 6 new news channels in Telugu are expected next few months (more of them however, seems expect viability) on. Some other news channel too have merged or new owners.

News channels have been exploring constantly with various options to cope with increasing competition and issue of viability. Once it was realized that TRP alone is not enough to cope with, channels explored different options. These include trying to attract investments from within and outside, revamp managements (resulting in criss crossing of senior executives), restructure programming pattern, reorder news priorities etc. Number of news channels continued to increase all through no matter what kind of rethink operating channels were going through. The desperateness was evident as a few had announcing close down, others added more in the same genre or different and some others diluted news contents or transforming into a mix of genre.

Two news channels in 2011-12 instead of limiting to news content had gone out of round the clock news by taking to entertainment, both such channels regained Maa and Zee in Telugu are an example. They become viable and also added on channels because of their strong hold with feature film and cinema personalities. Another twenty four hour news channel- I TV – on the other could not do so as it could not mobilize any other strength. It continues to languish.

The case of NDTV is no different. NDTV however continue to be on look out for an investor at home or abroad. None of its initiatives either with Hindi in South and metro news channels could not even take off. NDTV realized the peril of reliance on TRPs for generating advertising revenue. That was why it talked of "constant race for TRPs that lead to the deterioration in news content".[23]

NDTV is a pioneer of News TV in India. Many news channels in English and other languages and regions looked forward to NDTV's Prannoy Roy, Barkha Dutt, Vikram Chandra, etc as role models. It is rumored for more than a year in 2011-12 that this group too was on look out for "strategic investors" at home and abroad, as the channel finds itself in difficulties as it is on decline in TRPs? And then comes the big story of its suit in New York against TAM's principles who in turn accused NDTV that it filed the case as it was "loosing on TRPs and revenue". NDTV had already discontinued NDTV- The Hindu in South and metro news channels earlier. It had already sold its GEC Imagine to Turner which in turn closed that channel. NDTV had seen how it has become a victim of "complete reliance" on ad revenues going by TRP compulsions. In fact it had openly talking of "constant race for TRPs has lead to the deterioration in news content" (*Businessline, September 24, 2012).*

ETV group (other than in Telugu) are already concluded a "deal" of passing on some of these ETV channels. Although of GEC category, those channels are known news source.

Are these isolated examples? What message comes out of these three or four examples of news channels on wind up route? More such instances are in the offing going by the "market talk". There were a couple of other such cases earlier too. Is it that those news channels were not able to come up with distinct content priorities or is it because they relied too much on TRPs? Or, both? It has to be one of these two reasons?

In the meanwhile dilution process has started. Debt ridden, some news channels are looking for "strategic investors" others are looking for outright deals or mergers. "Negative outlook", although not dampened seeking permission for new news channels, that has put them in search for other ways and means. NDTV diversification into "business of guiding (regional) news channels" is one such way (although that has not given them any break – except a couple of instances as in the case of Saakshi Telugu news channel).

It is against this background that news channels should explore the possibility of differentiating model by taking to "needs based" content model. It is a good opportunity to unleash their creatives proactively as a better way of survival rather than taking to a more crime, more sex and more controversies.

Will Channels Ever Become Viable?

An insight we cannot ignore is that without participation of users, viewers or listeners we cannot evolve more appropriate news channels for Indian milieu. Today viewers are by and large passive (the notion that "remote" in hand gives option, empowers and ensures certain activism is not exactly how it works). How can that be ensured?

We know one of the reasons for decline in Governance and so many schemes for so long not achieving the outcomes is, the schemes are all Government driven, and Government made people depend on it as much, where as Indian model earlier at the outset was that people and community should share or contribute a certain part of the resources for common good. In the case of broadcasting the Government seems contend with collecting a one time license fees, without any obligatory conditions to do with viewer complaints or participation. This obligation could also be in different ways - a certain time / topics, locally produced material, etc. So that people feel the onus and take a stakeholder view. Media, particularly news media in public domain, are a public resource to be availed for larger good. What provisions are there to ensure that?

Like the electricity or water meters the user should pay for the extent of use of a channel / programme. Only then judicious or active viewing habit becomes a trait. The Government or a public Trust or even a corporate subsidizing viewing of certain news channels or certain contents could always be there to help certain section of viewers. This apart the old system of a onetime license fees could be also reconsidered (at purchase point itself).

With television sets being given free (tomorrow another political party would announce set top box free and also exemption from monthly subscription), can we expect active and discriminative viewership and stakeholder feeling. So that channels are motivated to take to serious programming. With digitalization process of television transmission already taken off in phases, we can expect soon (in five years) more authenticated billing by the extent of viewing when viability opportunity of channels could be expected to improve. Once TV viewing becomes pay - based, viewer expectations of benefit and relative differentiation between channels become a possibility.

The premise of content model of news channels is to inherently support and sustain the interests of investors and markets which in turn mean promoting consumerism. Unfold the proposition further; this model implies that viability of channels depends on advertising revenue. For getting that support channels in turn have to cater to the interests of investors and purvey consumerism. Consumerism depends on homogenizing consumption patterns of people as only then size of a market could be big enough for advertising. And bigger the market, bigger the advertising budget. TRP subtly keeps these (reinforcing) linkages. The stakeholders in this process being advertisers, advertising agencies, market researchers, media planners and corporate public relations, I called them as the "new gatekeepers" of media including the news channels.

A way out of this dilemma is not possible without addressing two critical issues. First is the notion of more the merrier. Without limiting the number of channels in a given segment / market, it is not possible to ensure their viability. News is bound to have multiple angles, but cannot have so many versions. One of the fundamental life philosophy of India is conservation – use to the extent it is essential – not to waste, do not over consume. But mass media's interests clash with that philosophy, because of the very premise of advertising and compulsions of markets.

An Alternate Model for News Channels

What could be an alternate model of news channels if one has to explore? An alternative to the current content model, based on driving greed in people, is needs model which opens new vistas and hopes to a much larger section of people. Ideally the model should be:

(1) As more is not merrier, better to limit, the number of players to be permitted or licensed in each "market" and with certain minimum obligatory conditions.

(2) The content model should be appropriate one for Indian situation, not replica of a model in USA where media is subservient to investors and corporates.

(3) Dependence on advertising for viability should not exceed fifty percent and dependence should not be limited to a few sources.

(4) Better if advertising on news channels are limited to "sponsor" and generic rather than to consumer brands (time ceiling of 12 mts in a clock hour was already suggested by TRAI).

(5) A decentralized news media has better chance to be more responsive and enhance scope and expand the very reach.

(6) Regulatory mechanism particularly for media content should be there. It should preferably be a three tier based with Government coming into picture in the last and if only and where necessary but the Government should not abdicate its responsibilities altogether.

(7) Cross media ownership in the case of news media has to be restrained and restricted to certain limits.

(8) Transparency in the operations of news media as to their ownership, conflict of interest, etc should be evident. And, they should come under RTI Act in their own advantage.

(9) It is in the interest of news channels in particular if they could save themselves from viewership measurement rating services and concern more about implications and impact of their contents. Such studies should be conducted independently and transparently.

(10) Redressal mechanism for viewers should be from within media and earnestly.

(11) Independent field research and analysis of trends particularly to keep track of impact should be conducted altogether independently of channels, advertising and even the Government of the day.

(12) It is perhaps time to take a critical review of the idea of round the clock news channels. A decade of 24x7 news channels and the way they had mushroomed and the line-up of new ones indicate a further decline both in viewership and their credibility.

(13) Television is an experimental medium. It is amenable for constant revamp, repositioning to strive for better and better. Channels should take to experiments constantly to distinguish individually. Channels which choose to experiments in so many respects reach a plateau much faster.

Endnotes

1 That there was unprecedented growth and changes in the media scene was amply indicated and amplified by so many reports, both of govts and independent agencies. The govt. one include those of TRAI, annual report of the Ministry of Information and Broadcasting, and the prominent private one include the ones in collaboration with FICCI, by KPMG, Macanzie, TAM, etc. please refer to these sites: http.www.trai.gov.in , http.www.ficci.in. , http://www.cii.in, http://mib.nic.in., and http://www.tamindia.com

2 TRAI was set up by a legislation in 1997 to be a regulator for the entire private sector telecom services. In January 2004 the govt notified that broadcasting and cable services will be treated at part of telecom services but to do more with carriage aspects.

3 Amir Khan's television serial, Satyamay Jayate(May 2012) interacts with citizens and discuss various social issues and tries to find simple alternative solution for contentious issues. The program was simultaneously telecast by different regional language channels. Soon its popularity tapperd off. But in the process it set a new model in the structure and content dimensions of TV Channels, including News Channels.

4 CMS Media Lab's monitoring of news media in New Delhi and Hyderabad as detailed earlier. Please refer to their websites.

5 CMS Media Lab analysis and the trends over the decade has unambiguously indicated the content priorities of news channels.

6 CMS analysis of the trends for the decade (2005-2015) indicated about trivia in the priorities of news channels and certain changes in the trend. News channels monitored on a daily basis over a decade include, Doordarshan, NDTv,

Ajtak, Cnnibn (now cnnnews18), Zee TV, Star TV Later ABN, CMS Media Lab in Hyderabad monitored and analysed the content trends over the years but only for 8 to 10 weeks but of most news channels in Telugu. Also see http:/ /www.cmshyderabad.wordpress.com/7/

7 More than 6o percent of advertising revenue of channels continue to come from consumer brands and services. CMS and earlier at ORG this writer was a foremost analyst of advertising outlays into different media by time and program wise. CMS brought out a publication initially in 1990, "an overview of media advertising in India", CMS, New Delhi, this was updated at least twice in the next decade. Various news reports have also indicated the trend. Also see "Why Media investments have dried up" by Vinita Kohli Khandekar in Business Standard 31 August 2010, also "soap channels lose share of ad pie" Business Standard 27 April 2006

8 Pitch-Madison Media Advertising, 2014, 2016 issues 3 to 9.

9 TRAI http://www.trai.gov.in 28 August 2012

10 As CMS Media Lab is monitoring channels on a daily basis and continuously for ten years or more, its track of shifts in content priorities makes the compulsions for such changes obvious. This review of shifts in the case of some channels and informal discussions with some of the concerned executives, as in the case of ZEE or MAA Channels, makes the conclusions here obvious. CMS had indicated much earlier that the idea of 24 hour news perhaps is not viable. The trend has been gradual. First the per cent of time devoted to hard news had come down and then that of entertainment or such other items has gone up. This media lab data had brought out that news channels had over 12 hours of hard news initially more than ten years ago which had come down to less than seven hours by 2011 -12, and further declined to less than five hours by 2015.

11 No formally declared information is available on ownership or stake holding pattern of channels, including of news channels. Unlike In the case of news papers, there is no obligation or compulsion to periodically declare stake holding. Even what is indicated to Registrar of Companies or stock markets, does not give indication as to whose Investments had gone into in starting the channel or later In operating the channel. Everything about news channels is in hush, putting things together of what is informally gathered from personal discussions with those who are familiar with such transactions or holding. To add to this CMS content analysis gives some more clues particularly at times of elections and in covering certain contentious issues or issues of conflict of interest. That is how this writer had summed up this scenario about ownership and control aspects.

12 "When politicians own the media" by Vanita Kohli Khandekar, in Business Standard 3 July 2012.

13 "Appetizer effect of t v news on newspaper readership" CMS, August 2005 Highlights of which were covered in most news media in August 2005. Also see "the resilience of Indian print media" key note presentation at IAMCR meet at Hyderabad, 19July 2014. Television, particularly. news bulletins, has helped

expand media market and more specifically news dailies. Even more so in the Hindi speaking states.

14 As earlier explained at 11

15 Subhash Chandra quoted by Rajeev Banerjee in Times of India, 24 March 2011. Chandra reiterated the view in an interview to Vanitha Kohli Khandekar in Business Standard 5 July 2011

16 TRPs of news channels after 2008 have indicated decline or stagnation in viewership to news channels. "News channels report poor showing" by Bipin Chandran, in Business Standard, 18 November 2005. This writer went (2013) to Banglore to personally see and enquire into operations of Public TV Channel and had extensive discussion with its promoter Mr. Rangnath

17 'AAMA KI AASH' of Times of India campaign intended to connect friends or families separated or missing across borders or conflict situations between the countries.

18 The undivided Andhra Pradesh state experienced in the previous fifteen years frequent elections. (in addition to at least three general and three elections to state assembly.), There were more than seven by -elections to one or more assembly seats in Telengana and continuous agitations for separate state of Telengana which eventually was formed on the eve of 2014 general elections and first Telengana assembly elections.

19 "Pipli live" was a feature film released in 2011. It was a satire on how news media particularly channels get fed by politicians as news plants. In this case the issue of farmer suicides and farmers debt were trivialised. It also depicts how Jugalbandhi between news media, politician and bureaucrats work.

20 More than, and in addition to Content analysis, it was personal observation for some days provocative love scenes (including un announced sex footage) and popular double meaning films were being shown by some channels, which on consolidating viewership gave up those midnight slots (or post prime time) in favour of some other type of programs. These observations were checked up with other people who either did Media review for news papers or supposed to know the content trends with some personal knowledge.

21 Promoters of TV 9, Telugu, news channel tried to pass on control (for reasons of conflict between the promoter and the content chief of the channel who allegedly building up his own empire within and outside the country). The channel continues negotiations as it could not reach a logical end and in the meanwhile the promoter had hit a bigger success elsewhere and was focusing on that venture.

22 Zee news www.zeenews.india.com

23 Business line, 24 September 2012,, "News Corp., Nielson settle dispute over TV ratings" Economic Times, 27, October 2006. "NBCU to buy 26 per cent stake In NDTV for dollor 150 million" Financial Express 22 January 2006 and Business line, 24 September 2012.

6

Trps and Awards Measuring Viewership: TRP Phenomenon

The idea of measuring viewership was mooted by advertisers to facilitate advertising outlays. Neither the scope nor the methodology of TRP indicates programme preferences or actual viewing of various programmes. The methodology of measuring viewership should depend on the kind of contents, genre and range of its reach. For example, the one designed to cater to ad agencies cannot be expected to dictate priorities of contents. The methodology in vogue cannot be expected to be relevant to know the viewership of news channels, and more specifically news bulletins. Yet, we have been using the same methodology to assess viewership of news channels. This is misleading. The dubiousness is even more as the number of 24-hour news channels have proliferated much after TRP methodology was devised and taken roots. How it could be explained that a channel classified as a news channel despite its preoccupation with "non-news" content is shown having high TRPs under news category even for a week or two?

"Rating viewership" of TV is a disastrous thing that happened with far reaching consequences. It has been playing a iniquitous role in the process of evolving and unleashing the power of television in India. In fact, it has been an amazing story of winning psyche and markets in a smart way with the help of a simple idea compared to the efforts put in by the East India Company to capture India. More than a decade ago, I described this phenomenon as a "TRP trap" and "hijacking of Indian TV".

Of course, no technology can be stopped from penetrating into societies irrespective of its political and economic basis. However, television was introduced (1964) in India with certain expectation that it would become an "instrument" and "facilitator" to refurbish India as a State, deepen democracy, motivate people, empower them and enable good governance. The television "flood gates" were not opened in one go, rather it was done in phases – experimentation (1964-72), establishment (1973 -1992) and growth (1992–2012) to realise and explore the potential of this media. Yet, no insights or learnings of that experimentation and establishment years of TV have gone into the electronic media in the later years as it underwent changes in its scope, structure, reach and implications.

TRPs started as a small idea, but ended up making big difference and changing the very course of TV, i.e., "rating of viewership" instead of measuring what is actually being watched or impact of such viewing. It was like losing the forest for the sake of wood... this is what rating of viewership in vogue is all about. Thus, it's important to understand how it became a factor, a cause and effect phenomenon?

With the increase in the number of centres of Doordarshan (in Delhi first, then Mumbai and other metros and state capitals), they also started increasing programme hours from three to six hours and then 24 hours, which advertisers celebrated. They wanted to speed up that process to scale up ad budgets. The ad agencies wanted some basis for justifying budget outlays on this new medium – as to how much and where to allocate. Initially, the basis was the number of TV sets sold. With Doordarshan starting a commercial wing to "market time slots" and taking to sponsored programmes, Mumbai-based ad agencies came up with figures as to how many would be watching (based on households with TV sets) film songs first, then serials such as *Hum Log, Nukkad, Mahabharat,* and so on. Soon, it was realised that a TV set was attracting a number of people and hence, its "potential for advertising" should be on that basis. To support that view, they needed figures and that is how the idea of "number of viewers" came in. With the increasing number of channels and diversification of programme, time specific and programme-wise viewership was sought due to variation in the number of viewers from one to another. To start with, for a short period, they tried to use first the "recall" and then the "diary method" for estimating viewers. Very soon, thanks to government's policy of opening the flood gates with 100 per cent FDI in services and sectors such as advertising and marketing research, foreign research agencies were looking for entry or expansion of their business in the country. Consequently, the number of "brands", particularly multinational corporates, being advertised on[1] TV increased to 500 from less than 100 by 1995, and advertising on "matching" programmes with high viewership was sought. That is when the foreign ad agencies and market research agencies imported this "meter" to try out on the Indian scene. This involved keeping track of time during which a TV set was on and who in the family was watching.

The idea of quantifying viewership was to cater to the needs of advertising and facilitate media planners in particular. It was not used to determine programme preferences of viewers or to decide content priorities of channels. Soon, advertisers wanted to know when or during which programme their commercials would have more viewers and then particular category of households. With sponsored categories of programmes and outsourcing of serials increasing and becoming a business opportunity, viewership qualification became a differentiator. It meant that the "popularity of programme" in terms of number of viewers at that time became an indirect yardstick. With the proliferation of channels and programme chunks by different genre, the idea of viewership of programmes was thought about by advertisers as a surrogate indicator. As outsourcing of programmes by channels increased, the need for time-wise and programme-wise break-up of viewership acquired more relevance as a guide to place ads and to have differentiated advertisement tariff. By then it was obvious that channels cannot sustain and survive without maximisation of ad revenue. It was also clear that they cannot achieve this without having content that help attract more number of viewers and advertisers. Simultaneously, media planning became a specialised function and sponsoring programmes became a preferred option. In this process, quantitative information on viewership became critical and an ongoing requirement of advertising planners from once a quarter (13 weeks) to once a month and then to once a week.

Initially, the media research (MR) service functioned within ad agencies. Later, rating service was promoted by ad agencies and for that, they pressed in service market research agencies to serve common interests. But as rating became a sought after service, it became a subsidiary service of a foreign MR firm. Then there was an impression of it becoming an "independent" service, and finally, a separate corporate entity.

Some specific questions that arise about TRP are: (1) Rating service is not an independent function, rather it came into being as a supportive service to serve the interests of advertising first and foremost and of channels in that process. (2) Rating service had not come into being from a perspective of programmes of channels. (3) More pertinently, there was no perspective of viewers and their concerns or interests in devising the measurement. (4) There is no transparency in the entire exercise of rating. There is certain conflict of interest all over to the extent of doubting the very objectivity of the outcome. (5) The way findings are used with claims by individual channels and even content producers. These ratings were used more seriously than the advertising community themselves for serving those interests for which the service came into being. (6) The question of methodology involving sampling, size of sample and selection and validation procedures of their representative character – all have questionable relevance and doubtful basis. (7) Neither the civil society nor the governmental agencies took serious view or review of any of the aspects of TRP service. Even when the rating service had slowly but steadily reduced the stature of Doordarshan (as if in a motivated way), the government did not bother to inquire into it. It was only at the end of 2010 that the government reluctantly undertook a review of the TRP system.

Nearly 25 years after TRP had taken roots to the extent of becoming the currency of the industry, the government appointed a committee in 2010 to review the rating mechanism and suggest correctives. The committee, however, talked only to channels and came up with a formulation related more to sample size of rating system rather than taking a larger perspective and concerns of viewers into account.

[2]Starting in 1993 in Mumbai with 250 meters, the viewership measurement experiment added 200 meters in Delhi in 1995 and by 1998 the four metro cities (Delhi, Mumbai, Kolkata and Chennai) had 250 meters (all were used meters imported from South Africa). When proliferation of channels started in 1998, more meters were installed – about 2,500 in all – in metro cities and between 2003-05 some more meters were added in a few Class I cities. But the "findings" of those meters were presented and projected as if they were representative of the national scene.

In the first 10 years, the number of "viewership monitoring meters" increased to 4,000, all confined to metros and Class 1 cities. Between 1998–2003, meter-based viewership made news as descriptive of the national scene, though by then TV had spread more into rural areas. With competition between channels, including 24-hour news channels, the findings of TRP drove news towards trivialisation and there was a paradigm shift in the media. That is how TRP took roots and became basis for programme priorities. A nation of critics otherwise, and despite more than 100 universities claiming to have journalism/communication faculties, there was no study of meter-based viewership measurement and its regular coverage in the news media. As more channels got added in regional languages, channels started claiming viewership for their respective programmes as TAM started giving TRP for individual programmes language-wise, even though the sample size rose only marginally to reflect viewership with any reliability for those language channels/ programmes.

I recall a very popular programme *Rajini*, sponsored by Mudra Ad Agency, which was making news for creating consumer awareness and preaching consumer activism, was not getting reflected in TAM reports. Sitting in A. G. Krishnamurthy's (the then CEO of Mudra) room in Ahmedabad, we wondered why that was the case. That was the first time, 25 years ago that I started analysing the phenomenon. I realised that the much talked about serial, *Rajini,* was not in consonance with marketing interests of advertisers. Even more curiously, no other similar serial was ever produced by other channels, which are, otherwise, quick to take to (copy) popular programmes. That was how my article questioning the TRPs appeared in the *Asian Age*, (12th September 2001) and Indiatelevision.com. It was the first article to question the very basis of TRPs and the irrelevance of this methodology.

Two market research agencies took to viewership measurement service – IMRB's INTAM and Neilson's TAM. They were also the ones who were conducting two readership surveys at that time. They gave an impression of providing competing service. But soon they ended up merging into one service, as they were giving conflicting viewership ratings, sometimes casting doubt on the credibility of TRPs. They both came together after 1998 and formed a separate company for viewership measurement to give the impression that it is an independent body, conducting measurement, when, in fact, the service is owned by two market research agencies that are part and parcel of foreign-controlled advertising MR conglomerate. As a result of this linkage, TAM was able to acquire a grip on channels, as they, in turn, have to depend on their advertising support. The more channels depend on commercials, the more their vulnerability to TAM's rating points (TRPs). [3]It is this close linkage that made TRP a benchmark. In this process, there were allegations of channels/producers "guaranteeing viewership rating points" to advertisers beforehand! How was it possible? There were also allegations with details in the news media on how the number of sample households in the panel was fudged to acquire a representative character and how the identity of sample households was manipulated to inflate the viewership points for various rounds. These revelations added to the "channel war" accusing one another for constantly getting higher rating points continuously or by turn! This media coverage of TRP sample led to the Research Agency adopting a "diplomatic stand" of appeasing whoever questioned its figures (of course, among the big ones), and its representative character. For example, Zee refused to take to TAM service for a while until one of their serials was given higher TRP. But that was more by way of bargain tactics to shackle the continued grip of Star TV's TRPs. That was how its "big TV" became "big" by getting TRP backup. Eventually, the issue was sorted out or rather it ended with both the broadcasters coming to an understanding on marketing TRPs.

In 1993, realising the inadequacy of TRP system at the very early stage itself and the kind of restrain it would cause to Indian creativity and concerns of the Indian TV, CMS, in collaboration with ECIL, Hyderabad, developed a rugged "people meter" similar to the one that was used by TAM, but could be indigenously produced and, more importantly, could assess rural situations and sustain certain power fluctuations. This meter was demonstrated in Delhi and Bangalore.[4]

However, until 2011, TAM's meter was neither shown publicly anywhere, nor have most of those who refer to the meter have ever seen it. I went out of the way to sensitise that Director General of Doordarshan (1993-96) what that meter service meant to Doordarshan in reflecting its reach in rural areas and across all socio-economic classes. Instead of encouraging, the DG did his best to scuttle that independent initiative of an alternative model, which includes rural India (he was negotiating a deal with Star TV to join them as their head was not known at that time). He asked me to "go to Mumbai's advertising agencies and get their approval before DD could consider" the idea of an alternative to TAM's TRP System. I tried to sensitise the then Secretary of I&B Ministry, Bhaskar Ghose and and the then minister K P Singh Deo (1993-95) about the DG, Mr. R. Basu's, insensitivity. But by then through push and pulls, the advertising lobby was successful in preventing my initiative. In desperation, the CMS gave up the idea after having incurred considerable expenditure.

In 2007, the CMS took another initiative to bring together two agencies, TAM and aMap, on one platform along with a cross section of concerned professionals to debate issues involved in viewership measurement at Delhi's India International Centre. Never before had any of these agencies made such a presentation. Even for this, they did not bring the meter to demonstrate.

While TAM is a subsidiary of foreign investors with interest in ad and MR businesses, aMap is a technology-driven company started by a former ad agency professional in India. That should explain why aMap, despite having marginally bigger sample, better spread and online viewership measurement, could not penetrate into TAM's clientele. In August 2011, there was a rumour that TAM had succeeded in cornering aMap to close down its India operations.

People Meter

At the outset, the meter used by TAM initially indicated only whether the TV set was "on" or "off". The "volunteer TV household" was expected to push the button on when the TV set was switched on and push it off when switching off the TV. It is not possible to know everything about real viewership from such a measurement. Since the data about the volunteer TV household was already available, it was presumed that they were watching the programme of the channel. It was with such mechanistic features that have nothing to do with any aspect of actual watching, that "viewership measurement" was formulated, popularised and made the basis for TV's future in India[5].

In mid-1990s the agency claimed that it had shifted to a "people meter" instead of the earlier one, for a more "specific" viewership data. The people meter (also imported and reconditioned) was an improvement in that it had up to nine on and off push buttons – one for each member of the household and two buttons for "visitors". In this "people meter", each member was assigned a number on the meter (husband-1, wife-2, child 1-3, child 2-4, etc.) to push when he/she starts viewing the TV and push off the button when not viewing. That was how TAM started giving TRPs by age group. Obviously, this system requires "motivated" participation (gifts or money being paid) for agreeing in the first instance to install the "meter" connected to the TV and then willing to push the button on and off each time and every day whatever that time is (in minutes initially of 15 minutes duration and later on to one minute duration). It assumes that every member in the household is equally motivated to participate in such a push-pull exercise every time, regularly and promptly and each time each family member comes in front of a TV set.

It was with such a clumsy, unreliable and motivated arrangement that viewership measurement by way of rating points was made out as the yardstick of the industry. Then, there are two other aspects – one related to sample size and representative character of those sample households. The second is what per cent of sample (households and individuals) actually push on and off every time while watching TV and as regularly that they are able to give an estimate of viewing duration for everybody. Another question is how do they compensate for errors arising out of TV sets not having electricity, out of order TV sets, forgetting to switch on or off or/and doing it at leisure or irregularly. Nothing is known about these aspects of TRPs. There is yet another aspect, that is the way the channels use/or quote TRP figures to falsely present viewership of their channel as "number one" for the week or among a certain age group or in a selected market area.

Weekly or Monthly Reporting?

The perils of viewership ratings were not formally questioned by any government or professional agencies until 2010. [6]There was also a revealing allegation/ accusation by NDTV by way of a legal notice against the principle promoters of TAM, Neilson-Kantar, in New York in August 2012. There was no effort to correct any aspect of TRP practices until 2010 when the I&B ministry appointed a pro-industry committee and it came out with the easiest and inane suggestion for enlarging sample size, ignoring more critical aspects pertaining to the methodology. Against that background, News Broadcasters Standards Authority (NBA) came out with an advice to channels that viewership ratings should be brought out monthly instead of weekly or even daily. Online availability of such ratings even in the case of news channel was considered as an advantage and it was preferred until 2011 when NBA advised TAM Media Research Pvt. Ltd., which has been doing TRPs, to bring out reports on a monthly basis from October 2011 instead of weekly reports in the case of news channels in English and Hindi. This was because NBA's member-channels were mostly in English and Hindi. But TAM was reluctant to bring out monthly reports and wanted the subscribing ad agencies to give such an advice in writing. The rationale for NBA's advice was what the author has been raising for more than a decade. TRP system has been promoting one-upmanship between channels to the extent of driving them to gossip, hype and instant popularity to the extent of affecting quality, relevance and credibility of news broadcasts. While advertisers and ad agencies were naturally in support of TRPs, as it was invented by them and for their advantage, not all programme people were in its favour. Some sensitive executives from different channels realised the fallacy of weekly TRPs and the trap they were falling in. While one of the agency (*aMap*), which came into market with the USP of "online" and "over night' ratings, had closed its shop by then, the other agency, TAM, wanted to resist it with the support of majority of "subscribing clients" and was likely to come up with a "new service" of "also a monthly" report as an option in addition to the weekly one. The very concept of TRP was based on the notion of cut throat competition and used as an instrument of advertising; quality or utility of programmes, whether entertainment or news, was not its concern. But it was interested in offering "advice or "consultancy" service on content priorities and programming strategies. Notwithstanding internal bickering, the NBA should be appreciated for correctly diagnosing "cut throat competition" being pushed by "Wednesday favour" and asking concerned agency to bring out the report monthly instead of weekly in the case of news and business channels for at least two years, to begin with. This was a much needed proactive initiative of the NBA. But it was not taken up until 2012.

The other advices of NBA were on reporting poll campaign and terrorist attacks. They were more in response to requests from outside.

TAM data has been under criticism off and on without the criticism gaining support and becoming a rallying point, even when it was alleged how metered household was changed for not viewing certain channel/ programme as advised. In fact, some channels debunked TRPs at one time or other, depending on their own score for that week. More than a decade ago, too, it was questioned when addresses of its sample households with meter were leaked and second time when the CMS challenged viewership rating agencies (TAM and aMap for a presentation before a group of independent experts at Delhi's India International Centre in 2007, which they did with reluctance.

Running after eyeballs even for a week is what all channels, including news channels do. These TRP scores are used for wooing advertisers and for popularity race among viewing public. That is how we have a situation where a couple of channels advertise themselves as the "most viewed" or "No. 1" channel for one or other week – as if that is what either by turn or all of them could claim sourcing TRP.

Therefore, Advertising Agency Association, Indian Broadcasting Foundation and Indian Society of Advertisers should come out of their shells and help the NBA in its initiative to restore the credibility of news and business channels that Uday Shankar of IBF talked about. This NBA initiative should make stakeholders of channels rethink about TRPs and come out with many more initiatives on their own to reposition the channels. This, however, does not mean that with bringing out the TRPs monthly, instead of weekly, the perils or adverse implications of TRP are gone. There are other equally critical issues related to TRP that need to be addressed and corrected. These pertain to the methodology, analysis and presentation of findings, the way findings are used, and transparency in the entire process of viewership measurement.

Misleading TRP Phenomena

Neither the scope nor the methodology involved in TRP measurement provides programme preference or the extent of actual viewing of pogrammes. The methodology of viewership measurement should be specific to the kind of contents and genre of the channel. For example, the one designed for viewing ads of 30 or 60 seconds cannot be expected to provide insights for programme of 30 minutes viewership. Also, a general methodology cannot be expected to be relevant in the context of news channels and news bulletins. Yet, we have been using the same methodology to assess viewership of news channels as well as entertainment and sports channels. Scanning through contents of channels, their programming pattern and schedules shows no evidence of a change that could have come out of TRPs. It is more of the same and targeting the same people. If there is any new initiative, it is from the foreign channels.

The Colors Channel is perhaps the only one among Hindi channels, in 2000-11, which could be viewed as a departure. And there is no evidence of TRP indicating, promoting, or prompting a different set of programme priorities.

On the contrary, one could say that TRPs have misled the channels and not helped them in distinguishing themselves and exploring their potential from a win-win framework. It has put channels on a race course rather than on a course for impact. TRPs contribution for expanding the reach of channels beyond the current areas and sections of people is minimal.

In the wake of NDTV filing a suit against Neilsen and Kantar, promoters of TAM in India for TRP service, an article of mine[7] was carried by some news media/websites in the second fortnight of August 2012. This is being reproduced here because of its relevance.

High Time to End TAM/TRP Era of Indian TV

NDTV's allegations against Nielsen-Kantar, sponsors of the TAM-TV ratings in India, for fudging data and deliberately publishing in return for bribe, received wide media reporting. Although such accusations against TAM were not new and the deceptivity of TRPs have been almost an "open secret" in the media circles for some years, the law suit filed by NDTV in a New York court created ripples. Prasar Bharati too, is considering filing a law suit against TAM on similar grounds. But the issues involved are not limited to NDTV or DD.

NDTV Claims

In its 198-page suit, NDTV is seeking "compensation" and "punitive damages" from Nielsen-Kantar for adversely affecting its revenue, reputation, profitability, capitalisation, stock prices and brand value - in the last eight years and "recklessly disregarding any responsibility". Most people would agree that NDTV is a pioneer on the Indian TV news scene. An analysis of NDTV contents produced in recent years brings out that it did come up with certain new initiatives in its programming, showing inclinations to deviate from a TRP-driven content model. Whatever be those compulsions of NDTV for filing the suit, the channel need to be thanked not only for mustering its courage, but for hinting at what the country has missed in that process. It meant that the "Indian TV" has been under the siege of TRPs; and it has been supporting a particular content model mainly because of the TRP system. I describe this as a hijack. Consequently, the country could not evolve a more appropriate "model" that caters and serves the interests of its people. The tranquilising effect of TRPs on channels is such that we could not avail of TV channels for national endeavours, cherished goals and needs of a majority of people. TAM promoted ratings suppressed the full play of Indian genius and creative talents. That is why apart from the "loss" that some individual channels suffered on account of TAM ratings, what the nation suffered and missed is much more.

TRP Implications

Among individual channels, the worst sufferer, of course, has been Doordarshan - much more than NDTV. But for that, TAM alone cannot be blamed, as DD has been submissive to such a situation for two decades even when the effect was so obvious. DD never did anything even to put the facts in perspective. On the contrary, it scuttled at the very outset, as early as 1993-94, a truly "independent" India rating service covering rural areas too, as if it wanted to facilitate TAM (and INTAM). It abandoned its own DART "rating" service covering rural and urban. Thereafter, the Director General of DD became the CEO of a "foreign channel", which overnight became the beneficiary of TAM rating service. I had written about this blatant lapse on the part of DD more than a decade ago. But that also shows that India did not envisage what such TRPs meant in the long term.

To understand the kind of content model that TAM prompted and promoted, one needs to know about sponsors of the system and their lineages. The general impression was that the rating service is independent and it seeks to facilitate advertising. The interests of the advertising industry are, by and large, driven by consumerism. Consumerism is determined by how the greed in individuals is pampered. That is a global phenomenon. That is how with the proliferation of satellite channels, it was ensured that the government allows 100 percent FDI into advertising first, and then into market research and later into public relations and media planning. Together, these functions serve the interests of global investors and promote consumerism to maximise returns on investment. That is how these four services work in tandem as "new gatekeepers" of Indian media in a jugalbandi way. Similarly, TAM is 100 per cent owned by foreign companies Nielsen-Kantar. By linking ratings to advertising rates and ad flows, channels have been made to adopt and go by TRPs and that is how TRPs have become the benchmark. TAM created its own outfits to advise channels and provide consultancy on contents and marketing of channels.

The negative implications of TRPs far outweigh whatever positive elements are attributed to it. Because of these "experimentation", the oxygen of TV medium, was never allowed to play a more positive role in the development of TV channels in India.

In 2004, [8]taking part in a CMS discussion on paradigm shift in media at Hyderabad-based Centre for Economic and Social Studies, the

CEO of a Telugu news channel read out a "prescription" given by TAM (on the letter head of one of its subsidiaries) as to which kind of programmes the channel should take up to stand out better in the ratings. Going beyond, the prescription explained that "since there are no TV sets in rural Telangana"; there was no need to waste channel's time for programmes of interest to that region. Over the years, at least two other channel executives told me how they go by TRPs every week to decide content priorities, including that of news bulletins. One of them told me how TRPs are "guaranteed" well ahead. That was how TAM was using ratings for prescribing content priorities and promoting a content model in lieu of advertising support to channels. The ratings service has come into being and has been devised primarily to optimise ads of big spenders, i.e. MNCs. That was how channels were lured by TAM to adopt a content model that could give boost to markets and consumerism and that is how the impact of TV has not been much on social development, governance and environment. Since the government allowed 100 per cent FDI into these services, as if it had not visualised what it meant for the country in the long run, to that extent, the government, too, facilitated the process of promoting a particular content model. As a result of all such calculated efforts of TAM, India missed an opportunity envisaged by Vikram Sarabhai.

Earlier Attempts & Claims

NDTV is not the first one to expose the fraud of TRPs. Zee TV had already tried it. It boycotted the service for a while and was able to "sort out" with TAM. Doordarshan tried with no "seriousness". I was invited (1998) as an expert by the CEO (K. S. Sarma) of Prasar Bharati to a crucial meeting with TAM/ Nielsen officials from Singapore. They agreed to announce that TRPs are not "national", as is being claimed, but represent only urban households. They never kept up this promise. Yet, the CEO went out of the way to settle "pending dues" running into crores to TAM.

More than 10 years ago, when the list of TV households, where the meter was installed, was "leaked" and it was obvious that the sample was neither representative as claimed nor all the meters were working, no channel protested or withdrew TAM service. One-sixth of the 8,150 meters installed were not working at any given time and as many were not representative TV households as was being claimed, but it did not bother anybody.

May be that is why NDTV demanded a ban on TAM (Nielsen-Kantar). If NDTV could ask compensation for losses on capitalisation, profits and market due to TRPs, what about the people of India? They, too, could claim several times more compensation and take punitive actions against TAM/ Nielsen-Kantar.

Despite a devastating role that the TRPs were playing in the country, there was never any effort independently or by the TRAI or the government to systematically assess its impact and study its use or to validate its methodology. We are made to believe that "TRP" is a surrogate indicator for viewing quality and impact. The then I&B secretary was present at the CMS round table on TRPs in 2007. In 2005, I had also briefed the minister about the adverse implication of TRPs and gave details on the conflict of interests involving Nielsen. In 2010, the ministry appointed a committee headed by Amit Mitra to please media barons, and leading to no intervention or corrective measures. NDTV did better by exposing the menace. Even TAM never tried to show its impact, except by way of rise in sales of several brands in the market. Nor were there any academic efforts to study the merger of two rating services. Nor did they consider Justice Verma's suggestion for monthly reporting of ratings by TAM instead of weekly. TRPs were never even scrutinised independently. The only thing that is often talked about is the sample size, when, in fact, more critical aspect is its relevance to the Indian scene and the conflict of interest aspect that determines the scope and methodology of TRPs. Another issue is how such channels were made to use TRPs in a misleading way.

A study by political scientists would bring out that despite proliferation of news channels, voters have not become any more active or discriminative. A sociological study would have brought out how the divides in the country on various grounds have been kept up by the content model being chased. A psychological study would bring out the linkage between viewership and increased crime, casteism, sex and similar deviant behaviours in the country, particularly among the young.

There is a much bigger case for the government to file a case against Nielsen-Kantar for the prolonged fraud. But then the government cannot escape the responsibility for facilitating that process over the years, however unwittingly.

The damages that TRPs/TAM has caused over the years is not of less consequence and comparable to the overnight Bhopal gas leak tragedy.

No wonder Justice Ranganath Misra described in a CMS seminar way back in 1997 the phenomenon of satellite TV as "an undeclared war on an unprepared people". The only difference being that the government remains passive and submissive in this case and ignores the tranquilising effects. Thanks to NDTV for the awakening.

The Broadcast Audience Research Council (BARC) was formed as a tri-partied agreement between advertisers, agencies and broadcasters. Indian Broadcast Foundation took the initiative and the ministry was looking forward for BARC to come into operation with an alternative rating mechanism. But Uday Shankar, Chief of Star India and also of IBF in 2012, blamed advertisers (and agencies) for making "bizarre demand" to delay the BARC project. ("vested interests delaying alternative rating agency", he told the *Business Standard*, 30th August 2012). What made Shankar to come up with such a revelation in a media interview? Shankar is credited for new initiatives at Star TV recently as well as at IBF. He had seen over the years what it all means to deviate from the content model perpetuated by TRPs and perhaps realised that the next phase of expansion of TV is possible only with focus on broadcasters' perspective and creative potential in viewership ratings.

News channels too, like the entertainment channels, take to thumping to position themselves distinctly. Idea of positioning distinctly is good in a channel-proliferated market driven by intense competition. For this they have been depending on "viewership ratings" as provided by TAM/TRPs for some years as a habitat. With TRP idea not taking them beyond a point of expansion, news channels are trying with "awards" as pops more recently. This chapter discusses how misleading these ratings have been and how awards have become part of the cheer up process.

An Alternative Framework

An easy and popular explanation given for continued reliance on TRPs is (even after realising the pitfalls and inadequacies of its methodology), that there is "no better alternative". Is it so? Let us first understand the compulsion for TRPs.

TRP approach was adopted at the outset for media planning (not for programme strategies or content priorities). With proliferation of channels and increased reliance on TV for advertising, agencies had to convince their advertisers of allocating higher percent of their budgets for TV channels. The "American model" adopted for that purpose had taken to "rating points" approach. In India it all happened "so naturally" as if we are unaware of the implications of that process.

Against this background there was no serious effort to look for an alternative system to TRPs. Because the effort instead, is for a quick solution which supports globalisation and pedals consumerism. Sample size was all that was ever considered as the basis for reliability of TRPs – not its very relevance. And the sample was being increased marginally time to time in response to criticism. [9]While that number was increased from 4500 in 2006 to 8000 in 2009, it was hardly increased next three years (2012) and to 12000 in may 2015 although the number of TV households in the country increased by almost 30 million. So also the coverage in terms of towns covered in erupted from 160 to 225 during the years (against total number of towns of 5161). The sampling has been unconcerned of the fact that TV is no longer limited to urban or middleclass.

An Alternative

An alternative for TRP system has to be considered holistically and together by stakeholders, not by the Government or TRAI or advertisers on their own. For the very idea of an alternative to TRP, the "mind set" of advertisers, channel operators and content producers have to be open and willing to explore. And remember that TV as a mass media thrives on experiments. In the alternative system, design, methodology would be decided by a representative body (could be BARC or MRUC) different from the one which actually conducts the field survey. And there should be responsible representation of viewers also in that body. First, it should be agreed that the very character of television and the potential of news on TV being what it is, the same quantitative approach is not enough and the need is for both qualitative and quantitative. So that it caters to the interests of advertising, channel planners and content producers. The methodology, analysis and reports should be omnibus – keeping the requirements of advertising, channels, producers and also viewers.

Why Rely on One Method?

I questioned sole reliance on meter for viewership measurement 20 years ago. Because of increasingly niche character in programmes and selective nature of viewership, on the one hand, and delink of TV ownership from socio-economic capacities, on the other, meter alone will neither be representative nor reflective for actual viewership with reliability – even assuring that all meters are operational, functional and each member in the family is equally cooperative in "on" and "off" of the button in the people meter. What I suggested as a more appropriate approach is to use three different methods parallelly – meter, diary and direct (recall) interview. To these I now add one more, self pitched responses (by mail, SMS, email, etc) of viewers. The selection of sample for the first three methods has to be structured and pre-selected both for representative and reflective features. The analysis would be desegregated way and also together and also cumulative for certain parameters (like time segment, age group, etc). This approach is cumbersome but allows validation and yields both quantitative and qualitative aspect of viewership. In 2015 TAM and BARC Formed in 2012, but came into operation in 2015. Came up for a joint venture with 34000 people meters. That is TAM got away vitiating view up scene and advertising priorities in the country with woo felly in adequate sample and methodology for two decades.

Transparency

Notwithstanding the motivation of some technologists (irrespective of Indian or European) in questioning the reliability of Electronic Voting Machine (EVM) being used in India for voting, the Election Commission of India (EC) has been grappling for two years (2010-2012) in so many different ways to show that EVMs are tamper proof. It had invited technologists and activists and allowed critics to prove their point. To satisfy the critics EC even conceded to make certain modifications (like voter verifiable paper audit trail). I have been asking every meeting that I took part on media across the country over the years whether anyone had ever seen "viewership meter". I yet to come across one. The point is that there was never any attempt to publicly demonstrate functioning of "people meter". The importance is even more because the metros in use are being imported from one country and manufactured in another and, more, they were used meters (for sure in the initial ten years). The question of why they cannot be manufactured in India when it could be cheaper and even better to suit the Indian conditions including rural was never asked.[10]

Instead, TAM has been lobbying for exemption of custom duties. When CMS invited TAM for a discussion at India International Centre, New Delhi, (2007) on TRPs, with a request to show the meter, its head came without a meter. And he was not even willing to tell how much a meter costs or how many of installed ones were actually operate at any point and every time by members of the sampled household. As such it need to be explored to get a "people meter" or even a better one manufactured locally, at a much cheaper cost and a more rugged one for rural installation.

How independent the agency that conducts ratings is important and knowing any "conflict of interest" is even more important. (Both Neilson and Kantar, sponsors of TAM, are in media, advertising, marketing and brand building business globally and they decide on how much to spend on TV advertising). Continuing the ratings further with same framework even if the sample size is increased will not make much sense. The change required is a shift in the very paradigm. Only then it could be a win-win back up for the Indian TV.

Sampling

Size of sample alone is not good enough; it has to be **representative** and **reflective** of nature of differences between people and range of variations in the context of different genre of TV contents. A third element of sample is its spread geographically. Then of course is how participative (cooperative) the sample TV households are objectively and under natural viewing conditions. The size of sample should not be top-down but bottom up way and what is measured should not be "promoted or induced viewership" as it happens with TAM sometimes. This approach is far more relevant because of spread of regional channels locally far more. TAM initially depended for the size of sample depending on the number of meters available / imported; later decided nationally and then desegregated cluster wise. Should representation of sample be limited to "TV household" as the number of households without TV is as high as 40 to 50 percent in some regions of the country, should not sample include such household too?

Sample size is only one key element. A bigger size sample, everything else remaining same, will make no difference but could in fact add to the erroneousness of the sample. The importance of sample size is hyped often because that is also linked to "affordability" aspect. That is the cost of subscription for the "syndicated service" will be higher. If the sample size has to be increased to 30,000 (as one Committee of the Ministry suggested), subscription cost would be several times more than at present. If TRPs are used to justify an expenditure of about Rs.15000 crores annually, is spending one percent of that (Rs.150 to 200 crore) for research high? Government or the regulator should underwrite certain capital expenditure for such an altogether new alternative.

Such services should be syndicated – anyone could buy the reports. Certain basic data should be available open for use by quoting the source. Source of funding should not be limited to advertising community or anyone. In fact, about half of the cost should be met by channels (assuming that methodology is not limited to the concerns of advertising) and at least ten percent should be by the State or the regulator.

Field data acquires its consequence only when it is analysed in an open ended way than limiting to a certain pre-determined way and /or excluding certain outcome of field data after it is validated (as it also happens with NRS/IRS?). At the user end, the use of TRPs has to be far more responsible. In the absence of transparency in conducting TRPs, each user particularly channels are having their own "field day" and that too without indicating fully and transparently – as if TAM endorsed such use. Based on weekly TRPs and quoting from it, news channels have been promoting individually as the "best viewed", "most watched", etc. They do that giving TRPs of other news channels by name in the same "market". Big channels have been claiming so often and frequently by way of advertisements in newspapers, magazines and repeat in their own channels. If one goes by those promotions, all big news channels claim the top slot for one week or other such an extent that such promotions are no longer taken seriously. The fact such misuse is not condemned spreads such an impression.

Reporting periodicity. The impact TRPs are making week after week on programme producers and planners in channels has been talked. That is why some months ago (much before NDTV's allegations) Justice J S Verma of News Broadcasts Standard Authority of NBA took the initiative of asking TAM to bring out TRP reports monthly instead of weekly as at present. (But this obviously meant decline in TAM's revenue and the very grip of TRPs on the market). The least TAM should have done was to consult the ad agencies and channels about such a suggestion. Instead it said it could consider that idea only if its subscribes ask for. Tomorrow NBA could suggest that viewership for less than two minutes viewing should not be given in the reports given to the channels.

A sustainable and better alternative requires to be developed with involvement of key stakeholders including the civil society and academics.

In the meanwhile channels may be better off to learn to live proactively without a "market driven currency" may be for one year until a more representative, reflective and relevant mechanism is in place (instead of continue to use TAM). That is what it would take to put in place on alternative.

Awards for News Channels/Programmes

As if TRPs need to be endorsed, some promoters have recently come up with the idea of awards. These awards idea was "prompted" also to cover up the decline in viewership to news channels. Some of them have taken to new initiatives in programmes even departing from TRP formula. Such awards are being promoted / sponsored by some of the channels which benefited most from TRPs. Awards have a role and should help differentiate good (from not-so-good) and to encourage initiatives by individual channels. They should not constrain or limit creative perspectives and perpetuate certain content models. In fact, experimentation character of TV should be kept up by awards.

Are Awards a PR Exercise or for a Healthy Competition?

More recently, television channels including news channels have been promoting and showcasing "awards" in the same way as they have been doing with TRPs for years as if awards are an evidence for a "great job" accomplished. Some news channels feature every morning the number of awards they have won. Against only a couple of awards until 2010, there are many at present. Now, some channels have taken to in-house awards annually, like "Star Parivar Awards". These awards are even advertised in newspapers and promoted as "news events" and covered prominently by the channels.

There have been many awards in vogue for television channels, and individual programmes of channels with fanfare. The way the awards are given shows as if they have made a difference and that contribution is being acknowledged. On the contrary, a critical analysis will bring out that the awards have become outlets of self aggrandisement. Awards are expected to help differentiate "good" from "bad" contents or not so good ones and promote certain standards or values or priorities as desirable.

If channels are not making a difference how are they getting multiplied? Is making a "difference" and being "popular" the same? Popularity is judged in terms of viewership rating. Likewise, making a difference is judged with regard to long standing social behavior on subjects, like social development, environment, child development, etc. Popularity in terms of viewership ratings is more likely to ensure the viability of a channel, rather than making a difference to the lifestyles or behaviors of people.

Awards are good, particularly, when they are given transparently by independent civil society or professional bodies. Awards could be for different features. It could be for technical value, acting skills, good script, proactive news coverage, etc. It could also be for making a difference to the lives of people, for example, CMS Awards for programmes on girl child, school dropout girls, against child marriage, trafficking, consumer rights, etc.

So far, awards have hardly made a difference to the overall standards and concerns of channels. The CMS award to Chetana (2008) of TV-9 in Telugu, or Prajapaksham (2009) of the same channel, for example, has encouraged other channels to adopt similar category of programmes. This is one good indication that the award has helped showcase the initiatives. But, on the other hand, CMS Awards for news channels for news bulletins and news and current affairs have hardly made a visible difference. Giving awards for three consecutive years and even involving role model personalities, is of course not good enough to make a difference to the practices and priorities of news channels.

The "National Television (NTV) Awards" for news channels are being showcased by most news channels, as if they are the "industry awards" and getting those awards is an endorsement for their being "the best" and "the most popular"; and news channels enthusiastically "participate" in the awards by sending entries together with "the fees" prescribed for each entry. It means that the more the entries from a channel to the organiser, the more the fees it had to pay. Moreover, these awards are not voluntary or held by viewers or civil society or truly independent organisations – as awards are expected to be an acknowledgement for inspiring initiatives for excellence in one respect or other. Awards are supposed to be for bettering the standards of programmes, quality of contents and the very credibility of a channel.

Whereas, earlier TRPs and now awards (like the NTV awards) are constraining or limiting channels, particularly news channels from exploring and experimenting with original ideas and initiatives. They serve more to homogenise contents for mass markets and further facilitate or sustain media to cater to the needs of advertising. In my view based on the kind of trends observed, such awards tend to promote the fallacy of channels. Awards are more for marketing channels and positioning certain programmes.

However, awards like "The Food Awards 2012" of Times Now, on the other hand, falls in a different category. It is more about others out there, outside the channel, but across the country in the real life. They give awards for best local cuisine, fine dining, best roadside *dhaba* and the like. Many channels are taking to such awards too of late. Zee News award for environment, or CNN/IBN award for "Real Heroes" are only a few examples. What I am concerned about is the way awards are bestowed on news channels; as if they are independent, objective and professionally conducted.

NTV Awards

The "News Television Awards"[11] are being given for some four years. They are organised by a Mumbai based commercial company promoted by a former journalist. Its main business is to represent media enterprises. It operates a fairly extensive website on Indian TV. Its awards ceremony, held in a five star hotel in Delhi or Mumbai, is showcased as an annual event. News channels showcase these awards on their channels prominently with claims of the "best" and the "most" for awards received in different categories. It is intriguing how these awards have become a kind of benchmark for news channels, who are supposed to be concerned about the credibility issues of what they cover.

An analysis of NTV awards on 28 March 2012 in New Delhi brings out that national awards were, in fact, given in only four languages – English, Hindi, Telugu and Marathi, as if news channels exist in the country in these languages only. Having started with English and Hindi, Telugu and Marathi channels were included in 2011. In this ceremony, 137 awards were given in all in four languages. Consider some highlights of these news TV awards. The sponsors of awards ceremony with glamour and glitter were CNN/IBN, Star and TV-9 and a host of others. Who received the awards? The sponsoring news channels were awarded two-thirds of all the awards. This sponsorship is in addition to what is paid as entry fees by these channels. Among these awards, 30 were received by IBN, 20 by Star, 15 by TV-9 and 10 by the Aaj Tak group. Many news channels including Times Now, DD News, etc. were nowhere as if none of their contents deserved any awards under any category or, perhaps, they did not send any entries with fees in which case that should have been indicated. Three English channels together received more awards than any other language channels got.

In the case of Telugu news channels, three of them got most of the 23 awards, including one channel, which was less than two years old, got eight awards. Half of 15 news channels got no award under any category. What is that mean? What is the message?

Hardly 20 per cent of 137 awards of "News TV" in 2012 have anything to do with the coverage of news of the day/week. Little over one-third of awards to news channels were for crime, entertainment, sports or business categories. There were no awards for any specific social issue that concerns the nation. For example, there were elections to State Assemblies during the year or calamities of one kind or other, but, there were no awards for covering such things. There were, of course, four awards given for covering the Lokpal (Anna Hazare) debate! So, there was an attempt to justify the kind of round of clock coverage of Anna Hazare events in Jantar Mantar and Ramlila Maidan in New Delhi, which, otherwise, was criticised by some, including senior editors of newspapers.

Enba Awards

"Enba Awards". Exchange four Media News Broadcast Awards are being given for last couple of years[12]. Although its focus is Hindi and English channels, it claims the awards as "national". How independent and important are these Enba Awards? Firstly, these awards were driven by industry people with conflict of interest being so obvious. For example the (September) 2012 awards panel was headed by Chief of Star TV and IBF and with most Jury members from media and advertising business. Second the awards are meant to provide yet another "marketing" measure as in the case of TRPs, with no implications to promoting standards or any content concerns. Third, those who are considered for awards are those who "apply" with entry fees. The fees in 2012 for example was Rs.5000 per entry. In 2012 some 400 entries in all were received. Less than ten are other than Hindi and English channels and mostly Delhi based. The awards are more a business proposition than a professional exercise. Not all nominations for awards were actually viewed by the members of the Jury. In fact, awards were not selected based on any analysis of contents. Nor any indicators or variables for the selection or the categories for awards were preselected on certain criteria.

In 2012, 24 awards in all were given. Aaj Tak, NDTV and IBN groups were given atleast five each. Times Now was given (although not "applied") an award as an exception. One of the award for "Best Public Campaign for a Brand", was not so much for the "public service" aspect.

What is the message these awards send out? What difference these awards expect to make? How is "excellence", for which awards are given, being differentiated?. The news channels which received the awards including the Times Now, showcased all through the following day or two describing the award as an acknowledgement for "being the best", for being "the only channel", etc.

Like the NT awards for some news channels, *enba* awards too are part of business proposition and marketing exercises – not so much for professional standards or guiding programme priorities of news channels in the country.

Some described the awards exercise as "bidding for awards" or "purchase of awards" as if only the "sponsors get the" or sponsor to get awards. That is the realty of these NTV awards. This is yet another mistake the news broadcasters are indulging in. Instead of truly unleashing creative potential on their own with their own "mission", they tend to indulge in short cuts and depend more on public relations exercise. Why is all this possible? What is intriguing is why channels, even the ones with record of initiatives, have to take to such (deceptive) measures!

In the wake of decline in viewership, news channels too took to "awards" route. Since "winning awards" is the new game, news channels need to understand the self inflicting deception that award's are being taken up. First, this exercise is viewed as a business and a PR opportunity, not as a standards upholding exercise or as an affair to encourage creativity in a competitive context. Second, there is no transparency in the process of going about choosing awardees or in deciding the categories that deserve recognition. Third, there is no objective or independent methodology to go about identifying the differentiators for awards. Fourth, there is no involvement of viewers at any stage in that process. Only a couple of film critics familiar with language TV were involved for assessing as to who should be considered for the award. Fifth, there is no larger context in the process, i.e., only those channels and those programmes or categories for which entries were submitted (with fees) are considered.

Sixth, how can these be positioned as "national", when the exercise was limited to a couple of language channels and even ignored prominent channels within a selected language.[13]

As against "*NTV* and *enba* Awards" bash for news channels, consider the CMS Academy Awards for news channels, but limited to Telugu language and held for three years (2009, 2010, 2011). These CMS Academy Awards followed a rigorous, transparent and objective methodology. First, it is based not on what channels nominate for each category, but on the total contents of channels for a minimum period of not less than three months to one year and an analysis based on monitored contents in such a way that categories selected for awards are identified independently of channels and such an analysis is used by an independent Jury of eminent people numbering not less than six to identify the categories for which awards should be given. The CMS Academy Awards are limited to Telugu language only and are described as experimental and were held in Hyderabad for all the three years. The methodology of selection is based on a four steps procedure. In the CMS Academy Awards, the role of news channels is limited to "come and receive the awards on announcement". Channel representatives are also invited for an open "focus group" discussion along with experts and concerned civil society groups to discuss the criteria for judging news channels. The organiser (CMS) has no role in deciding the awards, as it is done by an independent Jury of eminent specialists having no business interests in news television. Equally important, the CMS Academy Awards ceremony is carried out by CMS with no sponsors having anything to do with advertising or channels or their contents. There is no "giving and taking" of any money or favors, even indirectly. There is no "entry fee" of any kind to participate in the awards.

The high point here is that despite the fact that CMS Academy Awards are professionally and credibly conducted with no costs to news channels, directly or indirectly, prominent channels are not enthusiastic, as they are for ("NTV") awards! How come?

A channel instituting awards for its own in-house contents and on its own, as is being done by most channels is not the same as the deceptive *NTV* or *enba* awards. As Narayan Rao of NDTV said at the NTV Awards ceremony as chief guest that the "channels need to come out of deceptive policies for reaping the best of their potential. Such awards should not become yet another mistake in consolidating the strength of channels".

CMS Awards for News Channels

CMS initiated the awards for news channels in 2007 to acknowledge and appreciate positive powers of news channels. It started with the Telugu channels, as at that time, their number was getting multiplied every year. Apart from making an analysis of the contents of news channels towards sensitising larger pubic, we thought that we should take up the idea of awards. These CMS Academy Awards were being given annually to news channels more as an experimental initiative. The chief guest at the first year awards function in Hyderabad was veteran film maker Shyam Benegal, who made a difference to the feature film industry. The chief guest in the second year was the Founder Trustee of Public Service Broadcast Trust, Rajiv Mehrotra. Dr. P. C. Rao, a judge at International Court and a writer, was the chief guest during the third year to give away the awards to news channels.

News Channels in Andhra Pradesh were asked to select the best out of their own news bulletins and send them to an independent Jury for consideration for these awards. Only two channels responded. Perhaps, they were not confident or sure as to which one to nominate or, perhaps, they thought that since CMS Media Lab is already recording news bulletins on their own, there was no need to take the trouble of sending nominations (although it was without any entry fees).

A general feeling among experts and well informed people was that it is difficult to recall a bulletin or a programme of news channels for an award. In fact, a few also felt that as "bad and ugly" or irrelevant ones are often more evident in news channels, it is easy to name such examples.

Except in the case of one or two categories, the Jury felt that none of the programmes could be described "as the best". In fact, the feeling was that in a creative field, the "best is yet to come".

Nevertheless, we thought that we should go about in a positive way. The Awards are for the ones in Telugu news channels and for their programmes during the year. For inclusion in this award, a news channel has to complete at least one year of operation.

These awards were based on a rigorously developed methodology that was implemented transparently. This was developed to reflect the public concerns. Broadly, a three pronged effort was made for selecting the awardees.

A six member independent Jury had people, who were eminent and made a mark in their respective fields. It was headed by a retired Jurist and activist, the senior most functionary and had one eminent editor, one senior academician, and one lady literary and media personality, well known as a media critic.

The second input was received from a sensitivity analysis of contents of news channels and bulletins during a meeting of experts and civil society personalities. The summary of a three year analysis of trends, in the content of news channels, was made available to the Jury and the experts at this focus group meet of not less than 30. This analysis indicated the priorities of news channels and the kind of competition they were under.

The third input was a sample survey of TV news viewing households in three different regions of Andhra Pradesh to bring out the perceptions and preferences of viewers. 13 attributes for news channels were shortlisted, based on sensitivity analysis of contents, which were also enquired in to in this field study.

The independent Jury took into account the outcome of all these various exercises, saw the clippings more than once together and independently, and finalised the categories that deserved to be appreciated and also the specific programmes that deserve to be awarded for that period. Those clippings were from out of CMS Media Lab own monitoring independently of all news channels.

The Jury members felt that for the category of scientific temper, for example, no channel deserved to be considered in all the three years. In fact, the Jury expressed its disappointment that even news channels are competing to churn out programmes promoting blind beliefs and irrational programmes. They felt that the extent of such programmes is on the increase.

The three Jury members also felt that since the best bet for better programmes is the viewer, we should award a viewer, who symbolises activism by way of expressing views on good and bad aspects of news channel programmes. As there was no other way for the awards, initially, to identify such viewers, we wrote to the channels themselves, to give us the names of some people, who had been writing to them with their feedback. Only one channel responded with only one name even after a reminder request. The message was clear and loud. We needed to promote "active viewership" and for that sensitise viewers. We thought that the awards are one way of doing that promotional role, however limited that may be.

Also, apart from what the Jury decided, the CMS Academy, as the promoter, thought it relevant to recognise certain special efforts towards promoting concerns in TV programmes. With such a view, special initiatives by the channels as well as by the print media towards promoting sensitive television viewing, was recognised by instituting special award for such efforts.

Any lessons for TV channels from Sports people? Be sportive. Consider what Sachin Tendulkar said while presenting a BMW car to Saina Nehwal on August 19, 2012 in Hyderabad for her winning India a Bronze Medal at Olympics, London. He said that the world is "yet to see the best" of Saina. There are better days ahead and as a sportsperson, "you always try to believe that your best is to come"; praising Saina, he further said that "she has not got carried away and that is the beauty of being a champion sports person". This applies much more to those in creative fields and even more those engaged in operating television channels and doing a program under severe competitive conditions. Another sportive message from London Olympics (2012) is that the real heros are those who participate, try their best but may not get any medal. For the first time special efforts were made in Olympics, London, to highlight critical role "loosers" play for the "best to come" of the Olympics. News channels chasing TRPs and awards and promoting them need to ponder on the advice of Sachin Tendulkar. It is even more apt for news channels engaged in cutthroat competition and self aggrandisement.

This chapter reiterates that unless ratings and awards become transparent, independent and help news channels position themselves proactively and differently, they promote more of the same and may even speed up their sliding and decline.

Endnote

1 Down To Earth, of Centre for Science and Environment, 1990. see http://www.downtoearth.org.in

2 Presentations of L. Krishnan of TAM at CMS organised meet at India International Centre on ratings along with two other agencies. This writer had personally tracked ratings and had discussions with stakeholders, advertisers, advertising agencies, subscribers and media groups. See proceedings of "Television viewership measurement -dilemma and challenges" New Delhi, 7 March 2007. Also refer to Asian age, 12 September 2001 and refer to web site, www.Indiatelevision.com

3 Personal discussions with more than a couple of stakeholders on practices in gathering viewership data using meters and the way reports are prepared, arguments were put up by the research agency executives to news channels. How sample claims were made. Ravi Prakash, CEO of TV 9,then premier news channel in Hyderabad, himself said so in a CMS and CESS organised round table meet in Hyderabad on trends in media . see "opportunities and challenges : Indian media scene recent shifts in paradigm of media operations," two CMS national round table discussions first at India International centre, New Delhi, on 25 June 2004 and then at Centre for Economic and Social Studies, CESS, Hyderabad, on 31 July 2004

4 India Today., 31 march 1993 with photograph of TV Meter and system developed and demonstrated by CMS.

5 TRPs were criticised by some channels including NDTV for bias in report and some like Zee have boycotted TRP reports. One common criticism was about sample size, unrepresentative character of sample and fudged nature of data so collected some time or other. Also See "get set for overnight TV ratings" in Business Standard, 7 November 2006, "television ratings: peering beneath the hood" in Mint, 16 April 2008; Meenakshi Madhvani, "TV viewership: tracking it right" in Business World, 1 December 2006.

6 That NDTV legal notice to Neilson-Kantar was widely reported in the news media and some have given details of the legal notice. For details read lengthy article of this writer at that time in "Tripping over the TRP trap" in indiatelevision.com breaking news. 13 September 2001.

7 Dr N Bhaskara Rao in indiatelecom.com. August 2012

8 Recent shifts in paradigm of media operations, CMS round table in collaboration with Centre for Economic and Social Studies CESS m Hyderabad on 31 July 2004, also see Uday Shankar." Vested interests delaying alternate rating agency" Business Standard,30 August 2012

9 Starting with hardly 500 number of TV Households sample with viewership meter in two cities (Mumbai and New Delhi) more than two decades ago, this sample size reached 9600 in 2014 across 225 cities and added another 3000 to households in 2015 alone going by pressure by the Govt. it took that long for Govt. to realise what such a small and unrepresentative sample meant and many subscribers to even stopped taking to TAM service. That is when the newly formed BARC took over the task of ratings forcing TAM to collaborate with a much higher sample of 34000 in the first phase itself in 2016. One should guess what would have been the character of Indian television without that idea of such viewership ratings in a few cities and in a few households?

10 "CMS meter" in India Today, 31 march 1993

11 News Television awards (NT Awards) is an activity taken up in 2007 by journalist Anil Wanvasi, as an add on commercial activity to his website, indiatelevision.com a few years earlier. When NT awards were organised in 2012, its operations and the awards it gave away as "industry awards" were analysed by this author.

12 Exchange4media's News Broadcasting Awards (ENBA awards) are being conducted annually since 2008. This commercial agency organises a few other awards on other related fields particularly in advertising field that is where its primary interests are. Hence its awards are more to cater to those stake holders. This is

a profit driven agency having started as a publisher of a magazine, diversified into corporate public relations and communication. http://www.exchange4medis.com

13 TV channels do not look at awards as a way to bring in relevance, credibility and improve quality of programs as much as for channel promotion. In the current system awards are part of Jugalbandhi phenomena. Where everyone tend to or has scope to "claim number one" even if it meant that sometimes they do so parallel. Awards often been animated are deceptive. Awards are neither independent or objective or meant to contribute to standards and good practices. They are primarily commercial activities. Everything of course is in support of each other to maximize profit.

7

Society, Media and Influence

If one does not understand the difference between marketing support function and societal needs orientation of the news media, one will not be able to go beyond the usual and make a distinct mark in order to impact thought and influence people. Not all agree with this notion. This chapter attempts to explain this phenomenon of market domination, and how we assess and appraise changes in the role of news media.

Even as news on TV proliferates, the overall circulation of newspapers continues to increase. However, apart from that is there any evidence to assume that the influence and impact of news on society is increasing? There is ample evidence to show the increasing influence of media on markets, which involves primarily buying, selling, availing services, and consuming products whose shelf life changes constantly. But society is much more than markets and consumers. What difference has the boom in number of news channels made on society? What has been the influence and impact? Do we have any evidence for "more is merrier"? The correlation of data in some cases indicates more negative influence than positive. Take a big picture view related to (i) democratic foundations, (ii) processes of social development, (iii) good Governance issues, (iv) law and order scenario and (v) environmental issues – what has been the role of news media in the context of all these?

Despite boom, the overall reach of media in relation to total population expanded only marginally in the last decade, going by the NRS and IRS. This was perhaps so because content priorities of media are of no consequence to one-third or more people of the country. They remain outside the reach of all mass media. Professional and ethical standards of media are related to its "influence and impact" on society. Today, the concern is more with the markets, not with societal issues. Those who are concerned about society would like to see some restraint and responsibility on the part of broadcasters in particular. Those who are interested in markets are not in favour of regulations or restrains, including transparent self-regulations. Ad hoc decision-making suits such people. The reasons are obvious. The latter interested with the markets are united and also use news media to sway public opinion and even bully the powers as and when. The former, interested in society, do not have a unified, articulated and orchestrated voice. The so called choice and "power of TV remote" in hand is notional and not a good enough provision, particularly, in the absence of the promotion of discriminative viewership.

It is against this background that criteria and yardsticks are being promoted in a way that in the interest of the industry and markets, particularly big players, are protected and promoted. In that pursuit, citizens' end concerns hardly matter. That is how TRP has become somewhat like a currency. TRP system caters to the market needs and greed of individuals, not the interests of a society or a democratic and developing state. It is not just a question of the sample size, it is the very concept and methodology followed and the way TRPs are used (or misused) to consolidate the power of big media, corporate media, and boost consumerism. In this process, what interests viewers momentarily is promoted as surrogate for "what is in the interests" of people. That is how we have today "new gatekeepers" - to safeguard the interests of markets even at the cost of weakening the fundamentals of the society and that of news itself. The overall credibility of media to make a positive difference has declined, and the confidence in news media has declined the world over.

What Difference has the Proliferation of Channels Made?

The growth and proliferation of news television between 2000 and 2011 has been unprecedented anywhere in the world. This phenomenon has made considerable difference to the structure of consumer markets, stock markets, and lifestyle has undergone visible changes with regard to the consumption pattern of people. Nevertheless, one could still ask how extensive are the differences made by the proliferation of news media on practices and deep rooted attitudes associated with social behavior, social justice and social development aspects (like gender, caste, dowry, equity, etc.). Some news channels have taken to the coverage of health (cooking, yoga, physical fitness, etc.) and spiritual aspects in a big way.

It happened perhaps because there were sponsors for such programmes that have the elements to attract particular viewership. Whatever the motivation, it's good that some TV channels have taken to these programmes in a big way. But, at the same time, there are other issues like, for example, preference for male child, caste discrimination, dowry, corruption and blind beliefs, which are not covered prominently or strategically to have an impact. Whatever coverage is there on these issues is marginal, ad hoc and does not make much difference, as that's not perhaps the intention. In some instances, they have, in fact, promoted or spread the very practices that news is expected to decry. This is described as the negative drive of television.

[1]A quantitative analysis of crime, sex scandals, gender issues and practices like dowry, etc. for the decade (1990-2000) before the proliferation of television in the country and the decade after (2005-2015) would bring out a negative correlation more than a positive one.

Interestingly, there are no empirical research studies on what differences have the TV channels individually or together made on various sections of people or on their lifestyles or in special situations. Rather, the preoccupations have been with rating viewership, which is not the same as the "difference made". But presentations often attribute the increase in sales of consumables to television advertising.

Children's Channels

At the outset of the television era, [2]"children's programmes" were part of general channels during a particular day or a week or at a particular time. Later, with the growth of TV, "children's channels" proliferated. Against one children's channel in 1990, there were at least 14 children's channels in 2015 and another six or seven licensed ones to operate as a children's channel. How did they multiply if they were not making a difference? Are there any studies on the impact or difference that these channels made on children, or their education levels, for example. There are frequent and periodic studies on the time spent by children in watching TV and the kind of adverse impact such viewing has on their health, accomplishments, etc. Some of these studies on impact have been carried out by world's best medical schools and not media schools or sociologists.

Apparently, there has been no intention of children's channels of making any difference as to their knowledge, values, discipline, skills or to their growing up years. Most of the content of majority or all children's channels are of foreign origin with little or no relation to their surroundings, even though their language may be local, as dubbing into local language has become common now as if these channels are determined to lure children to TV watching as outlets of advertising.

Broadcast Model

The Indian television model, as it is positioned now, is based on a premise that what interest people, not necessarily what is in the interest of people, is what lures them to view television. The more number of viewers, even for five seconds for a channel, the better it is to make the channel viable and profitable by maximising the process of mustering viewers and being able to promote the channel with such claims.

Unlike in the case of newspaper and radio, investment and infrastructure needed for a TV channel is much higher and requires a different kind of maintenance as well as technology- driven modalities. The very compulsions of television are different. Once the television corporates are allowed as a part of "liberalisation, privatisation and globalisation" (LPG) policies, obviously, the broadcast media have to operate with the objective of reaching out larger number of viewers for viability first and then maximize profit, not just "Return on Investment".

Similarly, if a religious group or political party is licensed to own and operate broadcast channels, obviously, they cannot be expected to operate without priorities of their own and in their own interest, as they see it, particularly, when there are no specific public policies and no independent regulator to oversee the implementation of any codes and also programme effects. Similarly, if the interests of broadcasters are business of one kind or other, including real estate or politics, they will find ways of achieving those objectives. When FDI investments into broadcast enterprises are allowed, the investors are bound to expect a certain per cent as "Return on Investment", whichever route gets them that. As a part of LPG policies, the Government has been under pressure to consider increased per cent of Return on Investment beyond 10 to 15 percent.

In retrospect, it is obvious that the governments of the country have not fully understood or recognized the potential of TV as a mass medium and its implications to the national ethos and development pursuits. Even more glaringly, the government succumbed to ad hoc decisions of allowing and yielding to push and pulls of investors without safeguards, perhaps, because it suited the leaders in the government, who looked at TV as a medium to reach out to voters across the country, and the Indian industry's concern was more with expansion, corporatisation and maximisation of returns. Otherwise, how else, even after Supreme Court's landmark judgment (1995), can the government remain unconcerned of potential implications of TV even if it meant a few channels spoiling many? In fact, while decision makers were not enthusiastic about any restraints, the advertisers, advertising agencies and the rating agencies were even more open against any national policy (which would fix them to specifics) and an independent regulator for the content of channels (with possible limits or even conditions on content preoccupation).

Profit maximization, as in any other business, has become the concern of news media enterprises too. Obviously, most media cannot operate in losses, they have to be viable and sustain to continue and expand as in other businesses. But, when news media are viewed as 'fourth estate' and empowered with certain privileges, they were expected to operate with certain responsibilities and restrains in the larger national interests. (Those restrains enabled the news media or those in media to enjoy advantages, benefits and certain patronage of the State). The dilemma is whether in the changed scenario, the news media should continue to enjoy that stature of fourth estate and enjoy the privileges. This issue acquires significance particularly because it is not the journalists, who enjoy those privileges and benefits accruing out of that stature. With considerable foresight, Pandit Jawaharlal Nehru came up with the unique idea of a Wage Board for "working journalists" and a Parliament Act to ensure their freedom from favors from the management. Nowhere else in the world, there is such a legal provision. The fact that the recommendations of the Wage Board, which are obligatory on the part of the management to implement, were being ignored slowly first and then altogether, made that Act irrelevant. That was one of the effects of paradigm shift in media in the wake of the new economic order.

Research

Research is essential to realise the potential of media fully and benefit all stakeholders. Instead, it was the concern and interests of advertisers and investors, which determined the kind of research that got sponsored. It was not so much the concern for readers/viewers/listeners that dictated the scope of media research or for unleashing the full potential of media for positive outcomes. TRP and NRS/IRS are based on concepts and concerns that endorse and cater to the interests of the investors more.

Preemptive Reporting

One of the dilemmas that the news media in particular face is between "punditry" and "motivating" approach based presentation of news, current affairs and such public discourse based programmes. CMS studies over the years have indicated that the way certain programmes on contentious and need based issues are structured, formatted and presented, they tend to either daunt or snub or pre-empt viewer end sensitivities and initiatives. For example, in poll coverage when the contest is keen, the news reports give the impression that casting vote is not likely to make a difference as if the outcome is already more or less known.

"Self righteousness" of news media anchors that they know everything or they are always right is how things are presented, particularly on news television. This outlook is called by some as the "tyranny of media" or arrogance of media. Whatever the term, it amounts to preempting or demotivating people from taking an active view, unless the context is related to life style or markets.

Concentration of Media in Fewer Hands

Is it a trend good or bad in a country like India, which claims and cherishes socialism, secularism, plurality, equitable society and inclusive growth as goals? If someone or something is working against such national goals, should that be encouraged? This is one of many such dilemmas involving the news media that the country is facing today. One of them is cross media ownership. I first examined this trend in early 1970s. Dharm Beer Singh (Bihar) as the Deputy Minister for Information & Broadcasting (1974-76) was an active and articulate minister despite Prime Minister Mrs. Indira Gandhi herself holding the portfolio with I. K. Gujral as the State Minister and prime mover. He and I used to look into the trends in media scene and debate in close circles as to what all that meant to the cherished goals of the country. One sure issue was that of cross media ownership and corporatisation of media, a trend we envisaged in a big way once the sector is opened up for expansion, privatisation and the entry of foreign entrepreneurs. [3]Our analysis of CMS then indicated that some 50 media enterprises of all sizes were dominating 90 per cent of media news contents of. Twenty years later in 1995, I found that the number had come down to less than 40 enterprises. In 2005, with unleashing of LPG policies, the number declined further to less than 20 enterprises. This trend towards convergence and cross media conglomerates was too obvious by 2010. Yet, there were no specific legal moves against such a trend in cross media control. That trend, in fact, has gained ground. With proliferation of news media there is no evidence that this trend has changed much in 2015-16.

The Cable TV Act came into being in 1995 after more than a decade of consideration by the Ministry of Information &Broadcasting. It was not so much a proactive initiative; rather it was a result of public outcry from across the country. What difference has the Act made on the content, including TV ads over the years? Was any action taken as a preventive measure? What mechanism had the ministry set up to monitor the content of channels for timely follow up? In 2012, the ministry sent out once a while message to cable operators that violators could even be jailed. But this move was more against the cable operators illegally operating or those who were blatantly and consistently scheduling programmes against national policies. The ministry had set up a monitoring unit in 2009 with technical capability to monitor the contents of nearly 500 channels. But it did not think of an analysis of monitored contents for violations, nor did it institute a mechanism to take action. As a result, there were channels, who despite delayed notices, continue to repeat the content that was questioned, may be, after a gap of a few days or weeks. There were more than a dozen channels, and some of them were big ones in this category of violation. In 2010–11 some 40 violations, mostly by corporate channels, were issued notices with no effect. Nor was there any effort to promote discriminative viewing or active viewing.

Assessing Content Concerns

What are the *"universal criteria" or proof of pudding benchmarks* to say how credible news media are and how much potential do they have to make a difference. Four criteria are pertinent in this regard, although there could be more.

a. One is the *"reflective nature"* of contents of media –in terms of whose concerns or whose interests do the media voice?

b. A second one is *"how inclusive has the coverage"* been in terms of locations, kind of people, regions or parts of the country being covered?

c. A third benchmark is *"who and how many"* participated or are involved and responsible for the contents of news media and how well identified are they.

d. A fourth criterion is of course the *"reach of media"* and how *flat* is the base of that reach.

First, take the criteria of reach. Despite all that growth in India recently, *one-fourth to one-third* of people are dependent on the State, or a section of people continue to be outside direct reach of all mass media put together. They do not even get reflected in the news media of the country as if they do not matter or exist for the news media. The tendency is to reach those, who are already covered and have deeper pockets rather than the "unreached" ones.

Rural India and basic needs and issues like health, education, environment, etc. cover hardly four per cent of news bulletins of news channels, which set the agenda of the country. There is a challenge and also an opportunity in this dilemma. This means going beyond TRP led formulas of content and outdated marketing strategies. More than one-third of people's needs and aspirations are overlooked.

With increase in the number of newspapers and channels, theoretically the "choices" or "alternatives" should have gone up. But, it has resulted in more of the same and for the same people; as if plurality in news media is at stake. Have they become more like "marketing media" rather than retaining the virtue of being called "mass media", aiming at people across the country? The tendency is to reach the same people with "deep pockets". Why basic issues of concern to people have not been a priority of news media?

The priorities of media are guided by 'what interests' rather than 'what is in the interest'.

Effort is made to cover such issues interestingly, but those topics in the interest of people are covered hardly, occasionally and on ad-hoc and mostly in a negative context.

The distinctions are blurred – as to what is news and what is an advertisement; what is in the interest and what interests; what is civil society advocacy and what is market driven? Between people's voice and corporate interests, whose concerns matter more? Is centralization promoted in the scope and concern of contents in the name of decentralized coverage? The power of media, particularly channels, cannot be unleashed without transparency and differentiation. Earlier, *society* was the concern of news media, not so much the *market* as it is today; citizens mattered more then, today it is the consumer and the voter who matte more. There has to be certain locally relevant balance. One cannot lose sight of a concern for society.

This is also because of blurred distinctions: The change or shift in the paradigm is characterized by these dilemmas of distinguishing between:

- What is news and views
- What is news and advertisement
- What is advocacy and marketing
- What are people's concerns and corporate interests
- Centralization and decentralization
- The state and the government
- Government of the day and the party in power.
- Lobbying and advocacy

Media today are no longer public trusts, they are either corporates or they depend on corporates. That is perhaps why unorganized people and sectors hardly matter. Never before has India witnessed so much competition as today between all kinds of players – public and private, and foreign and Indian news media.

[4]This is despite the fact that today around 125 locations in India account for 85 per cent of news media against less than 30 locations three decades ago. With more than 600 districts in the country, the spread of media has not increased and expanded people's voice as significantly. But it is an important first step towards decentralizing news media coverage further. FM radio offers better scope for increasing the locations, spread and range of contents. The content model being followed by most news media is something to be critically analyzed. There lies a challenge and opportunity.

Framework

Change is an ongoing phenomenon that infuses vitality in a system. Change has been blatant, not subtle, in the case of the size, structure and substance of Indian media. Technological and demographical changes further add to its dynamics. But, these changes have not ushered in significant shifts in their content priorities and models (as in the case of volumes), except to some extent in the case of young. How could such changing face of Indian media be assessed and appraised? What criteria make sense in capturing the change in news media? The following broad trends could be identified to indicate the direction of change.

More Quantitative

Why has the media not made so much qualitative differences commensurate with the quantitative changes that have come about? Despite all that recent growth quantitatively, half to one-third of people, depending upon the district or section of people, are outside the reach of mass media. This aspect has to be a basis for the (re)appraisal.

With increase in the number of newspapers and news channels, theoretically, people's "choices" or "options" should have been a "lot more". Has it been so? Competition, freedom, privatization and new (miniaturized) technologies are expected to bring in qualitative changes in the contents too. But it is more of the same and for the same people, as if plurality is at stake. And at the same time, "freedom of press" is exercised far more today than ever before. Competition is here as never before, and it has given a boost to the growth of media of all kinds.

Dilemma of Contents

- The kind of content model being followed by news channels in the last decade is not helping expansion beyond those people, who were already covered.
- The society should be the primary concern of news channels, not the market with brands that promote greed in people where citizen should matter more, not the consumer and voter, which are the current practices.
- Conflict of interest in the content coverage and priorities is on the increase and more often no longer hidden.

Structurally, there are Changes in the Form of Media Organisations

News media agencies are no longer trusts; they are converging and becoming corporates. [5]Three decades ago, less than 50 journalists set the priorities of 80 per cent of news in the (print) media; today the number of those who set the priorities of news media is hardly 200 despite spread and proliferation of both electronic and print news media. Similarly, those who belong to one-third of people, whose concerns never get reflected in news channels, are not there in the news rooms. Only after 2011, some realization seems to have occurred, but, nowhere near to explore the opportunity, achieve equity and expand its own reach.

[6]A couple of decades ago, 25 newspaper houses had control over more than 75 per cent of all news media (not news) in the country. Does it mean anything? If that number goes down to 10 soon, for example, how conducive could that trend be for equitable growth, pluralistic nation, inclusive development and democratic foundations?

Then, of course, is the speed with which convergence is taking place in the ownership pattern cutting across the media. Unrestrained cross media ownership pattern is a key factor contributing to this phenomenon of "consolidation", i. e., when big become bigger.

All this indicates so much scope as an opportunity for the news media in particular to unleash them; distinguish from each other; and make a difference in so many respects and much beyond the present levels.

The [7]dependence of channels on commercials is anywhere between 65 to 85 per cent of total revenue, against 20 to 35 per cent more than three decades ago in the case of newspapers. This fact alone should be enough to better understand as to whose voice the media is likely to reflect and whose interests determine content priorities of news channels in particular. To what extent would this picture change, as expected with digitalisation, perhaps can be seen only after 2020?

Today in the name of research what is primarily focused is on instant surrogates for temporal interests, not concerned with impact and societal influence. Even the communication faculties of some over 200 Universities are contributing to research the basics and fundamentals of the fourth estate aspects.

Media no Longer Hidden Persuaders

Earlier, editors, sub-editors were the "gate keepers" of media. Today, we have "new gate keepers". They all operate as if in tandem - advertisers, market researchers, corporate public relations and media planners. They are all corporate, multinational mostly. Their number is increasing and so is their grip on the content priorities.

What per cent of news in news media is provided by independent journalists and what per cent is rewritten copy or moderated by public relations people?

A time series analysis of such trends supported by periodic impact research provides insights for the role of news media at a given point of time.

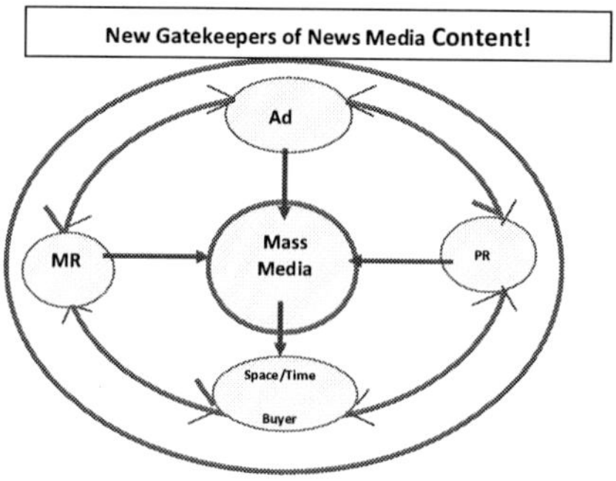

MR=Market Research; AD= Advertising; PR= Public Relations

Media are no longer "hidden persuaders". In the earlier years, editors, sub editors and reporters, as journalists with responsibility for what goes into media, were described as the "gatekeepers of media". Today, we have different "new gatekeepers". They function from outside media and they do not have the responsibility or accountability (as cable operators are for example). Their number has multiplied. They are not journalists more often. They operate as if in tandem, which is revealed when one analyzes their functions and operations. They determine more the content model relied by media, particularly television news channels.

[8]These news gatekeepers are: Ad agencies, Market research agencies, corporate public relations, and Media planners. 75 per cent of these "new gatekeepers" in operation in India are "globally controlled" and belong to one or other corporate conglomerate. Government policies have facilitated their functioning, leading to critical shift in the priorities and operations of news channels in particular. The content model promoted by these new gate keepers has not helped in the expansion of overall reach of mass media commensurately. The content model promoted by them has not been so much relevant to grassroots India. The content priorities promoted by them is more greed driven, not needs based.

That greed model titillates the individual ego more than the "we" or "community" perceptions.

Nick Davies of the Guardian (UK) too has written (2008) about this phenomenon in the book, *Flat Earth News (*2010). Only 12 per cent of what goes into the newspaper is written by independent journalists. The rest is rewritten content, agency copy or a PR moderated copy. What does that mean?

With government allowing 100 per cent foreign investment into these "new gatekeeper" enterprises in the last decade, we can expect no round about as to what matters or interests the news media. Adding to this are the blurred distinctions between State and the Government of the day, and the Government and the political party in power.

Lack of transparency in media operations and conflict in the interests of media establishments is increasingly coming to fore recently. In fact, who owns or who has stakes in the channels is not even known in most cases. This is because there is no obligation to declare annually such particulars as in the case of newspapers. (Even when it is hardly 20 percent oblige to disclose).

In this process of reversing the paradigm, 10 parameters matter for unleashing the potential of news channels or any new media:

- Reach/expansion beyond the present levels – to serve the unreached people/pockets.
- Easy access that does not require much skill or more devices to avail news sources.
- Cheaper, cost-affordability - both in the case of recurring and one-time costs.
- Proliferation should mean more options and choices, not otherwise.
- Responsive to citizen/user's concerns and ensure their participation, with user-end safeguards.
- Ease in the entry of new players.... level playing in access and in availing.
- Enrich, empower in such a way that concerns of citizens and communities are addressed in an inclusive way.
- Knit people together, not segment communities or ignore some at the cost of others.

- Promote decentralized distribution, particularly of content production.
- Interactivity in presenting contents, not merely one-sided or in a top-down way.

The emerging digital driven media should imply optimizing these various variables. That is when the better of Indian news media will unfold. This also helps deepen democracy and facilitates good governance. That is when media would regain the Fourth Estate character.

The Paradigm Shift is Irreversible

Some safeguards that could help such a process of shift are here. But there could be many more and not all relevant in all situations.

- Users are the best bet to take safeguards, not the Governments, but they have the responsibility.
- If market has to be the indirect regulator, then users, citizens and civil society groups cannot be passive, they have to be active and involved in such a process.
- Self regulation within and across media is good for everyone; it needs to be promoted and should become normative for all channels.
- Academic back up for innovation and experimentation is essential to be able to position distinctly.
- Research has to be independent, transparent and the concern should be about effects, not merely about "here and now" aspects based on top of the mind responses and indirect surrogates.

Concerned professional bodies should have proactive agenda and think beyond privileges.

Eternal Values Matter Always

Certain basic human values are eternally relevant for the news media while serving people and scheduling programmes. These include: (1) respect for all life forms; (2) reject violence; (3) sharing with others; (4) listen to understand; (5) preserve nature on the planet; and (6) rediscover the solidarity between people. Three basic elements run across these values - concern, care and compassion. How much or to what extent a channel reflects such elements through its contents over time is an indication of how well the channel has become part of life and how well it has entrenched or associated with people. These concerns and elements too should be considered instead of depending on *navarasas* only.

Is television bettering overtime mutual *trust* and *confidence* as well as *goodwill* and *faith* between people or is it contributing otherwise? These are the basics for building confidence or otherwise. These are the elements, which news television channels should rely upon more – to interest and lure people for making long lasting difference in the lives of people and society. It is in every one's interest that such virtues become the *basis* for relationships. Channels should not be accused for promoting jealousy, greed, grudge and hatred as virtues, even although such things are part of real life situations.

When he was the Prime Minister, Atal Bihari Vajpayee mentioned that the "fads and fashions of the rich and over privileged" are being "trivialized by media". He said that there is a "tendency to be habitually judgmental with a weakness for sensational headlines" and to "advertise lifestyles beyond the reach of the majority".

Two Prime Ministers pointed at television as a source and "mother of all cynicism" in people and country. President A.P.J. Abdul Kalam suggested that the media should become the "positive passion of many". These observations well explain the phenomena of television getting entrenched or the trap that it got into with all its immense potential otherwise.

Critical Context

Six critical contexts provide an idea for the kind of role news channels play and the difference they could make in the larger societal context.

1. Democratic foundations – Voting and electoral behavior are critical aspects that sustain democratic foundations. What has been the role of news media in this context? Some questions that come up are - has the voting percentage increased over the years with increased availability and coverage by the news media? Also, how free and fair are the electoral practices now with competition in news media? What has been the coverage by media of these aspects and has the Parliamentary debates enhanced on substantial issues? How appropriate is the poll campaign on substantial issues of concern to the people? A perspective of media coverage in

this context of these four dimensions should be good enough to give us an idea of its role.

2. Development process – If India lives in villages, to what extent do the media reflect that? If the problems of India are related to literacy, health, environment and poverty, then, to what extent do these aspects get covered in the media? Has this coverage gone up as significantly as the growth of media? Why has there been so much criticism of news media ignoring rural poverty, including farmers' suicides and other such issues related to development?
3. Social development – Women and children are the key to the social development of a nation. What kind of coverage do the media provide for women and children? How many issues and how well concerning women and girl child get reflected in the media? With the kind of boom in media, one would expect that coverage and participation of women, children and opportunities for them in media would have gone up. How could they be ignored? Children constitute around half of TV viewers. Has the recent increase in atrocities on women anything to do with the proliferation of TV and the kind of coverage given? To what extent are the channels catering to the aspirations of children?
4. Good Governance – India has been witnessing dramatic changes recently in its governance paradigm. There is rights regime and transparency era in the country. The Right to Information, Right to Food, Right to Education, Right to Forests, etc. are changing the very scope of governance. With these and other legal entitlements, has their utilization by the needy improved? Can we say that corruption is coming down – at any level - with the kind of potential media has?
5. Law and Order and conflicts – With the kind of spread of media and their proliferation, we could have expected, theoretically, a more unified country. And with better awareness and knowledge levels because of the spread of media, we could have expected better law and order situation in the country. Has the crime rate reduced or increased due to the pattern of deviant behavior in the country including drug abuse? Another question that one needs to ask is that with so many media and so much time spent on them, do we understand each other better?

6. Life styles – What kind of life styles and values does the media try to inculcate, promote or perpetuate and support? If they show, for example, in a glamourised way that "spending" is a virtue or criteria for public standing, not "saving" for future or for a productive purpose that makes all the difference. If media shows all the time that "I" is all that matters, not "WE"; that goes a long way in determining the kind of conflicts that the world is confronted with.

Technology Perspective

To help the channels unleash their potential, we now have newer technologies and new ways of utilising technologies. These are enablers. All technologies have double edged potential in the same way as television itself as a technology device. Sensitivity in the application of technologies is more likely to help their use in a positive context.

There is a feeling that having "latest" or "state of art" infrastructure gives additional advantage and helps distinguish the channel from others. That is how some channels promote themselves. While that is possible to some extent, technology by itself would not sustain distinctiveness in a competitive scenario. It is their use, application or adoption, which has potential to differentiate a channel even more even more.

Digitalisation Movement

The fast changing face of India on this front is bound to impact the media scene far more, both in scope and contents. [9]Going quantitatively in relation to telecom, broadband, access to Internet, broadcasting, websites and blogs, one will be misled to believe saturation in the reach of and access to mass media. Such a situation may not be far away once broadband and digitalization connectivity picks up. Competition will further offer a challenge to that process. The speed will be decided by policies and infrastructure. It is expected that in the next couple of years (by 2020), there will be more than: 1200 million telephone connectivity, 700 million viewers of television, 200 million television sets, 200 million internet users, 70 million PCs, and 1200 million "active users" between these various media. Think what it all means and how we could change the face of the country if only some efforts are made deliberately. The convergence process needs to be tracked for the effects in time for taking correctives when and where necessary. What would be the future of news channels once digitalization spreads across the country? How news channels gear up to those new compulsions as to their contents, structure, etc.

This chapter explains how news media should assess itself their own direction, priorities and perceptions so that it can expand much beyond the present levels of reach and impact.

Endnote

1 National Crime Bureau of Home Ministry, has been bringing out its annual report promptly and regularly last few years. This report for 2015 was presented early 2016.This report presents trends in a desegregated way state wise crime rates, particularly involving children and women. It is now possible to correlate over time crime rate and nature with exposure to channels and even in specific context of trends in the contents of channels. "Crime in India 2014 compendium", National Crime Records Bureau, Ministry of Home Affairs, New Delhi http:/ /ncrt.gov.in

2 Realising the significance of television, more specifically to children, CMS organised first ever national meet on the subject as early as November 1998 when alarming trends were indicated to watch out. See "CMS Round table on children and television" New Delhi 21 November 1998. Also see the book, "Social effects of mass media in India" by N Bhaskara Rao and G N S Raghavan, Gyan publishing, New Delhi, 1996. Number of children channels available in India has gone up from five in 2000 to 22 in 2016

3 Concentration of media continue in fewer hands despite proliferation vertically and horizontally. That 50 media enterprises dominated 90 percent of news contents in media was based on this writers analysis of contents of news papers (and All India Radio, TV was hardly there in 1975) including regional language news dailies. The same was updated with sample of a few news media for the later years. This summing up was this writers way to indicate concentration of news media in fewer hands perhaps also because there were hardly any cross media restrains and passive view of successive governments to implications of concentration of news media until more recently when the government asked TRAI to look into., pl refer to Report of Second Press Commission for which primary research was done by this writer, Second Press Commission (1978-82), controller of publications 1982

4 same as above

5 same as above

6 same as above

7 This was based on the writers observation over the years of journalists presence and moment between Shastri Bhavan's press conference venue and Press Information Bureau offices, Press Club of India, press gallery of Parliament and the kind of attendance at press conferences in New Delhi, matched with source of origin of contents of news media. This is also based on this writers analysis more than once during 1974-85 and tracking thereafter of the trends., including readership surveys, NRS, IRS etc. The content was analysed going by the byline, source

and origin or location indicated with the news stories. Based on these primary inputs, Personal Observations and discussions with stakeholders over the years, these conclusions in this chapter were arrived at. Some of these were reported in the news media either as interviews with this writer or in press meets or written as articles.

8 In the conventional terminology in media, those who decides with in media what goes into the media eventually are described as "Gatekeepers", that is editor, deputy or sub editors at the last mile desk. "New gate keepers" are those who are not a function in the media and have no responsibility to what eventually appears but are a factor in setting the priorities of media coverage. In addition to advertising agencies, market researchers, corporate public relations functionaries and rating agencies more recently are the new gate keepers.

9 Based on the growth trends in telecom sector by TRAI, Ministries of Telecom and Information and Broadcasting and many other agencies, this estimate has been made. Many other agencies have made such forecasts about the scenario of 2020. Also refer to this writers earlier publications, see TRAI Report, 20 June, 2016 " Perspective into the media scene :2001" published in 1988 and to "mass media and marketing communication: perspective into 2020" published in 1995. See Dr. N Bhaskara Rao's "changing Dynamics of media scene : rise of digitalisation", July 2014 and "rise of digital media" key note presentation at a conference at Symbiosis University, Pune, 11 September 2015.

Section III
A Framework for a New Think!

No new initiative or repositioning is possible without understanding the pros and cons of the reforms process – general as well as specific. Knowing ethical concerns, regulatory initiatives, mechanism and options is equally important. Can we harness India-specific news channels without providing for "checks and balance" in their operations? The different aspects are discussed so that together channels can explore the full potential of news channels in a democratic and pluralist society confronted with socio-economic divides.

8

Media Reforms: Missing Initiatives

The mass media scene in India was never as good as it is today in terms of growth, proliferation, multiplicity and importance in the affairs of the country. The electronic media scene is even better. Perhaps no other media in any country is currently witnessing so many qualitative and quantitative changes as the Indian media. While most of this may be attributed to technology, which for sure is the driving force, the government's economic policies have also triggered the process further. While the country is going through a reversal in several national policies, almost abruptly, the developments on the media front are happening on their own; in spite of any significant initiative by the government. There is, of course, a certain reversal in the thrust implied in its half hearted effort pertaining to the repositioning of Doordarshan in a competitive mode vis-à-vis satellite channels. The picture today is one of abrupt and haphazard media explosion. Also, the facilitative infrastructure, including viewing-end discipline has not evolved commensurately.

As a result, ambiguity in the scenario, contradictions in policies, and confusion about the future course is evident all around. It was against this background that the Supreme Court judgment in February 1995 rejuvenated hope of many people. In fact, the judgment, together with the development in the technology front, has shifted the debate from freedom and monopoly to autonomy, accountability, access and social impact. While issues related to the entry of foreign media and uplinking are more business-inspired, violence and vulgarity concerns of television cut across larger sections, including the judiciary. More fundamental issues like monopoly, cross media ownership, plurality, FDI limits, and so on have not received the kind of attention they deserve.

It is obvious that currently, there are no direct laws governing broadcasting in India despite committee after committee being set up over the last three decades, notable among them being the Chanda Committee of 1964 and the Verghese Committee of 1977. Two government initiatives in this context need a mention here - the Prasar Bharati Act passed by Parliament in 1990 after years of debate and consideration and the Cable TV Networks Regulation Act of 1995. Both, however, remain on paper and have made no difference to the scene. In fact, the Prasar Bharati Act is in a state of coma. The Cable TV Networks Regulation Act has lost its relevance with technological advancements and increasingly competitive and fragmented cable television market. The Supreme Court's judgment held that "the airwaves or frequencies are a public property. They have to be controlled and regulated by a public authority in the interest of the public and to prevent the invasion of their rights." The judgment laid down the principle of citizen's right to information and analysis from diverse sources and view points, and equal access to all citizens to avail of the medium. Earlier, the Supreme Court had ruled in March 1989 that censorship by prior restraint was not only desirable but also necessary as "the movie cannot function in a free market place like newspaper, magazine or advertisement."[1] In this case too, the judgment of apex court has not made any difference to cinema industry in India.

Despite the realisation that political parties in power, which had control over Doordarshan and AIR, have lost elections and that parties which had no control over these media have come to power, there is no persistent effort and follow-up to give the electronic media the much-sought after autonomy. The urgency is to constitute an independent commission or an independent authority for broadcast media. The Sengupta report of the government on the future of broadcasting endorsed the structure proposed in the private initiative taken a year ago by 30 eminent media scholars, including this author, Mr. Nikhil Chakravarty, Mr. Dilip Padgaonkar and Mr. George Verghese, after three rounds of deliberations with three previous I&B ministers and representatives of political parties. This privately initiated draft broadcast Bill suggested a Broadcasting Commission of India (BCI) which the Sengupta Committee named as the Radio and Television Authority of India (RTAI). Both the proposals recommend that Prasar Bharati should have independent executive boards for AIR and Doordarshan. Both implied that Prasad Bharati should be a public broadcasting operation with specific funding from the government as in the case of other social sector obligations of the State over and above what it could generate on its own, but without succumbing to the so-called market compulsions. The draft Bill intended to bring all forms of broadcasting and transmission – radio, television, satellite, cable and others under the ambit of the broadcast licensing authority. A strong Broadcast Complaints Council and a Standards Council with ethical concerns were also provided in the draft Bill. There was provision for programme advisory committees, both regional and sectoral, to aid and advise the broadcast stations and monitor quality of content at various levels. The licensing authority would strive to ensure that the market-driven channels are persuaded to accept certain obligations regarding the type and timing of programmes as well as responsiveness to community or audience.

Regarding the entry of the foreign print media, the September 1955 decision of the Union Cabinet against allowing it cannot continue to dictate the scene 60 years later despite the fact that several national policies of equal importance and with larger and long-term implications have been reversed. Central to the issue is the question: Should mass media be treated in the same way as any other consumer product? We seem to be avoiding this question and viewing it as and when it suits us rather than addressing it coherently, in a consistent manner. If we agree that it needs to be viewed as "public utility", then our approach has to be different. Similarly, with TV becoming a national obsession, we seem to have sidelined radio, a more cost-effective mass media, despite its undisputed positive potential and contribution. Cable TV operations have mushroomed in every nook and corner of the country, unconcerned with any legality and unaware of the larger implications.

While the visual electronic media has be at times accused of invading privacy, vulgarising culture, spreading stereotypes, destabilising political regimes in some parts of the world since World War II, the print media have not done that, at least, as blatantly. Because of the power of electronic media to cut across language barriers and political boundaries, there have been attempts to curtail its influence, whether successfully or otherwise across countries. In India, however, we seem to have remained by and large a mute spectator to the entry of electronic media and its haphazard spread until a couple of years ago, when the "business angle" became apparent. Those who are crying wolf now did not comment on that phenomenon, which has quietly taken roots in the country. Adding to the confusion, the then Prime Minister, Mr. H D Deve Gowda, hinted at the possibility of allowing uplinking, while ruling out any change in the policy with regard to the print media.

Missing Policy Perspective: The Challenge

[2]Despite proliferation of mass media in the country in the recent years, the percentage of "unreached" people has hardly declined in the decade, as is evident from NRS/IRS reports year after year. It means that 30-40 per cent Indians continue to be outside the reach of "any form of the mass media". What action is the government expected to take? Is it reaching out to more of the same people instead of connecting with the "unreached" and bridging the divide in access to information? This, despite the fact that today we have communication technologies with the potential to reach beyond the present levels. Then, why is it not happening?

In Retrospect...

Looking back at the government's ad hoc media policies during the last three decades, one wonders whether there was ever a serious concern to bridge the divide and whether there was a realisation pertaining to the challenge. For example, the Satellite Instructional Television Experiment (SITE) project, launched in India in 1975, was the most potential television experiment ever undertaken anywhere. The one-year-long pioneering experiment established the scope of using satellites for reaching villages in local languages. Yet, it has not made an iota of difference to our policies. The Kheda Television experiment, thereafter, well appreciated for the virtues, particularly about television becoming a decentralised and community media, was forgotten too. No government has since then showed any concern or commitment required to think big and beyond – as demonstrated by the late Vikram Sarabhai. Have the private channels ever explored that model for its potential to offer an "Indian model" of TV.

In 1983, China went ahead to reach thousands of its villages using satellite. A country where "wall newspaper" was relied upon as a medium of communication, excelled by adopting the most modern communication technologies and tripling the reach of TV as well as tele-density in a matter of hardly a decade. We are still struggling and reviving targets for rural phones year after year even when there's a glut of satellites and transponders and their prices have been reduced by half. [3]India has been talking of DTH – the commercial version of SITE – for a decade now. In the last couple of years, we should have seen a breakthrough in our rural coverage. The percentage of TV households in rural areas is hardly one-third of those in urban areas. Rural tele-density is hardly 54 per cent (against 82 per cent in the urban areas). In both respects, it is much higher in China.

The reach could have been increased three times by connecting television, Cable TV more specifically, with telephony. I have been talking of the need for such convergence of Cable TV and telephony for more than two decades now. There have been more than a dozen experiments across the country in this regard, but nothing serious has come out. Perhaps we have missed years waiting for a commercial proposition and a marketing package. The government has not taken serious interest to expedite such experiments for the convergence of voice, visual and data, until recently. But the process is slow.

Need a Regulator First

Take the instance of the Broadcast Bill. [4]Five precious years went in vain, despite a Supreme Court judgment and a wide range of deliberations, including among political leaders, we could not come up with any policy. To most people, a media or broadcast policy means FDIs or CAS. Then, the Convergence Bill appeared as if to bail out the Broadcast Bill. It is more than a decade and neither of the Bills is in sight. On the other hand, the Chinese success story happened during this very decade. All these years, the government could not come up with an independent regulator as in the case of the telecom sector.

Radio Model

[5]Over the last three decades, there has been certain stagnation with respect to the most cost-effective medium, radio. Take the case of FM radio. AIR first introduced FM in 1977 and did nothing to maximise the potential of FM for the next 20 years. In 1993, time slots on AIR FM were auctioned to private parties, but they were withdrawn abruptly in 1998, after those slots had became popular. The way the licenses for FM radio were decided is another issue. It is evident that none of the private FM channels would help expand listenership beyond the present level. Still, almost 40 cities would be crowded with FM radio channels when and if all the licensees come up. Some cities will have more than

six FM radio stations. Some have FM radio for a few years now without adding to the overall reach of the media or making any difference to content model. Thus, the potential of radio was sidelined with TV becoming the darling. Besides glamour, big money is involved in TV and now it has acquired political clout with proliferation of "news channels". Earlier, there was an opportunity to go beyond, when one transmitter a day "television expansion" phase was launched in the terrestrial mode. All this is happening without realising the potential of making [6]LPTs, such as "community media" – the Kheda type. For, no software capability was built at LPTs (over 800 of them) and they were used primarily as "top-down" media, despite insights from the experience of upgrading "auxiliary radio stations" to that of programme originating stations. The country, thus, missed an opportunity of having decentralised community television with scope for a three-tier structure and a more appropriate one for India.

Cable TV far More Appropriate

The next opportunity to adopt the most appropriate communication model for India was provided by some enterprising individuals, and not the government. In fact, despite risks, Cable TV operators went about connecting households and in no time, they achieved far more by setting up widely dispersed communication capabilities with a lot more potential than being availed – all in a matter of a decade. In spite of their innocuous background and no support from any quarter, except that of the viewers, Cable TV operators adopted and upgraded their infrastructure both in terms of reaching more television households and also delivering more channels with a lot more options and all that at the lowest price possible anywhere in the world. Thus, the Cable TV operators could be credited for the television boom in the country.

Cable TV communication model is the most appropriate model in view of India's unique socio-economic challenges. It is decentralised, community specific, most affordable, upgradeable in terms of technology and with least scope for media monopoly from outside the community. All that was needed was some discipline in operations, better customer service and origination of local programmes, which some Cable TV operators did take up on their own by way of news and announcements. I wrote about such initiatives more than a decade ago. All that the Cable TV operators needed was some financial support to upgrade their hardware. In fact, based on the CMS study of Cable TV operators, the

PM's Task Force on communication policies suggested that cable operators should be provided with financial assistance. But that panel's recommendations were forgotten too soon. Even Infosys founder Dr. N R Narayana Murthy regretted that neglect. He was the key member of that Task Force. However, in the last couple of years, Cable TV operations have come to a standstill with neither any new investments nor any upgradation because of the uncertainty of government policies. As a result, the penetration of Cable TV into rural India has received a set back after 2000; something which the government could have encouraged whole heartedly. This was because the government allowed foreign investment into the Cable TV.

As long as there was no government intervention, the Cable TV expanded and took roots across remote corners of the country. Whose interest did the government try to service by taking up CAS? If the ministry wants to retain control on television channels (as they have, of late, become primary "news source"), let that be part of a formal national policy. If CAS is advantageous, it will be taken up by TV households in the same way as they had gone for the Cable. Why should the government make it obligatory and go on fixing deadline and creating a controversy? Why should it fix the number of channels or even go about fixing charges when elsewhere and in every other field, the government claims that the market forces decide these issues. Why is the government anxious to formalise "pay TV regime" in the country? Should a government go all out in support of pay TV? Digitalisation, on the other hand, would have by now corrected the lapses and helped leapfrog. But, that process is lagging behind deadlines despite repeat pronouncement by the ministries.

They claim that the government has recently licensed(!) the Direct to Home (DTH) service. Star and ZEE as well as Prasar Bharati were the first to offer DTH service. As in no other country, in India, we already have seven DTH operators (2012) and more are lined up for 2012. Competing and luring offers have helped to expand the DTH base and make that a national next step. But for that, the government (TRAI) had prescribed compatible set top boxes more than a couple of years ago. But so far, it remains just an announcement. TRAI's tariff prescription has come into practice, and everyone knows that DTH requires a set top box in addition to a small dish, which costs much more and comes with much higher monthly subscription. DTH also implies formalising Pay TV regime. It is high time that the government institutes an independent regulator for broadcasting first and leaves the modalities related to CAS or DTH to it. The government should be more concerned about larger national issues related to preventing or bridging the communication divide in the country.

Where are the Priorities in Media Policies?

There are several examples of I&B ministry dithering for too long or/and, at the end, coming up with innocuous or delayed decisions. Private FM radio is one that the ministry has been the most concerned about. FM radio has not come into the country because of privatisation. It was there much longer as part of AIR network, but remained neglected. Privatisation, however, has given a boost to radio in general and FM radio in particular. But despite all that hype, private FM radio has neither added choice in the nature of programmes, nor expanded the overall reach of radio. What the government has done now is to concede to most of the demands of private FM radio operators, except allowing news. But, rebroadcast of AIR news is now allowed. Most FM radio channels are already giving news headlines; in fact, some even re-broadcast the same news bulletins. 26 per cent FDI is also allowed into FM radio. Thanks to this concern of the ministry, some cities will now have more than five FM radio stations (in addition to AIR channels), as if more is merrier.

Community Radio is a new approach to cater to local and specialised groups of people in a non-commercial mode and outside the AIR network. But, community radio took more than a couple of years to take off, in spite of its potential to reach out locally those, who are not yet touched by other media. Yet, community radio is not as fortunate as private FM radio to get the attention of the ministry, as if money making was more important (from license auction) than linking people and committees.[7] Despite more than 100 applicants for community radio, hardly one-fourth heard positively in the first couple of years as the process of licensing was too bureaucratic; and, in fact, it was difficult for genuine communities or groups to avail of the scheme. No wonder why there are hardly two dozen truly successful truly community radios in operation today. While both FM radio and Community Radio should receive the attention of the ministry, the latter should receive priority going by the *"aam admi"* focus of UPA government in particular and the potential for a more functional radio. Many suggestions were offered to the ministry by several fora as correctives in the policy formulated during the NDA regime. But, there were no powerful lobbies or media barons to backup Community Radio, as in the case of FM radio. It took another couple of years for the ministry to liberalise the scheme somewhat. The fact that "community radio interests" too need to organise themselves into a "lobby" explains the ad-hoc approach that the ministry took.

It took two years for grant of first license (2004) for community radio after policy was announced (2002). It took a decade for opening 50 and in 2015 there were hardly 200 community radio station operating.

Without having an independent regulator for broadcast sector as suggested by the Supreme Court of India, the government has been privatising and opening up the sector for foreign investment without first formulating specific guidelines towards protecting the concerns of all sections of people. The apex Court also said that airwaves belong to public and should not be used for personal interests. Earlier, messing up with CAS proposal, the NDA government had passed on the problem to the TRAI as an ad-hoc arrangement. As CAS continues to be in coma, TRAI is busy promoting the interest of investors, despite it not being equipped to deal with the issues of the media sector seriously and holistically. Consultations with a few people in Delhi neither lend legitimacy to TRAI recommendations nor could it be construed as in the larger public interest. Most of its consultation papers are formulated by foreign consulting agencies. The ministry's approach in this regard has been more passive in nature. Another example was TRAI's exercise for privatising terrestrial television. The basic premise was that more options were better for the viewer. Theoretically that may be true, but the experience in the country has been otherwise – both in the case of Satellite TV and private FM radio. That people are hungry to receive more and more channels is a myth that is being promoted. Studies have brought out that even those, who have access to any number of television channels, end up watching hardly ten channels at any time.

The issue is being deferred now for fifteen years. The ministry could not take a view whether it wants TRAI to be the regulator for broadcasting also or wants to bring out another regulatory authority for broadcasting. And, whether it would like to view licensing, carriage, content and tariff issues differently or together. If TRAI has to continue, it needs to equip itself with appropriate capabilities.

It took the ministry a couple of years to correct the loopholes in allowing facsimile edition of foreign newspapers as a way out of[8]

International Herald Tribune tangle. In this process, it had cleared the way for other international newspapers, of course, subject to certain formalities. Simultaneously, the cap for foreign syndication in newspapers was raised from 7.5 to 20 per cent of total editorial content. But there was no concern to do something to boost India's coverage abroad. The ministry had already raised foreign investment limit for non news publications from 74 to 100 per cent. But, now institutional investors as well as non-resident Indians can also invest in Indian newspapers, of course, within the limit of 26 per cent of equity, which the government allowed earlier. But, the demand to increase this limit to 49 per cent has already gained ground in New Delhi.

The Central Board of Film Censorship (CBFC), another activity for which the ministry of Information and Broadcasting is responsible, is crying out for a revamp of its operations to make it more credible and meaningful in the context of television and Internet. The guidelines being used by CBFC require a relook. Its procedure and methodology of certification, itself, requires to be made more relevant, keeping in view the proliferation of music channels and such programmes by other channels as well as various codes in the case of programmes and advertising in the context of channels of all origin and contents. Sensing the increasing public resentment about obscene contents and adult fare in some channels, the ministry has been coming up with one or other announcement without much difference. First of all, the ministry needs to understand the forces and factors causing such a trend. Unless the ministry undertakes an independent monitoring of channels' contents, it can never expect to be effective with its policies, no matter what legal provisions it comes up with. Issuing notice to one or two channels or suspending a channel for a month is neither a deterrent nor a solution for the larger issue. We need liberal laws, but with stringent enforcement and active involvement of citizens and civil society groups. A onetime registration fee of five lakhs and annual fees of one lakh for uplinking to foreign channels that too after some years of allowing operations as was being proposed by the ministry is too inconsequential. How will this measure remove shortcomings with regard to content and carriage needs to be seen? Simultaneously, the ministry should encourage independent social audit by civil society groups.

The ministry also needs to understand what is happening in the name of Children's Television. Almost a dozen foreign channels with foreign contents targeting children of the country are aggressively marketed, as if they have no obligation to anyone in the country. Also, music and remix channels have deleterious effect on children. Many research studies have indicated what this means to educational attainment of children, their predispositions, upbringing and life values. This subject is of significance to the nation rather than being left to broadcasters or bureaucrats. What has the government done to see that children programmes are more sensitive and that there should be locally produced programmes – even as a condition for down linking (as in some countries)?

The Geeta Krishna (a bureaucrat) report (2002 - 04) on media units of the ministry has been pending for nearly a decade now. After reviewing the functioning of units like Field Publicity, Song and Drama, the Directorate of Advertising and Visual Publicity (DAVP), etc., it recommended repositioning for better reach out to people, who need to be covered. In view of proliferation of media, particularly television, across the country including rural India, such a repositioning of these units is overdue. No one seems to be concerned about the efficacy of these media unites. Yet another pro-active initiative that is awaited is to bring the Indian Institute of Mass Communication (IIMC) "under the ministry". [9]IIMC has never been reviewed over the decades with regard to its mission, standing and contribution. Over the years, hundreds of institutions with similar syllabus, within the University network and outside, have mushroomed across the country. In what way does the IIMC justify and distinguish itself today to be an institute of "excellence" and aspire for a university status? Until 2010 that was the situation. What qualitative difference has it made to the media scene in the country or to the very functioning of the "information services" of the ministry of Information and Broadcasting? As early as in 1978, I did a report on IIMC and also on Field Publicity Units and raised the issue of certain contradictions in their functioning. But, the ministry was not as sensitive to either the "needs" of the communities or changing technologies as it has been to the investors, big operators and foreign corporates.

The NBR Report (1977), the "dumping ground of Shastri Bhawan" on IIMC was conveniently forgotten long ago, despite the fact that the institute continues to languish and the ministry continues to be riddled with its confused view[10].

As we keep talking about increasing plurality of views and choices, certain trends otherwise in the media scene of the country are gaining ground. For example, cross media ownership (of newspapers, TV, cable, radio) is crystallising too blatantly, which means media monopoly. In six or seven States, one media house already dominates the scene with nearly two-third market share. In fact, 12 or 13 media conglomerates are emerging in the country with such dominance. Yet, the policies are more facilitative for a further polarisation. There is also no debate in the country on such trends. The "Big Media", of course, do not want any policy in this regard and prefer "market forces" to determine the course. And market forces often mean "investors" and "vested interest groups". All this is happening as we have no national media policy.

High Time for a National Media Policy

At the outset of becoming the PM in 2004, Dr. Manmohan Singh called (in October 2004) for a "review of media policy",[11] particularly in the context of "information revolution" and "freedom of competition", as he described it. Further, the Prime Minister wanted the policy review keeping in view the "social justice concern" and in a meaningful way "for all players in the media sector". A Cabinet Sub-Committee was asked to review the policies instead of continuing with ad hoc and case by case approach of previous years. It was the most opportune time for India to come up with a "National Media Policy" based on a holistic and coherent view of old and new media. Do we have any publicly debated and transparently arrived at national policy, except in the case of Prasar Bharati as a Public Service Broadcaster? In the absence of a national media policy, we ended up having "reactive decisions" that caused contradictions and were devoid of any perspective as such, as the Prime Minister hinted at.

But the immediate issue which led to that review was limited to the publication of the Indian edition for International Herald Tribune by a local publisher "in violation of 1956 Cabinet decision", which continues as a "stand alone policy" despite so many conflicting decisions by subsequent governments. A reactive solution for such a violation was to go for an amendment or such other decision. Instead, the Prime Minister has rightly availed the opportunity to go into larger issues. But this Sub-Committee of the Cabinet made no difference, as it did not even consider the recent shifts in the very paradigm of media operations. Being limited to immediate issues like International Herald Tribune or CAS amounts to missing the wood in search of the tree and letting go an opportunity of empowering the people of India.

Core Issues

No government could be expected to do justice to the task without addressing three core issues. These pertain to FDI, particularly into "News Media" (radio, television, newspapers), and the conditions that need to go along with license; certain polarisation in the pattern of media holdings towards a monopolistic situation; and, of course, regarding emerging cross-media operations. Each of these issues deserves to be deliberated in the Parliamentary forum and outside. The deliberations of the Standing Committee of the Parliament on Communication under the Chairmanship of Somnath Chatterjee, in the 12th House, came close to deliberating these basic issues when the Parliament was dissolved.

A National Media Policy should help to correct the "increasing, but not expanding" dilemma of media. This includes doing something about continued and glaring regional divides in the reach of the media. We need another "tipping effect" as the country had witnessed with cable TV more than two decades ago, so that the reach of all media put together goes beyond two-thirds of population in all parts of the country and among all sections of people. To achieve that, do we need to encourage centralised media operations or decentralised media in the country? This is another aspect that needs to be understood. The recent spurt and qualitative changes in the media sector was mostly on account of regional and decentralised media by way of Cable TV and regional language newspapers and now regional language television channels.

Ministers for Information and Broadcasting have been rightly talking about the potential to have a few thousand community radio stations and even higher number of private FM radio stations in the country. But, in the absence of a clear perspective by a way of a policy as to the relative priorities of these media, we can hardly expect to make much headway. An appraisal of ad hoc decision taking over the years, including the ones related to community radio or FM radio, brings out the urgency of a national policy. Should we be concerned more about "commercial viability" of private FM radio or about the sustainability of community radio or with both equally? Also, had there been a deliberated national media policy, Prasar Bharati would not have gone for DTH as a marginal player in the country and without any implicit advantage, ignoring far more appropriate and cost-effective alternatives as a "Public Service Broadcaster".

Safeguards as an Obligation

An equally important issue that needs to be addressed as a part of national policy is related to "viewer-end safeguards" from market driven media operations. The licenses to private operators, irrespective of FDI, cannot be without obligations and responsibilities in the larger and long term interests of the viewers. It is rather difficult to understand how a government could have allowed television channels beaming into India initially without even registering in India and adhering to existing provisions, which are applicable to Indian media. By the time the lapse was realised, irreversible damage was done. "More (players) is not merrier", when it comes to media, as is often made out in the context of a State or region. Giving four to six FM radio licenses additionally for cities of ten lakh population would not amount to encouraging competition, but would make them unviable and may even destabilise radio operations itself. But, that was allowed and now (in 2016), after nearly a decade, operators within a city are allowed to merge. In the case of DTH, more than a couple of operators are neither desirable nor viable.

Initial research of CMS indicated (1995) that two or three DTH options are good enough for the country and also sustainable. But today (2016), we have already got seven DTH operators and as many are already in the queue waiting for a commercial proposition.

This "must carry" clause of certain public service channels (Doordarshan) is more than a decade old, almost forgotten by some flat forms, as there is no proactive monitoring and analysis mechanism. The ministry since had set up a mechanism for monitoring of channels. But, there is no evidence of any action or corrective measure that such monitoring has helped to initiate.

DD and AIR have the best infrastructure spread across the country, but for want of a vision, leadership and financial support, it is hardly being availed to take media closer to the grassroots and make them more relevant to people. National concerns and priorities in this regard have to be unambiguous. An issue related to this is the very positioning of Prasar Bharati (AIR and DD) as Public Service Broadcaster. They cannot be left to market forces and made to compete and then also earn to sustain themselves. The government, irrespective of which political party is in power, should ensure certain minimum level of budgetary support in the same way as for education and now for Lok Sabha and Rajya Sabha channels. The government should not look at licensing broadcasting as a source for generating revenue. The National Media Policy should take into account the Supreme Court's landmark judgment of 1995 that "airwaves are public", implying that they cannot be used to suit sectional or private interests. This judgment was for an independent regulator for broadcasting with specific "public interest" provisions as an obligation on the part of the operators. This also implies that "public service" and "public accountability" aspects should not be limited to a public service broadcaster, but should also apply to every broadcaster, private or public.

The government should have included in that review by the Cabinet Sub Committee the role and structure of the Press Council of India. For too long, the idea of reconstituting and empowering the Press Council is being talked about. There is no disagreement in any quarter that the Press Council, in its present form, is a toothless body despite being well represented; and that its scope needs to be expanded by bringing in electronic media. On the other hand, CAS was referred to TRAI overnight, and then the contentious issue of FM radio licensing was also passed on to TRAI as if the then government wanted to get rid of irritations it had created for itself by taking shortsighted ad hoc decisions. Since TRAI has taken on itself more issues to do with broadcasting as a carriage and was addressing issues like community radio, DTH, Cable TV and, in fact, wanted to take on even content related issues. The decisions on these can no longer be deferred or delayed. The government should deliberate the idea of having a separate Commission for broadcasting or enhance the scope of the Press Council itself. The I&B minister has been talking on and off about going for an independent Council. The idea deserves to be debated. The government should respect the 1995 judgment of Supreme Court for an "independent authority" to manage airwaves as "public property". Constituting a Cabinet Sub-Committee is a fire fighting way of going about it. The basic issues have to be taken by a mix of experts, Parliamentarians, technologists and operators. Like the Press Council of India, the "Broadcast Bill" of 1997 and "Convergence Bill" of 2001 should also be reconsidered. Both these proposals had gone through wide consultation process. Since communication technologies and the convergence process (irrespective of a government policy) have made it all the more urgent to have a national media policy with broad objectives.

Currently, digitalisation of broadcast sector is the buzz word. This is being talked by the government for a couple of years now. But, that is being looked at mostly as an opportunity to expand business opportunities rather than empowering and enabling people.

National Policy – Lessons from Telecom Sector

A national policy, first and foremost, is expected to end uncertainties in the country in the media sector and be explicit about government's resolve towards achieving certain national objectives with both short as well as long-term perspectives and role on regulatory and licensing issues. A national policy paves the way for transparency and makes instruments like citizen charter effective. Similarly, customer service standards and tariff and licensing obligations are the other features that a national policy provides. The National Telecom Policy 2011, announced on 26 March,[12] had the advantage of lessons from the first National Telecom Policy of 1994, which opened up the sector for private participation and its subsequent revision in 1999. The lengthy process that the government went through in the telecom sector is a good precedent for coming up with a national policy on media. The need of the hour for the country is to leapfrog in terms of availability of and access to new communication technologies imbalances and inequalities. Eventually it is customer awareness and activism, which would bring better and more reliable telecom service and also better use of technologies.

One of the handicaps that the policies and regulators seems to be facing is the lack of empirical field research on the use and role of telecom services among the various sections of users and regions. Management schools and social science faculties have contributed little in coming up with new insights for our present ways of looking at the telecom services, their viability and as communication networks. The National Telecom Policy provided for such periodic and independent research and evaluation as an obligation.

Should we Forget Checks and Balance?

Justice Markandey Katju, the newly appointed Chairman of Press Council of India,[13] has been hogging headlines for his views on the state of news media in the country. He was being accused (even asked to apologise) by big media representatives. However, what Justice Katju told quite directly to Karan Thapar, has been said in different shades of politeness in the last decade by two Presidents, two Prime Ministers and two Chief Justices, of course, without provoking and prompting a national debate as Katju and Karan did this time. I have also been writing since the last 16 years using facts and figures to demonstrate the same; still, it took this long to generate the heat. But, this is not enough; the debate needs to be taken forward.

Two visionary initiatives come to my mind when I think of the much talked about paradigm shift in media. The first initiative (1955), as nowhere else in the world, was that of Pandit Jawaharlal Nehru. As the first Prime Minister, he visualised at the very outset of the formation of Republican India that freedom of press (media) does not make sense unless a distinction is made between the owners of media and Journalists. The jobs of journalists should not be at the mercy of owners as also their wages. This initiative by way of a Working Journalist Act of 1955 contributed to the consolidation of media in India and nurtured journalism. It is because of that move that we continue to have assertive journalists and a flourishing profession that stands out as good as anywhere in the world. Nehru expected that the Journalist Act would ensure checks and balance for the emergence of an independent and vibrant news media. It took less than two decades to prove how wise Nehru was and how foresighted his idea was. By then, it was obvious that the freedom of Press and privileges extended were being availed of more by the owners, who were engaged in other businesses. That eventually led to summing up of the scenario with descriptions like "jute press". Two allegations were all over by then, including in the Parliament. One was on how profits from newspapers were being diverted by some to promote other businesses. A second one was how privilege of access and allocations were being used with conflict of interest becoming obvious. Yet, there was no way to go about with correctives, as there was no basis or data.

That is how the second visionary initiative (1973) was taken by the Prime Minister, Indira Gandhi. That was to find out the economics of newspapers first time in the country. She appointed Professor Bhabotosh Datta (he was a professor in the Kolkata Presidency College). Datta addressed two rounds of letters to newspaper establishments in the country appealing for income and expenditure details. Even after one year, he could get responses from hardly a couple of newspapers (none from the big ones). That was when I. K. Gujral, then the I&B minister, called me (1974) and posed the challenge whether I could ascertain the revenue and profitability aspects of newspapers. That is how, having just then conducted and analysed the figures of the first National Readership Survey (NRS) in the country (1970 -72), I ventured into the task.

Armed with circulation figures publication wise, I devised a methodology for constructing balance sheets, in four month time, for nearly 175 newspapers, including the prominent ones in the country, in different languages. Mrs. Indira Gandhi used the same to tamper the high spirits of media establishments (they were not yet accused as "media mafia").

After that, the argument - "not fourth estate, but real estate", as presented in my report, gained ground for some time. Moreover, the conflict of interest aspect of media came to surface. Even then, the government of the day did not come up with any measure to curb and curtail any of the privileges. But, this "give and take" as a quid pro quo practice between the political and media bosses started and the government found it mutually advantageous not to have a "media policy". The ad hoc or case by case approach suited both better. That is how we do not have a policy even though the Supreme Court had indicated it (1995). It has resulted in a series of decisions of long term consequence without any debate inside or outside the Parliament. That is when the concerns of media shifted from content to carriage and to growth aspects (and with that cross media ownership gained ground and media moguls were no longer limited to behind the scene maneuvering). They tilted the balance against the Journalists. The bargain has been more between the owners and the government with new gatekeepers tilting the scale. The civil society never figured in that process. Had the regional and national Journalists' unions not been there, the media in India would have become by now satellites of corporations, foreign and Indian. This is also described in the influential [14]*EPW* Journal as "fourth estate on sale" (2010) in the context of the paid news debate. Demand for increasing FDI further (from 20 to 40 and now to 64 per cent) into news media too is gaining ground now. When I analysed this phenomenon and brought it out for the first time in the country, it took me three years (1999 – 2002) to get an article (paradigm shift in media operations) published, as if the news media was not prepared to take a critical introspection. It was the *Frontline,* which published (2001) my analysis on the paradigm shift in media. Has the media changed further in this regard since then? (Only recently the last "Indian advertising agency" – Mudra has fallen and the likeliness of an increase in FDI into broadcasting from 49 to 64 per cent).

The ethical and legal angle of that paradigm shift is the conflict of interest for profit maximisation at the expense of the Fourth Estate. This is what I described as *Laxmanrekha* and organised a national roundtable in Hyderabad (in 2005) and at a few other places. A more likely difference between investors into media and others is that they too want to maximise their profits and privileges. Additionally, they also want the doors of the powers open for them, always. Further, they want to avail of "that connection" with powers for diversifying their business, vertically and horizontally. The other dimension of this phenomenon is from the perspective of a national policy. The concept of *Laxmanrekha* was thoughtfully adopted in our Constitution as "checks and balance" and it is what we need to remind ourselves today.

For the second time in a week (October 2011), the government was found in a quandary, indicating how weak the government is and how powerful the big media establishments have become. The government had to yield on two of its initiatives. One was on modality of license renewal of broadcasters and the second one was withdrawal of an important provision from the Press and Registration Bill 2010.

A more important amended guideline issued by the I&B ministry (October 2011) was that the "renewal of permission of channels will be conditional", subject to the channel having not been found guilty of violating (more than five times) the terms and conditions of the same old programme code and advertising guidelines as per the Cable TV Act of 1995. The government thought belatedly of some such provisions for the renewal of licenses. There should have been such a condition at the very outset of giving permission. Not all channels could be expected to avoid violation for whatever reason. As of early 2012, there was no evidence of withdrawal of permission of any news channel in spite of some of them receiving such notices for violating one or other clause and for more than a couple of times.

[15]Despite setting a monitoring mechanism (2009), the ministry has been neither able to promptly know of violations nor able to take action, even when required. There is no deterrence. In broadcasting, "retrospective views or actions" are of no consequence, as the damage has already happened. In the meanwhile, NBA should be complimented for its initiative for a self regulation. However, no self regulatory provision can be effective, particularly when such a body is hardly representative, though well intentioned. The Authority setup by NBA under Justice J S Verma did take some positive moves, like suggesting change in periodicity of TRP reports for news channels (from weekly to monthly) and guidelines in covering conflict situations.

Within 24 hours of this revised uplinking policy, the News Broadcasters Association (NBA) and Broadcast Editors Association (BEA) and all those representing investors' interests questioned the power of the government to issue such a notification under the existing guidelines. They also claimed that such a change in conditions for renewal of license amounts to infringement of "right to engage in business", "democratic rights", "freedom of press", "assault on media", etc.

According to the website of the ministry, it issued notices or advisories to 180 channels between 2004 and 2010. Whereas in just one month (June – July) of 2011, it received recommendations to that effect for nearly 40 channels, including 18 news channels from its internal Monitoring Committee. In the case of a news channel, the ministry even went to the National Human Rights Commission after issuing notices more than a couple of times. What does this all mean? Should permission to broadcasters be for life or routine even when the stake holding in the real sense in channels is not known? Perhaps, it is not too late for the government to consider, even now, the appointment of an independent Commission for broadcasting, as suggested by the Supreme Court in 1995.

These two instances remind once again what the country is missing - a national policy. Interestingly, in the same week, the Election Commission disqualified for the first time, a legislator in Uttar Pradesh from contesting elections on finding evidence for the allegation of paid news.

India has a national policy on a wide range of issues and sectors, which includes, marginal and mundane. Mass media is perhaps one of the few important services where we do not have a policy, despite several compulsions over the decades for a national policy. Why? Having a policy does not give this kind of flexibility! How else would we have free for all media scene as we have today? What else explains the government dropping an important provision from the Press and Registration (PRBP) Bill of 2010 in the last week of October 2011 before tabling it in the Winter Session of the Parliament? It was supposed to have been an outcome of Cabinet Sub Committee deliberation on paid news (*Financial Express, October 24, 2011).*

This provision would have saved journalists from the blame of paid news syndrome. Forty years ago, when I introduced the first NRS, I did not realise that I was laying the foundation for media research in India; and that I will be part of certain critical decisions of the time (1970-

95). But seeing the way important decisions were taken in the last decade without any rationale or a debate, I wonder where we are heading with two fundamental aspects of our democracy—free and fair elections and free and independent media. As I also pioneered election studies in India (1970-2010), I comprehend the critical linkage between the two.

Cross media ownership is another vital policy issue, which should have been taken up more than a decade ago before allowing "free for all to as many" and before it becomes too late to do anything, as we are witnessing today. [16]In 2007, the ministry referred this matter on cross media to TRAI for advice. As TRAI was about to submit its report, the ministry assigned (2008) the Hyderabad based ASCI for making another report on the same. Perhaps because neither of those reports were favorable (for the "growth of the market?"), they remain confidential until a couple of weeks ago! What is curious is that there has been no public discussion, not even in the media. How can this be understood?

[17]In August 2010, SEBI ordered that all media houses in the market should disclose their stakes in the corporates. They specifically asked them to disclose it on their own websites as well as newspapers or channels. The specific intention of market regulator was conflict of interest in and between media houses. But so far, hardly any media house is complying fully and neither has the media reported it nor did any government agency ask; and nor did the civil society remind about the desirability of such disclosures.

Fifteen years ago, when Journalists' Unions approached me to depose before the Wage Board on the performance of the media in the country (the establishments were arguing that press was operating in loss), I told them that unless unions close their ranks and leadership emerges out of them, journalists should not rely on the Wage Board for too long, particularly because editor-leaders were no longer around. Today, I see the situation even more delicate with no visionaries around to offer a holistic perspective or to take a bold introspection.

Every few years, journalists have to lobby for the appointment of a Wage Board and government obliges as if it was a favor to journalists and then journalists had to rally around again to get the Wage Board recommendations accepted and face resistance in getting them implemented by the media establishments. Had there been a national media policy, journalists would not have been in such a vulnerable situation today. The dilemma is best evident in the way paid news revelation was taken up and forgotten even after the appointment of Cabinet's Sub-Committee to consider the matter and a Parliamentary Committee looking into it. The Election Commission had, for the first time, disqualified a MLA from contesting an election as paid news was proved, and the Press Council itself proved blatantly that it goes by the interests of the big bosses of the media.

These recent two instances of October 2011 bring out the dilemma. That the provision for disclosing sources of revenue of news media has been dropped from the Press and the Registration Bill 2010 was hardly reported by any news media or countered by any leader either way, despite the Bill being in public purview for several months, awaiting introduction in the Parliament, obviously, because that is not in the interest of media establishments. Whereas the other notification making renewal of broadcast license conditional was all over in news media, - all that within 24-hours after the notification and in the next 24-hours, the government backtracked that decision, forgetting that today we are in a transparency era with RTI Act. Both the initiatives would have ensured some transparency and would have even enhanced the credibility of media.

Conflict of Interests

News channels have been under the grip of TRP culture and competitive compulsions. That is generally known by now. Despite concerns about channels' content priorities by civil society groups, no visible change is evident in the contents in the last decades (2000-2011). Two Prime Ministers belonging to two political parties - Atal Bihari Vajpai of BJP and Dr. Manmohan Singh of Congress had talked about the kind of priorities of news media. They talked at two different important occasions - 75 years of *The Tribune* and 150 years celebrations of *The Hindu*. Both called for introspection. Dr A P J Abdul Kalam and Pratibha Patil, too, did so as Presidents of India. In fact Dr. Kalam called on media more than once to reach out to a billion people with contents relevant to them. President Pratibha Patil, like Vajpayee, more recently (December 2009) lamented, while addressing World Newspaper Conference at Hyderabad, that news media tend to give preference to negative news and called upon editors to be responsible and reflect the needs of people. She even reminded the role of media for peace, stability, security and good governance. Even the Vice President of India, M Hamid Ansari, more recently lamented the trends in the content priorities of news media and favored a "media regulation framework". He posed the question, "Can the constitutional safeguards on freedom of speech be used to evade regulation of the commercial persona of media corporate and groups? Where does public interest end and private interest begin?"[18]

There are some who argue that as a Fourth Estate, media should not be institutionally and constitutionally responsible, as the other pillars are in a democracy. The assumption is that if media comes under the oversight of any of the other pillars, it ceases to be free in the true sense. This argument, firstly, is based on "old understanding" of media. Secondly, the argument ignores conveniently the framework of "checks and balance", which is not only inherent in the Indian Constitution, but it is also the hallmark of a functional democracy. The other missing aspect of understanding is "whose freedom? – the journalists', owners' or the ones, who manage or control media?" And, the old argument, otherwise, is based on the assumption that media is independent, but it is not so today from any angle.[19]

However, all such talk have neither provoked anyone in the media nor made any difference; perhaps, because none of their remarks pertain to the regulatory issue. But, a more direct talk (November 2011) by the Chairman of Press Council of India suggesting that TV should be brought under a Media Council has raised a flutter. An offensive against Justice M. Katju was orchestrated. Justice J. S. Verma, respected otherwise for his dispassionate views, heading an industry sponsored self regulatory group, too criticised the Press Council, when the spirit of issues raised by Justice Katju were altogether different. The controversy reminds the kind of power the news media moguls have acquired recently in the country by not allowing any criticism of any kind on their privileges and powers, from any quarter, all in the name of "freedom of press". It is in this context and against this background that Justice Katju's remarks and the controversy need to be looked at for a forthright introspection, not just by investors and big media, but by the government, the civil society and the professions involved. Justice Santosh Hegde, former Judge of Supreme Court and head of Karnataka Lokayukta, too, commented that news media should have some regulatory mechanism.

Justice Markandey Katju told Karan Thapar in an exclusive television interview, which was rebroadcast three or four times and covered widely in newspapers all over (October 28, 2011). The channels, in turn, carried discussions on the issues referred. What did he say? Katju said that media has become irresponsible; it's not working in the interest of people;

and it is diverting their attention from real issues by taking up news about cricket, films and the like. He accused media of dividing people, including on religion instead of promoting a scientific outlook and playing a positive role in transforming the nation into a modern State. To ensure all that, Katju called for "reasonable restrictions". He said no freedom is absolute and without "reasonable restrictions". As a reaction to those overview comments of Katju, News Broadcasters had gone offensive against Justice Katju, and they even asked him to apologise, when in fact, there is nothing in Justice Katju's statement that others had not said in the last one decade. He had put it more directly.

[20]But there is one thing that the PCI Chief had raised for the first time. In reaction to the offensive against him, Justice Katju wrote that "self regulation is no regulation". Dismissing the self-regulation mechanism adopted by TV channels", Katju said, "News channels are private bodies whose activities have a large influence on the public and they also must be answerable to the public.... How can electronic channels say that they are not accountable to anyone, but themselves?" he questioned. He further said that, "Even judges of the Supreme Court and High Courts do not have that absolute right (of self-regulation)." Lawyers and doctors, too, can face suspension or cancellation of license for professional misconduct. "Why, then, should you object to being placed under the Lokpal or some other regulatory authority," Katju asked. This is how a large segment of the country's public too feels about some channels.

Going further, the Chairman of PCI further wished to enquire the logic behind the news channels claiming the privilege of self-regulation. He asked the industry, "You claim the right of self-regulation. By the same logic, politicians and bureaucrats will also claim the right of self-regulation. Or do you claim to be so '*doodh ka dhula*' (clean as milk) that you should not be regulated by anyone else except yourself? If they are not willing to come under a Media Council, they should come under the proposed Lok Pal," Justice Katju said. What the government could not do over these recent years, and succumbed to the push and pulls of the media moguls, Justice Katju did that. No wonder why there is general appreciation for him in the country, even if not all of them agree with all that he said. What they look for is a way forward in such a way that there is transparency and also checks and balances in media operations.

From these deliberations one thing comes to the fore, i. e., the "content model" being followed by news channels has not helped expand the reach beyond, despite a boom in news channels in the country in the last decade, as if we are not unleashing the full powers of the TV.

The government is woefully equipped to do anything more and beyond what it is doing now with regard to its capabilities, infrastructure and resources. Over the years, it has, however, increased the consultation process on contentious issues, like content regulation. But the Advisory Committees that the All India Radio stations used to have for different streams (rural, industry, children, etc) have remained defunct or not constituted.

The I&B ministry is the nodal agency for dealing with film/cinema, print media, radio and television carriage and contents aspects. Despite growth, boom, expansion, proliferation of broadcasting and news media over the decades, the scope of the ministry has remained static as it was – with no expertise on any of the subject areas that it deals with; neither does it have any additional personnel to deal with nor any new agencies to help it except TRAI. In fact, during the Emergency (1977–79), the ministry had more "officials" (including from police and intelligence agencies) than it has ever after. Even its functional agencies, like the Press Information Bureau (PIB), Directorate of Audio-Visual Publicity (DAVP), Publications Division, Directorate of Field Publicity, Song and Drama Division – all of them remained static and under staffed. Even in the case of the Indian Institute of Mass Communication (IIMC), although it was declared as a Centre for Excellence, it was never added with any professional strength either in terms of faculties, courses or research capabilities - except opening two or three centres away from Delhi (Dhenkanal, Amravati and Aizawl). But, buildings were added. Even in the case of AIR and Doordarshan, there was a freeze for recruiting, but they were allowed to hire help temporarily or outsource in some cases. In 1976, I gave a report to the secretary Mr. Jamal Kidwai, "Dumping ground of Shastri Bhawan", but the ministry did so little to elevate the status or potential of IIMC, except appointing once or twice a professional from outside the ministry as its Director[21].

Neither the ministry nor any of these I&B ministry's units have changed or geared up to the changing times or scenario in the country in terms of technologies or global opportunities or the larger national policies related to economics, globalisation, privatisation, competitive compulsions, impact, etc.

The Prasar Bharati Act, the Cable TV Act or any other such legislative provisions of the last 25 years have made no difference to the functioning of the ministry; not even monitoring or any other analytical skills were added. Its monitoring (of foreign broadcasts) units were taken over by the Home ministry more than two decades ago. Only recently, in 2009, the ministry set up a (television) monitoring mechanism of its own, but without any capabilities to analyse of what is not monitored; nor has it come up with any such analysis reports.

One could notice the ministry's reliance on industry bodies, like FICCI, CII, etc. As a result of all that, the influence of personalities – interested groups – mostly of media owners – has increased, which is obvious too often. At no point in the last three decades, the ministry ever had creative or pro-active capabilities. There was no envisioning of emerging scenario. In 1996–97, the ministry commissioned CMS to come up with a perspective for Doordarshan based on a consultation process across the country. The report based on that, "Vision and Mission of Doodarshan" was never even taken up for a serious consideration because of frequent changes in the ministers and even secretaries. This report, although published since, was never even made available for any.

It was I. K. Gujral as minister and Jamal Kidwai as secretary of I&B ministry in 1973 at the very outset of the television era (although with only one (DD) channel, but going regional) who thought of gearing up the ministry with a "planning, appraisal and evaluation" division with two directors. The then Planning Commission even approved setting up of an Evaluation Directorate in the ministry. At that time, they approached me (in 1973) to join the ministry as an outside expert for setting up "appraisal and evaluation" capabilities in the ministry. It was the first time that the ministry inducted the then senior-most Information Service Officer (G N S Raghavan, who was known then as Genius Raghavan) to head the division in the ministry. As I never wanted to be part of the government, after discussions with the minister, I agreed to be an advisor to the ministry, but formally from IIMC, where I will also help set up a Research and Evaluation Department as a visiting Professor. In the next couple of years, I appraised the functions of each of ministry's units and also evaluated (like, for example, DD going commercial, coordination between AIR and DD, etc.). Emergency, however, changed the course of the ministry. The Shah Commission and the whitepaper on I&B ministry's role during Emergency took the ministry back to days of bureaucracy. And, worse, it never geared up thereafter with capabilities of any kind. This is because the ministry never had a "national media policy" to pursue or to gear up to pursue such a policy. As a result of that, the ministry succumbed and in (1995), the secretary yielded to the then Planning Commission's suggestion that DD/Prasar Bharati should earn from the market. The Finance ministry too pushed the ministry in that direction.

I recall that when I heard of I&B secretary succumbing to Planning Commission's suggestion that Doordarshan should earn from market to support its operations, I took (1996) B. G. Deshmukh, former cabinet secretary, who had retired, and Khushwant Singh (with whom I was having a meeting of Social Audit Panel for Communication ministry) to meet the secretary (Bhaskar Ghosh) and expressed that his yielding to the pressures of the Planning Commission was a hasty decision with grave implications for the very concept of Public Service Broadcasting. That is what eventually became the beginning of "neither here nor there" standing of Doordarshan.

[22]A second effort to add certain professional skills and objective outlook to the ministry was made during Mrs. Indira Gandhi's come back to power in 1980. As Mr. Vasant Sathe was reluctant to take over as I&B minister (He preferred Culture and Education portfolio), Mrs. Gandhi told him to rope me in for independent "strategic inputs" and also constituted a "Standing Advisory Committee" with good old G. P. (G. Parthasarathy), diplomat and former Vice Chancellor of JNU, and seven other members including me. The other eminent personalities included Dr. Narayan Menon, Alkazi, Mrs. Fathima Zakaria, Prof. Mutatkar, Kartar Singh Duggal and Dr. Mulkraj Anand. The heads of PIB, AIR and DD were special invitees. Mani Shankar Aiyer, diplomat on whom G.P relied for inputs, was also an invite for these meetings next two years.

This Standing Advisory Committee used to meet for two or three days every month to review important issues before the ministry and suggest appropriate course, particularly on contentious issues. The same Committee first formulated a news policy (for AIR and DD) after considerable deliberations, which the minister even tabled in the Parliament. The Committee also suggested reviving Advisory Committees for AIR and DD Kendras in different States with independent local people, who were experts in different fields. This Committee of I&B ministry ceased to function with the death of Mrs. Indira Gandhi.

Mr. Arun Jaitely too tried to constitute Advisory Committees for the ministry. But, before any of those Committees started functioning, he was shifted to another ministry.

The next initiative was taken by Jaipal Reddy as minister of I&B (2005) by way of an informal "consultation process" with about 40 representatives from different groups including the ones, who were critics of the government decisions. But, this exercise was an ad hoc one and was limited to what kind of regulatory mechanisms should be there. It was because, by then, the contents of private and satellite television channels had become a concern for women's groups, consumer groups and even political parties. Representatives of channels and industry were present prominently in this consultation process. The deliberations of these 40 people was reduced into a draft policy proposition by a four member informal group with P N Vasanti of CMS taking active role in drafting a three-tier regulatory mechanism (self, industry and the government). That is what the minister since then has been sounding on and off without actually taking any decisions. As the ministry keeps pointing out that the news channels (by then, important news media had already established their news channels) came up first with Indian Broadcast Foundation (IBF) and then series of associations of functionaries, (News editors, and then constituted Standard and Complaints bodies headed by retired Judges– as a pre-emptive intuitive so that the ministry could not come up with any other measures, ad hoc or otherwise.

The ministry remained political and bureaucrat driven with hardly any subject expert associated with it or with any of its units or with any creative support. Its approach remained ad hoc and crisis limited. In the last two decades, neither of its Media units had ever come up with any structural changes or review of the strategies. The classic example is that of Directorate of Field Publicity with more than 150 field teams. Twenty years later, I gave a report to relocate these units to far off and interior areas where no other formal news media exist, nothing has been done. Navin Chawla as secretary of ministry of I&B tried, but nothing could be done, as there was no national media policy for the country.

I recommended giving up "Fixed Point Chart" by DD and AIR stations; my suggestion to reposition Field Publicity Units in the country by relocating them in view of expansion of AIR and TV channels was liked, but never implemented and limited to occasional statements by a secretary or the minister.

I&B Ministry is Ill Equipped

An issue that needs to be debated is whether there is any need for a separate ministry of "Information and Broadcasting", as it exists, in the last four decades more particularly? There was justification in the initial years of free India. I had suggested more than two decades ago (Box newspaper clipping) winding up of the ministry and merging "B" (Broadcasting) with the ministry of Communication (and Information Technology) and "I" (Information) be made into a "Board" or a Commission somewhat in the lines of the Railway Board or Space Commission with the responsibility to handle public communication needs of all governmental agencies, so that the credibility of communication could be better and handled more professionally.

The genesis for this suggestion was my failure to bring together (1994) ministers for Communication and Information and Broadcasting to discuss better use of AIR transmitters (which were being used hardly one-third of time) in Himachal Pradesh, so that access could be increased to many more communities in remote areas and tariff could be reduced. Yet another reason for making such a suggestion was that there could be scope for more creative and credible communication strategies for reaching more and motivates more people. But that idea was never even debated. Instead, each new minister (there were about a dozen in the last two decades) quick starts with brave announcements and yields no sooner, coming under the pull and push of powerful lobbies and, in fact, does a volte-face. Some ministers are smart in talking of public consultations and others by setting up an expert panel or tactical in prompting industry bodies like the Indian Broadcasting Foundation to come up with an initiative in a pre-emptive way.

The P. C. Joshi (an economist) Committee Report of the I&B ministry on television outlined an "Indian Personality TV" taking a cue from Vikram Sarabhai's vision of communication technologies for growth and development of India and that of Mc Bride Commission of UNESCO (new communication order). That was based on insights from one of world's unique experiment of using satellite technology for reaching out to different language and climate zone communities. This one year experiment, Satellite Instrumental Television Experiment (SITE), operated for 2400 villages falling in six language territories. Thereafter, there was the Kheda Experiment (1978–80) as a follow up to SITE with four features - development concerns, participative approach, decentralised programming and entertainment education format in such a way that TV caters to the needs of local people in a motivating and empowering way. All that was forgotten. In fact, even those who assumed senior positions in the ministry in recent years don't know anything about SITE or "Indian personality TV". This is merely one glaring example for winding up of the ministry of bureaucrats; nor was there any sensitivity about the very potential of television in the Indian context. I know this as I am the person who evaluated various media units of I&B ministry (1974–78) and looked into its working over a period of 25 years (1974 – 2000).

Krishi Darshan (1967) which made a difference in many respects and at different levels was not the result of any I&B ministry initiative. SITE was not ministry's initiative. If there is one initiative it can boast of, it could be Humlog serial (1984), which remained a model for Indian television (including private channels) for a decade and which too contributed. It was S. S. Gill, the then secretary, I&B ministry, who took the initiative and pursued supported by Ford Foundation.

One has to do research to know any other initiative that I&B ministry had ever taken to change the course of Indian television towards realising its potential. On the contrary, such a research is likely to trace the origins of all the ills to the ministry. Some efforts were there, but they were never followed up to a logical conclusion. They were dragged on until forgotten by the successors at Shastri Bhawan. That is why even now (2012), I could not change my view that I&B ministry cease its avatar in its present form.

The ministry played a blatantly negative role and did a great injustice as if it was determined to reduce and demolish Doordarshan and even AIR as a great national institution. History cannot ignore the kind of innocuous role that the ministry played in the last 25 years.

This chapter traces twists and turns electronic media has passed through and yet achieved growth. All that with no national policy, no preparedness and mechanisms as if successive governments missed envisaging the implications and taking a perspective of the spread of television and take proactive initiatives. As a result the country ended up "missing the very mission" of availing television as a level player, support and sustain developmental endeavors. As a result of passive or pro-business concerns of the ministry over the years, news channels could not evolve in a creative mode and be more concerned of larger context as it was more an adopting mode competing to do more of the same. That is how we missed an "India TV", even more in the case of news channels.

Endnote

1 http://www.indiankanoon.org/doc /341773/

2 This writer made an observation in 1973 that Mumbai professionals were interested more in "reach" aspects of media and ones in Delhi were in the "Unreached" percentages. What matters for future outlook and planning is the extent of Unreached people whether it is in family planning, or any other campaign and for the conventional mass media. An analysis of various primary sources on the direct reach of mass media specifically news papers, Radio, cinema and television. This percentage is derived by this writer based on his analysis of the data available from various primary surveys including that of NCEAR. Until proliferation of television into rural the combined reach was within 60 percent. The phenomena of duplication that is same people who are reading are also the listeners and viewers and vice versa. After such an analytic exercise the writer concluded that the percent of Unreached by conventional media was more than a quarter of adult population in general. But it varies specific context to context. For example, the Unreached would be much less In the case of entertainment than in the case of health aspects, solar power etc.

3 Satellite instruction television experiment (SITE) initiated by ISRO chairman Dr Vikram Sarabhai with the cooperation of USA space agency was a pioneering experiment in the world between 1975-76. This experiment's commercial version is Direct to Home (DTH) 35 years later . China and Indonesia used satellite to communicate in a Multi language regions a decade later.

4 Origins of Broadcast bill (1997) goes back to land mark Judgment of Supreme Court in 1995, when it viewed airwaves as of public and advised the government to go for a regulator for broadcasting. The govt could not defer or delay any further When it came up with this draft bill. No other bill on any media has ever been discussed in the country as this Bill (1996-2007) and over such a long period. CMS too played a key role earlier by coming up with a draft after consultations with more than 24 media experts in the country but it suggested a three tire broadcasting system. CMS also had two round table discussions with the chairman of Parliamentary Standing Committees and then with the minister. After all that the government shelved the bill assuring to bring out a more comprehensive Convergence Bill which the govt did bring out but that too was allowed to lapse. See "Broadcast Bill in Budget session" Business Standard 10 October 2006

5 In July 1999 the government announced 150 new FM channels in 40 cities. But of 108 licenses issued only 22 operated and one was even closed down. That is when the same media bigs got In to since there were only minimal cross media restrictions and pooled as many F.M Channels in as many cities. In 2016 there were 243 FM channels in 86 cities. This they could achieve with the rallying of advertising industry. See TRAI annual report, and annual report of the Ministry of Information and Broadcasting, New Delhi.

6 The Ministry of information & Broadcasting Annual Reports.

7 Low Power Transmitter (LPT) were set up for receiving relayed programes. The Minister HKL Bhagat had taken to the task of one LPT a day and to cover every district. But ISRO development group with Professor Yeshpal, Prof Chitnis and Kiron Karnik went beyond to demonstrate that broadcasting could be for local communities with locally relevant and produced programs.

8 International Herald Tribune is unique example for indecisive and ambiguious approach of the Ministry of Information and Broadcasting. In such a vacuum

, M J Akbar then chief editor of Asian Age and Deccon Chronicle group tried out by going ahead printing International Herald Tribune in India in May 2004 by having an understanding with that paper .but soon there after the Ministry had issued notice and got it closed. In 1974 when the Minister and Secretary of Information and Broadcasting invited this writer to join the Ministry to head its newly initiated evaluation wing, he chose Indian Institute of Mass Communication (IIMC), to base evaluation department and also be a visiting professor. In that capacity he had witnessed over a two year period its operations and also discussed with the faculty and students

9 On IIMC seeking additional grants in 1975, the Secretary of the Ministry Mr. Kidwai asked this writer to conduct a quick review of IIMC operations. The report submitted was titled as "Dumping ground of I and B ministry" with a hope that the report will provoke the Ministry to take IIMC far more seriously and prompts a critical view of structure of courses. But soon after the report was submitted, national emergency was declared and secretary Jamal Kidwai took early retirement and the Minister was shifted to Planning Ministry.

10 Same as above

11 "Review media policy, says PM" Tribune news service. New Delhi 5 October 2004. http://www.tribuneindia.com /2004/20041006/ nation.htm

12 "Highlights of draft national telecom policy 2011" by Joji Philip, Economic Times, 10 October, 2011 http://articles.economictimes.indiatimes.com/2011-10-10/news/30263359_1_spectrum-act-grievance-redressal-mhz

13 "Justice Markandey Katju clarifies", in The Hindu, 16 February, 2015. Press council of India.

14 http://www.epw.in

15 Electronic Media monitoring centre was setup in 2008 by the Ministry of Information & Broadcasting to track contents of channels and identify deviations of program and advertising codes. This centre claims monitoring nearly 900 channels, including 401 news channels. http://www.emmc.gov.in

16 Trai 2007, http://www.trai.gov.in

17 SEBI, August, 2010. Website http://www.sebiupdates, blogspot2018/08/media-companies to disclose

18 *(The Hindu, 16 November 2011).* http://www.thehindu.com/news/national/article2633148.ece

19 *The Hindu, 22 November, 2011*

20 The Hindu 16 February, 2015

21 Same as in 9 above.

22 Some Govt. committees come into existence in unusual contest. Vasant Sathe preferred to be a ministry for culture, rather than for Information & Broadcasting. The portfolio offered to him on Mrs. Indira Gandhi's come back to power in 1980. Mrs. Gandhi suggested to Sathe to have standing advisory committee for the Ministry to help him on an ongoing basis. That is how this 12 member committee was appointed with senior diplomat and former vice chancellor of Jawahar Lal Nehru University, G. Parthasarthe as its chair, This writer was an expert member of that committee (1980-83) and was involved in drafting news policy.

9

Ethics and Regulations

Independent Regulation as a Compulsion

A public hue and cry over certain TV contents a decade ago focused on violence and vulgarity. We now seem to have reconciled to that fact. For, the concern now is about immoral and obscene contents. With the multiplication of music channels and launch of DTH platforms, more civil society groups are joining the chorus for some pro-active initiative to curb such uninhibited tendency of TV channels. With such contents getting added now in regional languages, as if in competition with "foreign music channels" being down linked in the country, the I&B ministry itself has taken initiative by holding consultations with stakeholders to find ways of curbing such trends. With more political leaders and parties taking to news channels there is increasing realisation that channels do need to have some regulation not only to curb certain tendencies in election time coverage like paid news, but even otherwise.

Compulsions for Moderation

As a nation we need to realise that television as a medium and its contents, more specifically, have far more implications on viewing public with long term impact at individual and societal level. As discussed earlier, peculiarities of TV are different from print media in terms of use, contents, and influence, particularly on vulnerable sections, women and children, who constitute three-fourth of all viewers in the country. The double edged character of TV is known. But that its negative drive is far more because of the kind of contents that channels tend to hype is not so well realised. In the process, impressive positive potential of TV gets marginalised or negated. As such, contents of television channels, particularly in a competitive environment as we have today, call for larger concern. TV empowers and enables positively, provided it is moderated in favor of such ends. Several researches have been undertaken in this regard (on the effects of TV) over the years world over. Although conducted mostly in US, there are several insights from all that for India.

Responsibility Towards Society

Responsibility of TV to society gets reflected in its concern about implications of its contents on the society, at micro and macro levels and on disadvantaged sections and interior regions in particular. Such a concern should be expected not only from a public broadcaster (Prasar Bharati), but by all broadcasters. In fact, all channels should do something about basic "national issues" (like illiteracy, health, children, etc) or even global issues as an obligation and in their own interest. A list of such concerns or issues can be formulated by channels themselves from time to time taking cue from the country's constitution, national policies, development goals, local compulsions and sensitivities, etc. But it should be left to individual channels to use their own ingenuity as to what, when and which issues to cover and how. Some of the channels in fact have been doing so at one time or other. Decency (of programmes) is concerned with sensitivities of people of various sections – both the viewing public and also the larger society. If telemarketing on cell phones is viewed as "invasion into privacy and amounts to harassment" of subscribers as the Supreme Court had (2010) observed that TV programmes could be several times more harassing or irritating to the viewers. Creativity without concern is a misnomer and could even be futile. They are two sides of the same coin. The landmark judgment of Supreme Court of 1995 that "airwaves belong to public", hence, their use need to be independently regulated and that broadcasting should not be used for "private profit" is something which the governments have ignored despite declining trends in the last couple of years.

While upholding 26/11 convict's death sentence, Supreme Court bench consisting of Justice Aftab Alam and Justice C K Prasad questioned the argument that "any regulatory mechanism for the electronic media must only come from within". The two member bench observed that "any attempt to justify the conduct of the TV channels by citing the right to freedom of speech and expression would be totally wrong and unacceptable" as "the freedom of expression, like all other freedoms under Article 19, is subject to reasonable restrictions".[1]

The Press Council of India Chairman Justice Markandey Katju reiterated to the government while appealing for bringing electronic media under a "media council", that "an unregulated electronic media is playing havoc with the lives of people". He dismissed the assertion of the broadcast media that their "own self regulatory measures are sufficient without any further governmental over sight". He reiterated that, "self regulation is an oxymoron" which of course was promptly criticised by IBF, NBA and some other media organisations.[2]

Which criticising PCI's resolution for bringing in channels under its purview, News Broadcasters Association (NBA) stated that "self regulatory mechanism has been in force for the last several years" and that "had a very real and positive impact" in improving broadcasting standards" (NBA Press release of August 30, 2012). Whereas NBA initiated self regulatory mechanism irrespective of the fact that hardly one-third of news broadcasters are its members), is hardly three year old and that there is no evidence to claim that channels had "positive impact" on standards.

Speaking at a meet of Editors Guild of India[3], both Union Law minister Salman Khurshid and BJP's Ravi Shankar Prasad (also a former Minster for I&B) argued for media regulation. Both of them of course were talking for content regulation. Khurshid in fact said that "self-regulation by the industry" was not working. A two Judge Supreme Court Bench (July 2012) questioned the electronic media's argument that it has self regulatory mechanism to get away from whatever coverage unconcerned of national interests.

Existing regulatory provisions in the context of TV channel contents (programme and advertising codes) are out dated or irrelevant or inadequate to tackle and address the issues arising out of today's television scenario in the country. In addition, there is the anomaly between Cable TV channels and those of DTH. Even the Cinematographic Act of 1953 needs to be modified urgently with demarcation from feature films. There are no studies on long term effect or impact of various media in the country. In the absence of an independent monitoring of TV contents, TRPs have become the only driver of contents, despite realising that it is more often misleading and is adding to the problem, perpetuating and echoing all that is condemned by concerned citizens. In fact, the best of creative talents in the country have been suppressed unwittingly because of TRP criteria. TRP is advertising driven, not so much concerned with the editorial or viewers. Also, at present, there is no reliable mechanism in operation to enforce either of the existing provisions, not even blatant violations of whatever regulations are there, as if the governments is helpless in this regard.

Inadequacy of Existing Regulations

Existing laws/regulations in the context of broadcast contents (programme and advertising codes including) are either irrelevant or inadequate to tackle or address the issues arising out of today's television scenario, particularly satellite channels, music channels, news channels and DTH platforms. Whatever regulations are there were formulated before the market driven TV era or even before the proliferation of satellite TV, and without taking into account the "popularity" compulsions of channels. "Market forces" approach may be good for optimisation of commercial revenues. But, its relevance is marginal where equity is a bigger concern in national policy, particularly with so many divides and disparities all across the country.

Various decisions taken by the government to do with broadcasting are ad hoc, in isolation and some of them are even contradictory. This is because we have neither a national policy on broadcasting nor a holistic view of emerging technologies. As a result, broadcasters are having a field day as if it is only their interests, which matter – it means concern for "Return on Investment", "consolidation" of business interests and "expansion of enterprises". But, at the same time, over regulation is also not good. In fact, unrestrained regulation could be worse than monopoly and market force view. Nevertheless, the State has a responsibility to be concerned about the effects and implications of broadcasting on larger sections of people. Broadcasting should be free from the control of both the government of the day and self interested dominant sections. Self regulation or voluntary regulation, whether individually or together by the players, is far better and desirable, particularly in the case of *content*. The scope for government intervention, as and when, should be exceptional. Government's role should be more related to policies and in supporting an independent regulatory mechanism. The best bet is by way of self regulation, from within by each channel and media. Not all broadcasters could be said as responsible and concerned about effects or consequences at any point of time.

TV channels need to follow certain restraint on their own as responsibility with certain dos and don'ts guidelines, on hours of broadcast of certain type of public interest programme/announcements, etc. Broadcasters could have annual public hearing as a pre-condition for license renewal. At present, there are no reliable mechanisms in operation to enforce either of the provisions of any Act, not even blatant violations, as if the governments are helpless. Monitoring has to be done by an independent body involving eminent citizens and professionals with no links with advertisers, advertising agencies, producers, channels and even the government. Even now, when broadcasters have taken some initiatives, there is need for a National Policy and a more transparent and independent monitoring mechanism.[4]

(P N Vasanti's article, Mint, May 27, 2011)

Fine Print | PN Vasanti

Self-regulation revisited

NBSA found that TV9 had violated clauses 5, 6 and 9 of the NBA code of ethics and ordered TV9 to display an apology for the story on its channel for a fixed duration during peak hours.

The first half of this year has seen a significant triumph for self-regulation initiatives by Indian broadcasters. Industry-led peer groups have taken up initiatives that have given new momentum to the sector.

Recently, in response to numerous email complaints sent to the channel as well as the News Broadcasters Association (NBA), the News Broadcasting Standards Authority (NBSA) took "suo motu" cognizance of a programme titled Gay Culture Rampant in Hyderabad, aired by TV9 in February and accused of having sensationalised the issue. After receiving TV9's defence, justice J.S. Verma of NBSA issued his decision on Sunday, holding that TV9 had violated clauses 5 (sex and nudity), 6 (privacy) and 9 (sting operations) of the NBA code of ethics. TV9 was ordered to display an apology for the story on its channel for a fixed duration during peak hours. In addition, TV9 was also fined Rs. 1 lakh to be paid to NBSA.

Even though NBSA is not an "official" adjudicatory body, the order is a welcome move for citizens' rights to privacy and dignity. Another reason why this order is so important is that it demonstrates the viability of NBSA—a voluntary self-regulatory industry body—as an expedient channel of redress for the public. By delivering its decision within a month of the date of the incident, NBA has succeeded in inspiring the public's confidence in its mission to serve as a truly impartial regulator of broadcast news in India.

Constituted in 2007, NBA has 20 leading news and current affairs broadcasters (comprising 45 news and current affairs channels) as its members. NBA presents a unified voice before the government on matters relating to news and current affairs broadcasters in India. It was formed to promote and protect the interests of India's television news broadcasters and was the first to adopt a voluntary code of ethics.

Discussions on broadcast content standards have been on since 2005, when the ministry of Information and Broadcasting constituted a formal committee to draft conventions for the sector. This committee was created after immense pressure from the courts and civil society groups who felt that broadcasters were testing the limits and the law of the country through provocative and sensational programming.

After a comprehensive consultative process of over three years, this committee, consisting of 40 stakeholders from government, civil society, non-governmental organisations and industry, submitted its report, along with suggested self-regulation guidelines for the broadcasting sector. As a part of this committee and the subgroup set up to draft these guidelines, I had the privilege to be involved in this debate since inception to submission in 2008.

However, since then, there has been a stalemate on efforts to formalise or accept any content regulation. The good news is that the Indian Broadcasting Foundation (IBF) announced earlier this month the adoption of the committee's work and unanimously approved a "self-regulatory content guidelines and complaints redressal mechanism" for all non-news and current affairs television channels, including general entertainment, children and special interest channels. The guidelines will be applicable from 1st June and will provide the channels guiding principles for content programming along with a redressal mechanism for bona fide complaints from viewers.

Established in 1999, IBF is one of the earlier associations set up to promote the interests of the Indian television industry. IBF comprises major broadcasters running more than 250 TV channels and enjoys a unique position as the accredited spokesman of the broadcasting industry.

IBF has been, from time to time, taking up various issues affecting the broadcast industry with the concerned authorities.

The self-regulatory content guidelines and complaint redressal mechanism sets out principles, guidelines and ethical practices to guide the broadcasting service provider in conforming with the programme code prescribed under the Cable Television Networks (Regulations) Act, 1995, irrespective of the medium or platform used for broadcasting the programme.

The redressal mechanism will be a two-tier process: providing viewers an opportunity to complain first at the broadcaster/channel level and in the event of no response or an unsatisfactory one by the broadcaster/channel, the complainant can approach the Broadcasting Content Complaints Council (BCCC) at the industry level, which will have 13 members. The council is headed by justice A.P. Shah, a former chief justice of the Delhi high court, and will consist of four non-broadcaster members, four members from national-level statutory commissions and four broadcaster members.

The two major broadcasting associations—IBF and NBA—have reiterated and demonstrated their commitment to self-regulation. Of course, there is still a long way to go—many broadcasters are not part of these two groups, and, more importantly, the guidelines need to be implemented. Most media professionals, specially regional and local broadcasters, are still unaware of the guidelines. Public discussion among peers on the norms, with illustrations of ongoing violations will help orient other broadcasters towards becoming more responsible and accountable members of the media.

P.N. Vasanti is director of New Delhi-based multidisciplinary research organisation Centre for Media Studies (CMS). She also heads the CMS Academy of Communication and Convergence Studies.

Active Citizenry a Better Bet

No legislative provision to regulate broadcast contents is good enough if not backed by larger public concerns and initiatives. To achieve that, the public needs to be reminded of TV's long term implications in the context of children, family, community, etc. Active citizens should be able to talk-back to channels in multiple ways. Such skills and opportunities need to be promoted and provided for. Parents have as much responsibility in moderating their children's television viewership and disciplining them by discussing it at home, even viewing TV programmes along with them and in promoting active viewership.

Educational system and teachers individually, at primary and secondary levels more specifically, have a role in promoting skills for discriminative viewing as a part of curriculum and for advocating certain desirables from time to time and as and when content trends call for. The Civil Society has a responsibility to come up with appropriate measures locally – by way of advocacy, discourse, sensitisation and by taking up grievances and suggest alternatives wherever necessary and even by taking up field studies on their own.

Once again, we should consider the Broadcast Bill by taking into account newer technologies that should provide for an independent regulator. This Bill should recognise the role of self regulation. Twice in the last ten years, the Bill could not get through the Parliament. The Convergence Bill is nowhere in sight. TRAI itself could be formally entrusted with the responsibility, including the licensing function. A citizen centric regulatory mechanism is what the Bill should envisage. There should be no more delay in this direction. A better way of going about this is for the government to come up first with a 'National Media Policy'. But, without waiting, the broadcasters should set up their own mechanisms as self regulatory initiatives, both reactively and proactively. Their endeavours should be to preempt the government interventions. This is what the IBF and NBA did in 2011.

The initiative of consultations by the I&B ministry was timely (2008-2010) and deserves to be appreciated. But, unless such a meet is followed up with much needed specific and concrete measures towards restraining TV channels' contents in particular, it will remain a futile exercise. No legislative provision is good enough, if not backed by larger public concerns and initiatives. To achieve that, the Public needs to be made sensitive about long term implications of television contents for children, for example. Once it is achieved, the channels would not remain as passive as they are today. Parents have as much responsibility in moderating television viewing habits of their children; so also the teachers and the educational system in promoting discriminative viewing. The Civil Society has a responsibility to come up with appropriate measures locally and be active and alert about certain contents of television channels.

There is no one legal authority today to actually regulate the contents of broadcast channels comprehensively. Despite that, none of the provisions of Cable TV Regulation Act are applicable to the broadcasters or producers; too much is expected of it. In any case, there is no mechanism to enforce any of the provisions however outdated they may be. Several initiatives in this regard are called for. First and foremost, the channels themselves should come up with their own codes and compliance mechanisms of self imposed standards. But, since not all channels available in the country are even registered in India, they cannot be expected to do anything like that. Also, because their sole concern is to "maximise viewers" somehow, not all can be expected to do so. As such, there must be some public policy and responsibility provisions applicable to all channels, including the down linked ones. And, there must be legal provisions to make broadcasters and even production houses responsible. Since "self regulation" approach in the present competitive and free-for-all situation has not worked, it cannot be depended entirely. Simultaneously, there should be legal provisions and procedures for enforcement and complaint redressal procedures as an obligation. All that is not possible without an independent and competent authority for content regulation and for their compliance. This authority should address all contents – programmes, advertisements and even news in such a way that it will not amount to or lead to day-to-day interference by any government department or curbing the creativity of producers. Music videos should be shown on TV only after they obtain a certificate as a mandatory condition. Monitoring has to be done by an independent body involving eminent citizens and by professionals with no business links with advertising, producers and channels. But their participation in the process is desirable and would facilitate the process. By waiting for a Convergence Bill and a Broadcast Bill earlier, we have, perhaps, allowed the situation to deteriorate. During that decade, channels mushroomed from all directions. Broadcast scenario today calls for a separate authority for content regulation. But the government should first assess how the initiative taken by the industry bodies are working and whether they have made any difference. And, how can they be made more effective? Presently, the initiative taken by the news channels is more than two years old; that should be a good enough period to appraise the efficacy of the self regulatory mechanism. Justice Verma, chair of that body, himself should be requested by the government to give his appraisal and suggestions as correctives.

Apart from the issue of responsible broadcasting of contents, another issue that requires attention is that there is hardly any coverage from the grassroots. It seems that the broadcasters have nothing to cover from the grassroots. Or, is it because of their inability to prioritise the basic issues and the processes behind it? Almost 60 per cent of news in news bulletins is repeats. Television channels are taking up more and more "reality shows" as if real situations do not interest them; they hype life styles as news. "Fake stings", "staging events" even by big media, including in the nations' capital, are echoing everywhere. There are more copycats as if imitating and adoption has become a model! The regional channels copy from the national channels and they, in turn, copy from the ones in USA or UK.

"Fake ratings", dubious analysis and claims ("we are No. 1" like promotions) quoting TRPs is, perhaps, *what we have been witnessing recently?* Further, the roles of "hidden persuaders" are no longer hidden. The influence and impact of "new gatekeepers" on media is yet to be viewed with concern. On the contrary, there are people, who think that the "market forces" will take care of the anomalies (as if a few channels are spoiling the many).

All this reminds that TV has the potential for immense positive influence. But, we are not able to avail the best of that potential, which needs to be harnessed. Professional and ethical standards, regulations and research should exploit that potential of television.

Peculiarities of Broadcasting

Some argue why broadcasting should be under some kind of regulation when print media is not subjected to similar measures. There is a need for a separate regulator for television because of its peculiarities, which are distinct from print media in terms of usage, contents, influence, etc. More specifically, because television's:

- reach is far more, includes vulnerable sections simultaneously;
- more than two-thirds of the viewers comprise women and children;
- impact of audio-visual is far more and in so many respects;
- airwaves belong to public and they are not unlimited;
- origin of broadcasts are not always under national laws;
- responsibility/accountability for contents is not always possible to establish and separate between carriage and content providers.

- compulsions of technology are different and are changing fast;
- it's not always possible to retrieve, reverse and correct contents as and when necessary;
- It's driven more by real time compulsions and remotely measured viewership.

The potential implied in these distinct features of television is often described as its *double edged* character. The drive of negative influence is far more active because of the kind of contents that it tends to prioritise and hype. In the process, many of the positive potentials of TV often get negated or remain latent. TV empowers and enables more when it is moderated for such ends. As such, the need and compulsions of restrains are far more in the case of broadcasting. In fact, there has been so much research on the effects of TV over the years. TV's significant influence has been established empirically on violence, numbness, alienation at individual level and on certain basic values to do with family, society, public agenda, etc. Should we ignore all such research? TV as a *carriage* and its *contents* call for larger concerns.

A basic dilemma related to the contents of broadcasting today is lack of subtle difference between "what is in the interest of the public" and "what interests the public" momentarily. Unfortunately, the latter has become the yardstick and basis for content priorities and strategies of channels. Indian needs and values are unique and hence the model of broadcasting has to be country specific particularly because there has been a wealth of originality and creative talents in the country. But all that is not apparent in the priorities.

Yet another fact is that media enterprises, particularly television, are not as transparent as they should be to their organisation, conflict of interests, share holding, balance sheet, etc. In fact, much less is known about the media enterprise than what corporates in other sectors are made to reveal fewer than one or other regulation. The Right to Information Act (2005) should help public media improve their credibility.

Broadcasting is complex because players are from different technologies, from different origins across the globe with different concerns (known and unknown) and objectives, and often without anyone being identified or accountable for the content, unlike in the case of newspapers. Because of proliferation of channels, there is intense competition between broadcasters for one-upmanship, often, at any cost. Competition, of course, becomes healthier when channels are bound by codes, guidelines and self restraint than when they are without any such restrain. In the absence of any codes and unquestioned viewership measurement system, television tends to lose its reflective and representational features and character.

Certain codes or guidelines are needed because of peculiarities of broadcasting in India and in the larger interest. Codes enhance credibility of contents and universality of their appeal. Professional standards imply a certain code from within and outside. Codes are needed for all types of contents – news, advertisements, serials, music, etc. Such ethical practice implies distinguishing desirable from what is not (for the many) and having concern for such subtle difference. In the case of news channels, self regulation is far more desirable. Realising this desirability and respecting the increasing public demand (and perhaps apprehending pressures on government to come up with regulations), the broadcasters, both news and general entertainment ones, themselves had come up in 2010 and 2011 with their own arrangement by adopting what was earlier being considered by the ministry, of course, with certain modifications[5].

Promoting Positive Potential

It is high time that we have some initiatives to promote the positive potential of TV. Of course, the best bet is for channels themselves to observe restraint on their own and explore that potential not just in the context of certain individual programmes or time chunks. Some specific provisions given here are only indicative: (1) codes/standards for various contents, programme timings, etc. Some of these provisions could be by way of licensing conditions and linked to license renewal; (2) alerting viewers in advance – with pre announcement by giving advance description of programmes just before telecast or/and channels could also have a fixed time for such advice to parents/teachers in the case of children; (3) channels themselves could follow certain restraint as an expression of concern in the interest of viewers. Devoting certain hours of broadcast for certain type of programmes in the interest of certain public is one such way. Many channels are already doing that. In fact, channels should come up with their own "restraints" or "responsibility code" (as to what they will not do, etc). Had there been such restraint, a news channel would not have telecast for over a fortnight "pornographic contents" in the garb of news, bulletin after bulletin, in the name of a "sting operation" or as "breaking news". In fact, channels could hold periodic public hearings on their contents when complaints from responsible public bodies could also be responded to; (4) Independent research on viewership, and also on its implications on various sections of people should be carried out.

Professional & Ethical Standards

In no civilised society, the mass media is without societal compulsions, restraints and responsibilities. Unfettered news media without societal concerns could be a threat to a free society and to its very independence. Freedom gets enriched and becomes more responsible with ethical concerns. The issue of ethics and responsibility is no longer limited to editors or journalists. The problem is one of a few spoiling the credibility of many. Ethical practices strengthen the core values and foundations of free media. They rarely restrain or constrain freedom as it is made out.

Press Council of India Chairman, Justice M Katju, a former judge of Supreme Court, and the then Union Law minister Salman Khurshid have been arguing that self regulation efforts have failed and such efforts are not good enough (Indian Express, August 2012) . They were particularly referring News Broadcasters Association's Standards "Authority" under the chairmanship of former Chief Justice of Supreme Court of India, Justice J S Varma. More recently (April 2012), Supreme Court bench consisting of Justice Affab Alam and Justice C K Prasad, which declared death sentence on Ajmal Kasab (September 6, 2012), questioned "electronic media's argument to have a regulatory mechanism for itself". In fact, they concluded that "electronic media has done much harm to the argument that any regulatory mechanism for the media must only come from within". Going further, the Supreme Court bench said that "any attempt to justify the conduct of the TV channels by citing the right to freedom of speech and expression would be totally wrong and unacceptable" in situations involving national security. But the bench also felt that "freedom of expression, like all other freedoms under Article 19, is subject to reasonable restrictions".

Myths About Regulation

Freedom of speech is a much talked about concept. But there is no absolute freedom anywhere. Regulations need not be preventive or restrictive of freedom. There is no country without some kind of regulation. Privatisation, globalisation, corporatisation, competition and big becoming bigger call for certain regulatory mechanisms, not necessarily by the government. In fact, the less the government is involved, the better it is.

Ethics and Regulations

Ethical concern is nothing but some kind of a self regulatory culture. What are ethics? The characteristics inherent in ethics include:

1) Concern for society
2) Concern for long term implications
3) Interest in the larger good
4) Based on eternal human values

Ethical practices distinguish rights from wrong and motives from ends. The codes of ethics are described as "conscience of journalism". Regulatory mechanisms do not reduce relevance of ethics and need not imply erosion of freedom or independence of media.

Regulation is not necessarily restrictive in scope or intentions. In fact, regulation is indicative of responsibility, accountability and credibility; and even enhances the universality of appeal. Also, it does not always mean "government regulation". Regulations could be more than a couple of types:

a) The first and foremost regulation in vogue more often is within a media as self adhered codes, practices and precedents.
b) Second, the one decided by professional bodies/associations, etc together.
c) Third, is by the civil society - by way of pressure groups, advocacy initiatives – no regulation works without the backing of larger public concerns.
d) Fourth, by independent bodies, academic or research bodies. For example, TRP has become a regulatory proportion – dictating what is good or what is desirable, etc.

Self Regulation is Better and Indicative of Better Professional Standards

Self regulatory initiatives work better with some regulatory mechanism from outside; but it will be even better when these are supported by some legislative provisions. Some regulation is inevitable, but with win-win provisions; particularly in the case of television, because of its peculiar characteristics. It should also include promotion of certain concerns, priorities and standards. Independent research should be an essential element for the working of a regulatory mechanism. Certain regular reviews in public media like that of Amita Malik's column in The Indian Express in the early 1970s, Sevanti Ninan's in the Hindu, P N Vasanti's in Mint are some such examples.

There are several laws encompassing media and their contents including advertising, directly or indirectly. Yet one could say that despite the penetration of TV all over India, there is no comprehensive law today. In the earlier years, the concern was the impact of media on society. And, that is how certain instruments, like Children's Film Society, were promoted with a hope to make qualitative difference in the society.

- Cinematographic Act 1952 – certifies films for public exhibition Based on the contents, it has the power to censor and certify as A for adult and U for universal screening, etc. Notwithstanding criticism, it restrained and ensured the emergence of creative talent.
- Children Film Society –Promotional body initiated in 1955 to cultivate good taste and good films by taking into account the special needs of children. Today, there is no such concern, particularly with regard to television.
- Cable TV Networks Regulation Act 1995 – registers of Cable TV operators; responsibility for service standards and codes amended.
- Telecom Regulatory Authority of India (TRAI) assigned, on an ad hoc basis, the responsibility for carriage functions.
- News Broadcast Standards Authority (with Justice J S Verma) - But only 20 – 25 per cent of channels are its members. This body is controlled by big, corporate media; the complaints have to be accompanied with Rs. 1000 as fees. There are hardly any complaints in the first two years. However, on a couple of occasions, this unofficial "Authority" issued guidelines to members on covering poll campaigns and violence and even about periodicity of TRP reports.
- Indian Broadcasters Foundation (IBF) - Not all broadcasters are members of IBF. It is managed by the same big broadcasters mainly to safeguard their commercial interests. The IBF constituted (2011) a Broadcast Content Complaint Council (BCCC) with a former Chief Justice of a High Court as its chair. Channels have been informing viewers about the arrangement and seeking complaints.

- Taking cue from these two national bodies of the industry and after some differences with them, the regional language channels have now (2011) formed their own bodies. But they have not yet come up with any initiative.
- Registrar of Newspapers of India – As a government department registers title and ownership, etc. Newspapers are required to file annual returns with all such details. It also brings out an analysis. But compliance rate is on decline.
- Press Council of India – after wider consultation/involvement, it has the power to indict newspapers (but not to prosecute) for their contents, but mostly based on complaints. There is no precedent of suo-motu action except public statements. It has no power to prosecute errant ones. Nevertheless, it tries to promote standards, administer ethics and inculcate self regulation.
- Readers' Editor – The Hindu is the first and so far the only news daily to have a Readers' Editor to consider, respond to queries and be an intermediary.
- Advertising code prescribes guidelines for what should not be towards maintaining responsibility, fairness and standards.
- Advertising Standards Council of India (ASCI) is an industry body that promotes self regulatory initiatives, acts on complaints and also as a suo motu. More recently, it is active and visible with initiatives. In fact, it has become an example for self-regulatory initiatives.
- Ombudsman – Times of India (TOI) (1996-98) was the first daily newspaper, which hadgone for an ombudsman in India, but made no difference during the one year of its presence, despite Justice P N Bhagwati, former Chief Justice of India, was the Ombudsman. The Hindu model, on the other hand, provides for more transparency. Despite being a new comer, HMTV, Telugu news channel, was the first TV channel to go for an ombudsman on its own with a senior Journalist, Varadhachari, heading it with monthly open reviews. HMTV even made operations of ombudsman transparent.
- Several other Acts – with implications for what appears in media, but made no difference therein. There are many such laws and for too long, as no implementation mechanism exists. Some of

these are: (1) Food Drug Adulteration, (2) Juvenile justice, (3) Cruelty to animals, etc.

Correctives

No wonder why the I&B ministry between 2008 and 2010 took the initiative of consulting the stakeholders, including the civil society groups, about the measures to regulate the contents of television channels and even cancelled the uplinking license of one TV channel and issued notice to another for the "indecent contents" they telecast. Both the Houses of Parliament also discussed the issue specifically in the wake of news channels too going all out in chasing TRPs even if it amounted to reducing themselves to broadcasting obscene or porno as part of prime time news bulletins and as "breaking news". The TRP mania has caught on the news channels and newspapers because of frequent "market surveys", mainly because it is a no-holds-barred competition, which is dictating the choice of contents, not so much the concerns of the people or the basic issues before the nation. This explains the chase "for what interests" people, not "what is in the interest" of people. In this order, presently, the marketing people in the media are setting the priorities. News media are not so much journalist driven as in the earlier years and as the Fourth Estate concept implies. Further, virtues, values and criteria cherished all along by newspapers are under a push-pull to fall in line with the "new order". It is against this background that *lakshmanrekha* becomes relevant, even in the case of media. That is how the news daily, The Hindu,[6] had put it in its editorial way back in 2003, *"The buoyant growth of Indian newspapers in recent times is a new combination of pressures on the core values of journalism, pressures generated by intensifying competition, by business success, and sometimes by political ambition. In the name of the omnipotent market, a new kind of demand is made for manipulating news, analysis, and opinion to suit the owners' financial and political interests – and for tailoring editorial product to subserve the marketing goal"*. As expected in the current transparency era in the country, media should be in the forefront of this movement. But who in media would do that? Users? Journalists? Civil society? Carriage people or content people? Ideally, all of them should be concerned about and also do something. But, the owners, managers and marketing people may not be interested in this and may even oppose it!

Should this situation be allowed to drift further or should we look for some correctives, which are more reliable. CMS has been advocating a three tire system where neither the independence of media nor the rights of the civil society are sacrificed. A *lakshmanrekha, however,* should not mean curbing or curtailing freedom of press. But if an independent body could help promote responsibility and standards in contents and bring out the potential of media, it deserves to be encouraged and strengthened. That should be a win-win opportunity for everyone. Such an inclusive coverage goes a long way.

What emerged from that two year long exercise was a three tire based mechanism to regulate media in its various dimensions, but particularly the electronic media.

Policy Initiatives

No one initiative is good enough for ensuring a responsible and responsive news media. A series of parallel efforts are needed at different levels. Some of these are:

1. First, a national policy should be formulated with desirables for the country, how they are addressed and the course on core national issues, options to go about and methodology of realising the objectives including the instruments. 1995 Supreme Court landmark judgment should be an input in framing the policy. The present ad hoc decision making needs to be ended.

2. An independent regulator, both for carriage and content – as a part of the State (not the government) should be in place at the earliest. The rules, regulations and mechanisms should be widely known.

   a. Promote and strengthen self regulatory practices and make the process transparent and decentralised. The industry together and individually should rely far more on self regulation. There could be independent initiatives too.

   b. Public service obligation should be a licensing condition. Such an obligation should not, however, be restrictive of initiatives and representation.

   c. Also, grievance redressal mechanisms should be built into the regulatory system. This could be done by the industry, individually or together or both on their own as well.

3. Media should be brought under the Right to Information Act to make this sector more transparent, particularly on matters to do with conflict of interest.
4. Civil society groups, professional associations and academics should play a proactive role to take on media literacy and media activism in such a way that eventually sensitive consumers themselves take the initiatives.
5. Objective and independent research, much beyond TRPs, should be promoted as an ongoing concern. The need is for studies on impact on society, not just on market. This should also be a concern of the independent regulator.
6. Educational system promotes more "bolts and nuts" for more of the same and copying, rather than exploring newer concepts, approaches, alternatives for the models in vogue. There is an urgency for revamping "educational business" and reposition its very scope and structure.

It is more like a few spoiling for the many. Wondering whether there are any professional codes of conduct in journalism, Prime Minister Dr. Manmohan Singh raised the issue of ethics and responsibilities of news media in a provocative way a few years ago at The Tribune's 125 years function. In no civilised society, not withstanding its political system, mass media is without some societal compulsions and moral obligations nor is it without any restrains and responsibilities as in the case of freedom. Ethical foundation is what gives stature and strength to a societal role, particularly where credibility is a principle criterion as in the case of mass media. Ethical practices and norms distinguish rights from wrong and motives from ends.

As ethical standards are constantly under question not just in India, but all over the world, it is important for the media profession that they are discussed and reiterated from time to time. That is how ethics in general and in the context of mass media in particular are constantly debated world over. With the emergence of electronic media – television earlier and satellite broadcasting more recently – media ethics are being viewed in a newer context and have become more complex, as operational compulsions of the new media are different. That is why issues related to media ethics require serious deliberation at various levels within and outside the profession. Even in a competitive scenario such values are derived either from market forces or from self imposed standards and codes that are evolved over the years by the players themselves, as in the case of the newspapers. Even a regulatory mechanism by the State does not reduce the relevance of media ethics.

With tremendous growth and expansion, mass media is being viewed as more powerful than ever before, but at the same time, the level of public confidence in media has been on decline, as studies have indicated over the years, including in the USA. News media in particular are being accused of arrogance, insensitivity, bias, inaccuracies, sensationalism, stereotypes, and trivialisation as well as conflict of interest and the disappearing line between paid advertising and news on the one hand, and between news and views, on the other. This, in turn, has led to certain decline in the role and stature of journalists in news establishments, but increased the role of corporates in setting media priorities. Competitive compulsions and continued dependence on advertising has sustained such a trend and added to this concern for ethical standards. In such a scenario, market forces are being relied more and more, as if what attracts people in the media is also in their interest. This is an underlying dilemma today.

One associated aspect in this context is the growing corporationalisation of media, causing certain shifts in the paradigm of media operations. This, in turn, has increased societal concern for declining ethical standards in media. In that context, it is better that media constantly encourages the public to voice grievances against the contents of news media in particular. Such a practice implies ethical concern. To give an example of the concern within, consider what many dailies in USA print prominently every day, "If you believe that we have made an error, or you have questions about The Time's journalistic standards and practices, you may contact James Gold, Reader's representative, by email at …., by phone at … by fax to … or by mail to …" [7]Recent examples of practicing ethics by mass media as in the case of The New York Times or CBS are also worth mentioning. While the New York Times publicly apologised for publishing fiction as fact, CBS dismissed six staffers in the Dan Rather controversy after an open enquiry about misleading reporting. They are setting standards. The endeavour for ethical standards is related to more responsibility. There cannot be specific rules for every situation. Nevertheless, each opportunity should help make sound decision and empower people in that process to set their own standards, styles and priorities in such a way that it becomes a good precedent to help consolidate freedom with responsibility and further the very credibility of media. Overall and by and large, the Indian media in today's global media scenario may not be the best, but certainly not a bad one as per its concern for ethics. In fact, some individual newspapers, like The Hindu, The Tribune, The Mint, are as good or even better as anywhere else. These are only a few examples. The same cannot be said in the case of television channels. All this, however, should not overlook or undermine the positive contribution of news media.

Towards sustaining media ethics, there could be certain broad principles. First and foremost concern that should become bedrock for media ethics is a realisation that media has effects on the concerned and larger public and also has long-range implications of what appears in media today. A second corrective is the separation of advertising function (and interests) from that of editorial. In this regard, the US television channels, although their model is not something that fits the Indian socio-economic scenario, have recently taken a good initiative. For, unlike in the earlier years, they distinguish a "paid programme" from the rest prominently and specify when a commercial looks like news or a feature as a "paid ad" or a "leased access" content and, in fact, even simultaneously disclaim questionable contents. In India, we are increasingly facing this dilemma - both in the case of news channels and newspapers. A third area which often prompts an ethical dilemma and increasingly so, is the mix up of interests of media corporates with those of the editorial. Taking responsibility for the contents, which includes owning lapses of any kind and correcting promptly is another ethical practice, which helps set good atmosphere for media credibility. There are very few examples one could recall of media acknowledging something adverse they were responsible for and which they could have avoided or corrected. This is despite that accountability to readers or viewers is something that most media have accepted in principle.

Media Ethics do not Fetter Freedom

In no country, not withstanding its political system and state of economy, mass media is without some societal compulsions and moral obligations; nor is it without any restrains and responsibilities as in the case of freedom. As ethical standards are constantly under question not just in India, but all over the world, it is important for the media profession that they are discussed and reiterated from time to time. This is how ethics in general and in the context of mass media in particular are constantly debated world over. With the emergence of satellite broadcasting and newer media, media ethics are being viewed in a newer context and have become more complex, as the operational compulsions of the new media are different. That is why issues related to media ethics require serious deliberation at various levels within and outside the profession. In the present context, as Mahatma Gandhi said, [8] "*True ethics to be worth its name must also be good economics.*" Their balance is what debates help fine tune.

Every profession implies certain core values, which shape its functioning and performance. However, in a democratic country such values are derived either from market forces or from self imposed standards and codes evolved over the years by the players themselves, as in the case of the press. Even a regulatory mechanism by the State does not reduce the relevance of media ethics.

Media Ownership is a Backdrop for Revised Debate

Media need to constantly encourage the public to voice grievances against the media contents and that of news media in particular. Such a practice implies ethical concerns. In the last couple of years, there has been tremendous growth and expansion of mass media. With it, they are being viewed as more powerful than ever before, but at the same time, the level of public confidence in media has been on decline, as studies have brought out. Even in the USA, 41 per cent think that media has too much freedom. One associated aspect in this context is the growing corporationalisation of media, which is causing certain shifts in the paradigm of media operations. This, in turn, has increased concern for declining ethical standards. Bill Moyers, a champion of objective journalism in USA, alerted his country that "media concentration threatens freedom" and that media ownership is increasing. If there could be Ethical Committee for elected representatives, whether in USA or in India, then, why media and journalists shouldn't have ethics panels.

Participation of readers or viewers actively in whatever manner is yet another more lasting way of coping with this eternal issue of media ethics. Another change that I noticed in USA recently is a deliberate effort to elicit readers' feedback for every section of a newspaper and give them more space. In fact, some of them now position readers' views prominently however critical it may be of what the newspaper itself has published or is known for. A recent example is what The New York Times did in the wake of media reporting of New Orleans calamity.

It devoted half a page to admit a critic's view as to how the newspaper failed reporting about the possibility of such a flooding. Such a self introspection is rare with Indian media. Without such initiatives at various levels on such instances, it amounts to missing an opportunity to further confidence in media.

Media ethics get reflected from their role individually and together. In a given socio-economic and cultural conflict situations and processes, certain concern that coverage of such conflicts should not add to the problem even unwittingly, should be evident. Big media have added responsibility to set examples for others in such situations with regard to the levels of professional standards and the best of values that need to be emulated. Since big media dominate the industry bodies, they are in a better position to take initiatives by going beyond their own bottom line interests.

The issue of media ethics is becoming increasingly complex. It is no longer confined to editors or journalists. In fact, media corporates are becoming the centre. As the problem is one of a few spoiling many, professional associations and bodies have a particular responsibility to minimise the scope for such a tendency. Initiatives and interventions are needed from three different levels, simultaneously. Apart from those from within the media, the civil society and the educational system should be concerned about and also do something about restoring ethical concerns.

More specifically, in India, we need more forums for discussion on the role and impact of media in the society, media watch groups, nationally and regionally, for the news media and the media at large should operate. They should monitor conditions under which media operate.

The best bet for any issue to do with media is active and more discriminative readers and viewers. This also amounts to breaking the trap of ratings in which the media is often entrapped. This trap of TV content rating makes the country believe that what interests the people momentarily is also in their interest. This vicious circle could be addressed by an informed and engaged citizenry. Media literacy in a more serious and sustained manner at different levels helps such a process.

The educational stream in the country, including at the University level, does not offer any scope to be sensitive about media use and media effects. The journalism schools owe to the country to do something in this respect. They need to assess ethical practices and come up with posers on contentious issues based on case studies and experimentations. These faculties need to have more active linkage with practicing professions than at present.

The University of Southern California's Annenberg School of Communication, a premier institution in USA, has introduced Walter Cronkite awards for excellence in political reporting by television channels. An objective of these awards is to promote objective and ethical concerns in covering politics. I was fortunate to be invited for the 2005 Awards function and also for a luncheon meeting with Walter Cronkite. Cronkite made certain interesting observations about the concerns and priorities of channels affecting their very credibility and moral standing. On that occasion, Walter Cronkite, the most trusted broadcast newsperson that USA ever had, observed that news media should guard against entertainment in the news, otherwise "it would amount to cheating the public". He cautioned that corporate broadcasters are paying more attention to Wall Street than to the health of democracy. The more such introspections, the better it is for ensuring ethical concerns.

Even more important and urgent is that various functionaries and their professional bodies have to be more visible with their concern for ethical standards and practices. Only then, the "a few spoiling it for the many" tendency could be addressed. They need to take interest in so many different ways. They could take on projects on ethics in specific contexts; and undertake introspection of media's functioning more than what other professions do. The Press Council of India, Press Institute, Editors Guild, Media Professional Group and Centre for Media Studies (CMS) occasionally do so. A few individual editors and journalists periodically do raise the issue, but never get followed up. In fact, even when the Prime Minister or the President of the country refers prominently to such issues related to media performance, it hardly provokes any response. Perhaps they tend to "overdo" that. For example, how apt it is for the PM to say that "media should not indulge in "sensational reporting at a time, when he and his government is under severe criticism for a series of corruption accusations. "The desire to be sensational should be avoided", the Prime Minister called upon media at a meet of Kerala Union of Working Journalists. Self scrutiny is the next best bet for ensuring and sustaining good practices and ensuring ethical concerns in the media. Eventually, it is the degree of professionalism and responsibility being exercised by those in the media, which tell upon the level of freedom and independence of media.

In conclusion of this chapter, it could be said that ethical practices are never a hindrance for growth and credibility. More often, ethical concerns strengthen core values and foundations, although sometimes, it may appear limiting the options in an immediate context. Ethical considerations rarely restrain or constrain freedom at any level. On the contrary, freedom gets enriched and becomes more responsible. The media sustains its credibility and societal status from being concerned of ethical implications.

This chapter discusses pros and cons of ethical and regulatory aspects concerning broadcasting. Peculiarities of broadcasting particularly of news channels to justify regulatory provisions are explained for tapping positive potential. Importance of self regulation together with active citizenry is a better bet. Certain myths about regulatory arrangements are debated.

Endnotes

1 The Hindustan Times, 30 August 2012

2 The Hindu, 28 August 2012

3 The Indian Express, 6 July 2012

4 P N Vasanti in Mint, 27 May 2011.(http://www.livemint.com/Opinion/eOPrNCzZurdrWm4VdyGE0M/Selfregulation-revisited.html).

5 P N Vasanti in Mint, 27 May 2011.(http://www.livemint.com/Opinion/eOPrNCzZurdrWm4VdyGE0M/Selfregulation-revisited.html).

6 The Hindu, 13 September 2013

7 See Controversy involving a Pulitzer Prize winning journalist of New York Times (2002)

8 Quote of Mahatma Gandhi from Press Council of India annual souvenirs, quoted at several places over the years.

10

Corporatisation: Challenges and Opportunities

Despite so much talk about a relationship between *"media and corporates"*, very little about it is in public purview, barring some recent bits on "private treaties" (now brand capital). Based on extensive research, we have been writing for the past 15 years, about a shift in the paradigm of media operations. An analysis of that emerging scenario was published first in the[1] *Frontline* (2001) and then in *EPW* (2002). We have expanded that understanding further in our 2005 publication titled, "Media Scene as India Globalises". Even more recently, [2]"A Handbook on Poll Surveys in Media" (2010) described how political and corporate interests get hyped and camouflaged without transparency in electoral processes. This chapter discusses these processes further.

There are two emerging issues: one, the relationship between media and corporates, and two, media becoming corporatised. The latter has to do more with obvious paradigm shift in the media operations in recent years. The former is more about media's dependence on corporates for their support by way of advertising. Both are interrelated. This is a cause and effect relationship. However, which one is cause and which one is effect is difficult to pinpoint. One thing is sure that the role of corporate sector is getting consolidated in the context of media.

The driving principle of a corporate is profit maximisation. Return on investment to share holders is a differentiator. Media, on the other hand, is supposed to operate without conflict of interest. Traditionally, in democracies, the media function is viewed as a service. That is how they are considered the "Fourth Estate", "people's voice", and a watch dog on powers and "establishment". But whose voice is the media today? Is it more corporate voice than that of citizens? For corporates, the consumer matters more; therefore, understandably, they are more concerned with the markets. At this, point, the question arises - with the corporatisation of media, have they become "marketing media" rather than "mass media"? The "corporate culture" is all over and entrenched into media. In 1995, I titled my article as 'Marketing Media – Perspective into Media' for capturing the emerging scenario. A finer point in that process is how much "means" matter for the "ends".

FDI Issue

Foreign Direct Investments or FDIs have lured media institutions to turn themselves into market-driven corporates. How well a media is corporatised is a criterion for foreign investors, which means marketing and advertising of media as a "brand". To attract FDI, news media have turned themselves into corporate entities and "products" to serve the "markets". According to the Registrar of Newspapers' annual reports,[3] the per cent of newspapers, which are "corporates", has gone up to about 30 from less than 15 per cent in 2000. As broadcasting is capital intensive, most television and radio operations are owned by corporate groups. FDI into media, particularly into news media, has to be viewed together with whether there are any regulations and obligations for foreign participation and of what kind, not just in terms of equity pattern, but also contents. No country is without some restrictions on foreign investments and content related obligations. With FDI in media and media related services being allowed as part of economic reforms, the "global media moguls" have been taking interest in the Indian "media market". For pursuing that interest, they needed "cheer leaders" as advance party to facilitate their entry. That was how initially, 100 per cent FDI was allowed into businesses, which "support and sustain" news media. These businesses include advertising, market research, public relations and, more recently, media planning. In 1995, we described them as "new gatekeepers" of media. These businesses today dominate Indian media and the policies about media. That is how FDI into news is being consistently increased. All this implies further corporatisation of Indian media.

Has Corporatisation Helped Media?

Corporatisation of mass media has helped both its horizontal and lateral expansion – the very impressive growth story that is lauded worldwide. To achieve this impressive growth rates, corporate agencies have relied rather heavily on advertising in media and also on market research. The regional language media have benefited even more. Corporatisation has attracted new crop of youngsters into profession, created many new job functions and better opportunities. Corporatisation has also made media marketing and media management as distinct specialisations. India is going to see even more "corporatisation" of media in the coming years. There were no efforts or arrangements at any level to adopt corporate principles and prepare better, so that media's privileged position (as Fourth Estate) is not threatened, but continues to play positive role in deepening democracy and better serving the Indian Constitution.

What Does Corporatisation of Media Mean?

What do we mean when we say that the media are corporatised? Some of the features of media corporatisation include: enhanced capital investments; expanded reach; bigger content package; a more attractive and a more market orientated "product"; more advertising support; adoption of new high-end technologies; and aggressive marketing tools. Corporatisation has brought in competition and competitiveness. All that process has helped explore untapped markets and reach some unreached sections. For investors, Media has become more attractive than ever before. In the process, media has become an "attractive" business opportunity from that of a "service"- a business to make profit and also derive "other advantages", including political and society 'clout'. For example, businesses like real estate, which make faster money, have ventured into a newspaper or a TV channel to arrive at the local political scene.

In this process, the role of editor and journalist is no longer what it was. They have become "employees", not so much stakeholders. With Wage Boards becoming ineffective, in spite of an Act of the Parliament, journalists no longer enjoy the independence of earlier years. Some are there as an exception. Marketing and advertising functions have become more important. Share value in the stock market has become a priority concern than the "fourth estate" or watch dog functions. The big media have become bigger and are becoming even bigger and aspiring to become monopolistic "industry". Thirty years ago, about 30 media enterprises dominated (75 per cent) most of the media in the country, today, hardly 15 media houses have that share. All this is happening without strictly coming under active legal and regulatory provisions that apply to corporates, as if media are "super corporates". A more recent example is that Securities and Exchange Board of India (SEBI), despite acknowledging its concern about "private treaties", could not directly notify its directives to the media prominently engaged in such practices. Instead, it suggested the same to the Press Council of India (PCI) knowing well that PCI has no teeth to take any action.

Corporatisation implies maximisation of profits and optimising outcomes. The "Freedom of press should not be turned into commerce," said Ravi Shankar Prasad, BJP leader, who represented the party at the

4

Election Commission meet in October 2010. At the same meet, Jayanti Natarajan, Congress Party's representative also talked about democracy and freedom of press. Former Chief Justice of India, Dr. A. S. Anand said, "While commercialism has a legitimate place in the business office of the newspaper, it becomes a danger when it invades the editorial room." Further, stating, "Today, there are some genuine concerns about the way in which some sections of the media function," Anand said, "the liberty of the press cannot be confused with its licentiousness." Successive Presidents and Prime Ministers have been saying so at one point or other during their tenures, but of course, making no difference to the ongoing process of corporatisation of media and their increasing hold on the media.

Equity Business is now Brand Capital!

[5]Private treaties perhaps epitomise this nexus between the media and the corporate world. It is also the precursor and another reminder of a "corporate media" regime. SEBI chairman has expressed his concern about private treaties that the media entail with corporates as they "harm fair, unbiased news". SEBI felt that it will lead to "commercialisation of news reports". Private treaties are the ones that some media houses enter with companies listed or proposing to come out with public offers and, in return, promote the companies with positive reports and/or advertisements.

To gear up treaties for a larger role, The Times of India has renamed this "equity business" as "Brand Capital" (October 2010). It hopes to generate "advertising capital" for corporate businesses and growth in advertising revenue for news media. What are its implications to the scope and structure of news media as equity business and the like take roots and expand? What checks need to be ensured?

Can There be a "Right Balance"?

The challenges and opportunities involved in this process are nothing, but the pros and cons of corporatisation. In either way, considering the global trends, there is not much choice - corporatisation is a compulsion today. That is why the effort now should be how to retain the virtues, rather than how to minimise the effects of corporate compulsions. Five features that illustrate the "fourth estate" and "watch dog" standing of media are: 1) conflict of interest on content, 2)transparency in the operations and priorities, 3) reflecting plurality of voices of people, 4) reflection of certain self imposed discipline and concerns of people, and 5) a balance of information, communication and entertainment based contents.

The Profits Issue

As a Fourth Estate activity, the mass media has certain trusteeship standing where the pursuit of profit or margin (between expenditure and revenue) has self imposed limits. A certain profit or margin is essential. But that should not be a limiting or restraining factor for the very scope of media, i.e., for the very survival or sustaining to the extent of upholding the independence of media.

The strength and differentiation of media as a unique institution comes from that balancing. Increasing dependence on anyone source for survival obviously threatens that very stature. Increasing share of advertising in the revenue or continued reliance and declining revenue from users of the particular mass media or subscribers does not auger well. Transparency and self imposed discipline, in that process, matter. A couple of decades ago, revenue from advertising of leading newspapers were less than half of the total revenue and the rest was received from the readers. Whereas, today, television channels and many newspapers, too, depend on advertising to the extent of getting three-fourth of the total revenue; which, in turn, determine the very scope of the channel's contents and its very credibility. For example, in 2010, 73 per cent of Zee News revenue was from advertising against 60 per cent in the case of other Zee group channels.

FDI and DD

The content model of channels including news channels also depend on the extent of FDI in the channels. Interesting viewers and luring viewers is what every channel tries to do. But that will be an all out in the case of foreign and FDI channels. One may not find contents driven by "national concern" (concern for issues of the country in the larger context) that, in turn, is TRP driven content – unconcerned of whether the content is in the interest of certain sections of local people (and not merely interesting to watch). That is why there was so much debate in the earlier years of proliferation of satellite channels, whether FDI should be allowed into and in what extent. Some channels, which opposed FDI into Indian media initially, have turned around after a couple of years and become advocates of higher FDI. Most of premier media houses owning TV channels had changed their stand on FDI, once they realised that they could have windfall gain by divesting the holding to a foreign party. Government looked at FDI into media as into any other sector, except that for news channels, the FDI ceiling was kept lower than what goes into non-news media. It is pertinent to know the arguments about FDI into news media. A shift from the existing (greed oriented) content model to needs based model may not be easy.

The present (greed oriented) model is to the advantage of foreign players not merely in terms of investment, but also as an opportunity to influence markets, public policies and also public opinion, both political and social. In any case, some convincing is there of those foreign investors, particularly if the change proposed is.

I recall the debate in 1976 when the idea of accepting "commercials" by Doordarshan came up. At that time, myself and the then Deputy Minister of I&B (Dharam Vir Singh) opposed, although we know that the Minister (Vidyacharan Shukla) was in its favor. The alternative that I have suggested in writing to the Minister was for "sponsorship advertising" by corporates, not advertisements of consumer brands. I argued taking a cue from the US experience that Indian TV should not go for the model in vogue there.

The minister very practically put the ball back in my court and N. L. Chawla (then, the Director, AIR and DD) and asked us to go to Bombay (then) and consult some advertisers and ad agency leaders, where I failed to put forward my arguments. The Minister took the decision to open the flood gates of DD for advertising (with the same code that was applicable (then) to Vividh Bharati (Commercial Broadcasting Service or CBS of AIR) – as if that was good enough. He did not even agree to put in the office "order" open up for commercials an upper ceiling on the time for commercials, which was included much later.

In fact, [6]when the issue of FDI was first taken up by a Standing Committee (1998) of the Parliament (with Somnath Chatterjee as the Chair), it was against even a minority stake of foreigners (below 26 per cent). The feeling of the Committee was that there was no guarantee for the absence of investors' role in the affairs of the news media. Interestingly, the Standing Committee at that time was more concerned of FDI into news papers than into channels, as they did not expect that 24X7 news channels would proliferate so much and become the primary source of news in the country so soon. Majority of the members of the Standing Committee were concerned about the "threat of destabilising India's democratic systems" and "destabilising the cultural ethos of the country" by being "hostage to manipulation by outside powers". When the 1955 Cabinet decision was taken, there was no television in the country, so the fact that the satellite channels will proliferate as much as nowhere else in the world was not even thought of.

The scenario related to FDI into channels could be explained by taking the case of DTH. India has six DTH players and two more are likely to be added by 2012. In 2011, 49 per cent was allowed as FDI into DTH. But, the Ministry and the Regulator (TRAI) proposed (in August 2011) 74 per cent (and another Minister, later, may be after a couple of years, will argue for 100 per cent). Expecting that decision, Reliance DTH (Big TV) with no FDI earlier, was planning to sell 49 per cent of its stakes. Comsat, the largest cable operator in USA is expected to acquire controlling interests. Tata Sky has the Star Group and Singapore based PE Temsek as partners and it, too, is expected to download more to its foreign partners. Another one, Sun Direct, has partnered with Malaysia's Astro Group. Dish TV and Airtel Digital TV, too, have foreign partners and will increase that holding to 74 per cent once the decision is announced.

In mid-2011, Doordarshan (DD Direct), on the other hand, was in the process of bidding out of its DTH operations to private players (like Dish TV, Tata Sky, etc). This was presumably decided "to cut costs and maximise revenues". "Why should the government offices manage DTH services at a higher cost when private agencies can do it more efficiently," was what the Ministry officials were quoted as saying by the news media[7]. How did such a situation arise?

By increasing the FDI limits into DTH from 49 to 74 per cent, the government is making it difficult for DD (Direct TV) to compete with other DTH players, who are all diversifying or increasing the share of

FDI into their operations and adding more (attractive) channels to offer and give keen competition to others. Obviously, public service broadcaster cannot be expected to compete and cope with such tacit support of government to private operators. DD is being compelled to "surrender" itself or yield its infrastructure for the advantage of private operators under the pressure of media moguls.

Envisaging such a situation in 2005, I went out of the way and opposed the very idea of DD going for DTH and proposed, instead, argued for strengthening its already existing decentralised operations across the country with local programme production capabilities. Going beyond meeting the Minister with such a proposal, I issued a press statement to that effect. I sensitised the Minister about what going for DTH was meant to other DD channels. What explains DD closing down its news channel, thereafter, (they reopened the news channel after a gap is a different story). To my surprise, the Minister found that the Prasar Bharati officials had already went ahead and committed Rs. 300 crore for DD DTH without even having a formal discussion on the issue.

[8]The Parliamentary Committee of HRD Ministry on Foreign Educational Institutions Regulation of Entry and Operation Bill 2010 had recommended (2011 July) safeguards against the "possibility of the foreign education providers poaching Indian institutions of qualified and experienced faculty." The Committee report with such a suggestion was tabled in the Rajya Sabha (August 2011). If such an apprehension could be realised and even included by the Parliamentary Committee of HRD Ministry, then why the hesitation or shying away from a real and more serious problem of satellite channels, whether unregistered or registered with no obligations to declare or to include or from where the certain broadcast is beamed into without any advance indication of the nature of contents and for whom such service is meant, like some "pre-designated people"? Let us take another example. Without a discussion, the government allowed 100 per cent FDI in the pharmaceutical sector in 2001. Realising that as a result of takeover of Indian pharma companies by multinationals, the government's national Health Policy, particularly, that of making basic drugs at affordable prices, will no longer be possible, the Health Ministry went for "safeguards to be built into FDI process" and even it meant review of allowing 100 per cent FDI.[9] Low cost generic drugs are unlikely to be produced in India as that will pose competition with parent companies. How come there was no such a realisation ever in the Ministry of I&B? Even for a debate?

Market View of India

Media is viewed as more than a double dhamaka opportunity for investors. As in no other business, they could expect a return, sooner or later, and in one form or other and if it is a foreign investor, the return is even more assured! Besides the return on investment, media could be used to peddle politics, promote market interests and also gain social standing. This "conflict of interest" aspect is becoming so complex that it is not easy to untangle and bring it to fore under a specific legal or accountable framework. Even more so with news channels. More and more investors and entrepreneurs associated with media units are engaged in businesses, like real estate, chit fund business or other such quick liquid money operations, "export- import" and, of course, political- business people. Foreign or Indian broadcasters, all view opportunities and challenges similarly and that is why they compete, cooperate and converge after a brief attempt to resist (such as any road block attempts). There are channels which appear to have come into being only to explore the opportunity of being "taken over" by a big corporate, preferably a foreign one. The Ministry "facilitates" such a "hoarding" or "parking" of licenses.

India is viewed as a "market", a potential market, for broadcast business. Broadcast business is viewed as something like a bore well, where the more water you draw, the more it gives (as if it never gets dry).

In the case of foreign investors, even basic identity of original investor will not be known easily. A few years ago, a Union Minister asked me an innocent question – Who owns the "TRP Company"? Although it is known that it is a 100 per cent foreign owned enterprise. Who owns TAM? Who controls it? Who promoted it? Who takes decisions about the TRPs? Who took the decision when the two rating agencies merged? I took a fortnight to figure out the corporates behind it, although not for sure. The investors associated with media rating companies are the same, who have the major share holding or control in advertising business and also in market research and even public relations corporates – with the primary interest of promoting mass markets for consumer products or services. A. C. Neilson and Kantar are global corporations entrenched in influencing markets, public policy making and engaged in homogenising life styles of people. That is what "maximisation" of profits meant and that is how multinational corporates operate across nations to support other multinationals. To them, societal and cultural aspects matter only to the extent that they help in entrenching, expanding and penetrating deeper into societies, systems and lives – to the extent of replacing older influencing institutions, like "family", religion, education, etc.

In this process, there are interventions and initiatives, which are frontline; there are others from above and behind, from sea and even sky. These services or businesses support and sustain each other. They all coverage somewhere after twists and turns and are traded in New York or London stock exchanges. Tracking all that is worth a research project by itself. The nature of merger and acquisition process is not always transparent and amenable for immediate tracking and understanding.

Their prime objectives are to maximise reach and returns, influence public policies, dominate markets and economies and push life styles and aspirations of people. To initiate all that process, "reach" is the basis and an essential first step. If "somehow" you could expand and increase the reach of media, you have consolidated the business. To expand and establish that reach, you need TRPs (both as a cause and effect) and all those elements that enable media contents to lure people and hold them.

To achieve this, you need the support of the advertising industry that, in turn, makes their clients believe all this with the help of "TRPs" as the basis. For that purpose, market research comes up with entrenching strategies to facilitate and lubricate the process of maximisation. At policy level, in that process, the public relations corporates are there to pursue further – at both ends of policy level and consumer end.

Media planning corporates/advisory services support broadcasters, who are big, drive the same content themes for peddling the model. That is why these agencies and their services are being described as the new gatekeepers of media. Most of these corproates are foreign controlled multinationals. They function more and more as embedded services for corporates to ensure the maximisation of their interests.

This chapter discusses challenges and opportunities of corporatisation of media particularly in the context of foreign investments. How news media more specifically is being availed for vertical and horizontal expansion of businesses for profit maximisation and for creating new business as in the case of "equity business" or "brand capital".

Endnotes

1 Frontline, 14 September 2001, and Economic and Political Weekly (EPW) 2002.

2 Handbook on Poll Surveys in Indian News Media, by Dr N Bhaskara Rao National Book Trust. New Delhi, 2012.

3 Annual report of RNI...... Http://www.rni.nic

4 Election Commission Meeting of political parties .....".. http://www.eco.nic

5 Private treaties, pursued by Times of India group, is its controversial Investment arm. It is a business proposition riding on the strengths and privileges of media. About which SEBI observed "harms fair, unbiased news" The Hindu, 12 June, 2010. But that made no difference. Press Council of India linked private treaties to paid news in its report on paid news.

6 Parliamentary Committee of Ministry of Communication headed by Somnath Chatterjee, Lok Sabha Secretariat.

7 The Govt. raised the FDI limit (as of 2016) in news channels and for radio to 49 per cent up from 26 per cent, against hundred persent in non-news channels. But the demand continue to allow 100 percent in news channels also.

8 Parliamentary Committee of HRD Ministry, Lok Sabha Secretariat.

9 The Hindu 4 September 2011

Section IV
A Way Forward

The book discuss a way forward for news channels in specific context and with examples for a new order of priorities. What a "needs model" of content should include is indicated. However, no one can claim such suggestions or initiatives are applicable for all times, in all situations and at all contexts of socio-economic-political backdrop. The examples are neither inclusive nor comprehensive. Such an approach should eventually be specific to a context or channel and in a spirit that "best is yet to come", and that it is a chase even more in the case of news channels operating under intense competition.

11

Critical National Contexts for News Channels to Excel

This chapter takes a look at the way the media has taken up some of the critical areas of India's developmental endeavours, whether all that has made any difference; and if so, then, in what way? It has been acknowledged that the phenomenal growth of media has brought about significant changes in the consumption priorities and purchasing behavior and time use patterns of people. But, the same cannot be said about social behaviours. We are not sure as to what difference media has made on attitudes, behaviours, values and social development aspects. There is not much research or empirical evidence to talk about it at any level. The examples at micro level are also isolated. There are no systematic time series studies matching the growth and proliferation of media, or the difference they have made at the community and citizen levels and in the context of the basic issues of the country. There are, of course, a number of studies on markets, consumer behavior or advertising. This is despite India having so many (600) Universities and even more colleges. The Indian Council of Social Science Research (ICSSR), which came into being more than three decades ago to promote research on issues, like social impact of media, cannot boast of one national study that they took up or promoted on media.

Consumer Protection Act is 25 years old and has been much advertised over these years. But, more than half of the states are not aware of it or its provisions or what they are entitled as buyers in the market.[1] Swami Agnivesh, a well known social activist working on child labour in the field as well as at the national level, came to meet me some years ago (2007) and raised this question about the "minimum wage"? No one knew it (including those in the news rooms). If the government has notified a minimum wage, but no one knows about it or implements it, then, what is the use of so many news channels, particularly, when the size of people who would be interested in such information in the country is sizeable?

It is not so that media has not made any difference or impact at all. It has, but the concern is whether they have made as much impact on social, environmental and development issues as they did on markets and consumerism; and whether they have made a difference that is needed the most for the advantage of more people and in the interest of the basic goals of the country. Based on my field research and personal experience in this area for over four decades, I can say that television has been an important contributor to whatever changes have been brought about in the country at the micro level as well as in rural and urban areas. In fact, the most significant contribution of TV has been that of being a "level player" – the exposure to channels has cut across the socio-economic and educational differences. The exposure across all socio-economic strata has been simultaneous, and there is no more need of "trickles down" model of development. That is all the more a reason for my anxiety. Because of television's potential to reach most sections of society simultaneously, and simultaneously, cutting across the barriers, it has the potential to bring down the divides between people and achieve in a shorter time what the government could not achieve with its policies and intervening programmes spread over a period of 60 years.

Further, it was expected that the media competition between newspapers and news channels would have made some of them carve out a new path, excel and explore full potential of television. At least, one would have expected some of these channels to do some experimentation with larger national concerns. Out of these more than 500 channels available in the country (2011) and half of them telecasting news and current affairs (not necessarily 24x7 news channel), can we name any channel that engaged in such a pursuit overtime? This however does not mean that a channel doing so would by itself make all the difference. But together channels could start the process and even trigger the change. [2]Harsh Vardhan in Jaipur is well known for his crusades in Rajasthan for few decades – earlier to save engendered Bustards, famous vulture and then, tigers, etc and more recent years to save Mausagar Lake, Amansimhan nalla in Jaipur and Duvathi river. He made an interesting presentation at a CMS roundtable in Jaipur on Environment journalism (September 4, 2012). He showed how he succeeded in the earlier years before 1995 in his crusades because of the interest news media took and their support. And how he could not make any head way recent years with campaigns involving a much larger section of people and the very heritage of Rajasthan and yet news media is not taking interest and even tries to snub as the interests of one or other business group is involved. Rajan Mahan, NDTV correspondent in Jaipur, who himself pioneered television taking interest in covering environmental issues, endorsed Harsh Vardan's views by narrating his own experience in more recent years because of "TRP priorities". Narayan Bareth, BBC correspondent in Rajasthan too regretted how journalists who are otherwise concerned of such issues are finding it helpless of late in making a difference in their work.

An immediate poser that comes to my mind is the revelation of 2011 Census – how female sex ratio is declining or female births are averted – despite an Act of Parliament penalising such behavior. This phenomenon was recognised as an undesirable practice more than a decade ago and the government has been campaigning about it. It was during this period that the news media proliferated in every nook and corner of the country and they also competed with each other in terms of coverage

In the light of such issues, what changes have been made in the content priorities of channels, for example? With the presence of multiplicity of channels, have they tried to distinguish their content from others? They could have considered children and women concerns in a special way. That would go a long way, particularly because more than half of the viewers of these channels are women and children. Have they considered this fact? Yes, some channels have done so. "Colors" channel (2010 -), perhaps, is one such example among general entertainment category in Hindi. And there are news channels too with individual programmes, like *Chetana* of TV-9 and *Batuka Jataka Bandi* of Zee Telugu TV. These are only two quick examples. That I am fully aware. They have made an enormous difference. For example, the weekly programme, *Batuka Jataka Bandi* (life is like a bullock cart), united 150 couples in distress and in more than ten cases, it was responsible for leading to marriage and uniting separated couples in many other cases.

The role being played by news media, particularly news channels, more recently signals certain realisation of their power, individually and together, to influence public policies and public priorities. The expose of scandals at various levels and the way they went about indicates a rethink on their own content priorities. RTI Act, series of serious scandals and Anna Hazare have made such a rethink a real. If all that could be proactive it would be a new beginning.

More than two decades ago, *Rajani* (DD) and *Helpline* (Zee TV) were two such experiments, which made great impact. There were a few others, too, during that pre-media boom period. But the question is - going by that experience or experiments, why haven't more channels, which are competing with each other in terms of the TRPs, taken to such successful programmes?

Similarly, consider the voter turnout at Assembly and Lok Sabha elections! Voter turnout being a critical indictor of the strength and maturity of democracy, it is relevant to ask - has the growth of news media and the extent of political coverage made any difference to it?

Even a more critical issue is the menace of corruption, particularly, corruption involving citizens. With news media devoting so much of its time or space to corruption coverage and also increasing it in the recent years, has corruption gone up or come down? What has been the trend in this respect? Of course, it is known that many scams have come to light because of news media. But that is more recently. And we do not know how many more scams have not come out.

Another similar example is the sensitivity about the country's environmental concerns at various levels. Recently (2005), news media has been increasing its coverage of environment and wildlife issues. What difference has they made? It was against such a background Satyamev Jayate tried to show case the difference the 13 episode of Amir Khan did.

Literacy is another issue with which the country has been grappling for decades and implementing several initiatives, culminating in the Right to Education Act, 2010. What has been media's role in this context? With the kind of reach and potential that these channels have, they could have reduced illiteracy levels much more. I know some regional newspapers like Gujarati Loksatta have taken initiatives to do something about it. But why such efforts were not pursued or scaled up?

These are some of the national concerns where the media has not taken any deliberate interest in the previous years (prior to 2000), before the news media boom in the country. This chapter tries to review the role that media has been playing in the context of such issues.

Notwithstanding all that, one could argue that crime rate in USA has not come down or declined over the years despite so much news media, their extensive reach and exposure for much longer periods – than in India. But, then does that justify what is happening in India. That exactly is the point that I am trying to make. The content model of US TV is such that it contributes and perpetuates however indirectly, or even unintentionally, crime culture and deviant behavior of young and of children even in good schools, and "good families". Any number of research studies over the years has indicated that linkage. The "content model" pursued by US media, the television channels in particular, is such that it needs to be viewed for its appropriateness to India, particularly since in India we could evolve a different model of TV – more appropriate one – one based on lessons from countries like USA and needs and compulsions of our own people. And yet we seem to be reluctant to learn, to realise and devise our own "needs based content" model. That is what this pursuit is about. That would have meant unleashing the power of TV.

Law and Order

The proliferation of television channels regionally and the spread of television viewing in rural areas has not made much difference to the law and order situation in the country. It has not impacted the crime rate and other crime related behavior in a positive way. Take a look at the extent of farmers' suicides in India. In 2000, 16603 farmers committed suicides and since then, the annual suicide rate has remained between 16000 and 17000 and crossed 17000 in 2004. In 2010, it was 15964 according to the National Crime Records Bureau (NCRB) Report, 2010. The NCRB data showed that the suicide rate has not come down in the last few years compared to the previous years. The five States where these suicide rates are high are also the States with comparatively more local/regional TV channels.

[3]The NCRB 2015 report was released in October 2016. This government agency brings out data for crime, violence, law violations for the year along with those for the previous years, going back to 1995. News media covered on the front pages how crime, violence against women, etc. went up in 2014 and how they have been increasing in the past few years. Similarly, the regional media presented data for various States showing how the crime rate has gone up in these States.

Crime against women has been on increase in the last decade all over the country. Theoretically, one could expect that there would be some positive influence of so many television channels on such deviant behavior. But, the reports of NCRB indicate otherwise. Such a trend is even more visible in Andhra Pradesh and West Bengal (the two states where the number of local language channels is higher). This increase is reported despite the fact that many violations go unreported and remains invisible. The 2015 report indicate increase in juvenile crime rate more than marginally.

Crime involving women (1995 – 2014)								
Crime	**1995**	**2000**	**2005**	**2010**	**2011**	**2012**	**2013**	**2014**
Rape	13,754	16,496	18,359	22,172	24206	24923	33707	36735
Dowry death	4,648	6,995	6,787	8,391	8618	8233	8083	8455
Molestation	26,856	32,940	34,175	40,613	42968	4535	70739	82235
Sexual harassment	4,689	11,024	9,984	9,961	8570	9173	12589	9735
Cruelty by husband	28,579	45,778	58,319	94,041	99315	106527	118866	122877

Source : NCRB 2011,15

The news media of Andhra Pradesh, too, has considered this phenomenon. The case of Andhra Pradesh is special because this State has the highest number of local (Telugu) language channels in India. The number of these channels, including news channels, has doubled between 2006 and 2016. As of end of the year 2015, there were 18 round the clock news channels and as many other channels in Telugu. Some of these other channels, too, telecast three or more news bulletins every day.

Such an unprecedented proliferation of news channels should have, theoretically, made a positive difference to the law and order situation and gender based crimes, such as violence against women, dowry deaths, rape, etc. in the State. At least, there should have been some indications to that effect. On the contrary, the 2010 – 2011 law and order situation in Andhra Pradesh reflected the same trend as that at the national level.

The following tables show the data provided by the crime department of Andhra Pradesh covering seven months of the year 2011 (January to July).

Crime Cases concerning women : AP 2005-2011			
	2005	**2010**	**2011 (Jan - July)**
Dowry deaths	140	149	108
Dowry killing	522	570	318
Dowry suicides	1171	1247	822
Women killed	728	677	451
Rape cases	1147	1308	858
Kidnap of girls/women	1171	1239	805
Multiple wives (?)	485	404	308

Source : NCRB 2011

Criminal cases involving women registered : AP 2005-2010		
	2005	**2010**
Registered cases	21437	23702
Cases under enquiry	1208	4695
Cases charge sheet filed	17042	16838
Cases sentenced	539	207
Cases of court settled	6567	2846

Source : NCRB 2011

It can be safely inferred from this table that on an average, 17 cases are registered daily for criminal assault on women; one rape occurs every six hours; and one woman is killed every nine hours. It also shows that although cases registered for atrocities against women are increasing, the number of cases prosecuted and sentenced is lagging behind. In this respect, some people are of the opinion that violence against women is increasing because action against the perpetrators of such violence is slow.

There is no empirical research to establish any causal relationship between crime and deviant behavior pattern in the country and the content preoccupation of channels and exposure to such contents. The more the channels shows such occurrences, even isolated ones, as “news”, the more such incidents are happening and the more young ones are adopting such behavior, or getting lured to such behaviors.

Three types of arguments could be presented in this regard. Firstly, there may not be any empirical study to establish the linkage, but it is obvious that such deviant trends are unambiguous and they are increasing, coinciding with the proliferation of media, particularly the TV channels in the state.

Secondly, the content analysis of news media and news bulletins, more specifically, brings out in unambiguous terms that such behavior has been getting priority. That is, the more such "news" is purveyed, the more people are taking to such behavior. This however, does not mean that all media contents are negative. In fact, there is also evidence that exposure to media also impacts people positively.

Thirdly, there is ample research elsewhere, particularly in USA, to indicate that high media consumption is positively related to negative social behavior pattern, more in the case of children and youth. In fact, it is also known from anecdotal evidences that negative traits are taken more from the media, particularly by the youth and children and that negative behavior and messages spread faster through media than the positive ones.

What is curious is that in a country with people of such high intellectual caliber and, at the same time, argumentative,[4] there is no research to analyse the impact of media exposure on different sections of people, even when it is widely felt. Whatever research has been there is in the form of isolated case studies, or quantitative research on the "reach" aspect of media. That too, in any case, is more from an advertisement centric point of view, particularly as a part of consumer campaigns and brand culture that measure viewership by way of TRPs swaying the concern or drawing temporal attention.

Based on my own 40 years' experience of conducting field research, analysis and consultancy in the country, I could say with confidence that there was never any deliberate effort to find out the social impact of media. Interestingly, there is no research of significance on media impact even after the spread of television in every nook and corner of the country and the media boom in 2000. (Raghavan, GNS & N Bhaskara Rao's: Social Effects of Mass Media in India, 1996)

The only person, who thought of social impact of media, was Dr. Vikram Sarabhai, who initiated the Satellite Instructional Television Experiment (SITE) in 1975. In fact, he did encourage some such qualitative research in the 2400 SITE villages in six States. Before that, there was hardly any example to show the impact. The Pune case study on community radio (1955) was another such research (Vinod Agrawal's book). But, there is no such interest after the boom and competition that has come in a big way in the last decade. My book on social impact (along with G N S Raghavan)[5] could, at best, serve as a baseline, as that was based on field data just before the media boom in the country.

Intensive Agriculture Cultivation Programme (IARDP), 1964 - 70, (popularly known as the Green Revolution) also brought out case studies on the impact of media and interpersonal sources of information on farmers. In fact, at one time (during 1965-70), faculties of Agriculture colleges undertook such studies. Another set of such studies were conducted in the context of family planning campaigns in the country during 1970–90. I was personally involved in both these movements during these periods in different capacities. But, most of those studies offer insights for the situation and scenario today in the country. But who cares?

In December 2011, the Director General of Police of Andhra Pradesh caused a nationwide furor by attributing changes in the dressing behavior of women as responsible for recent spurt in the number of rapes in the country. That being the case, he contended that the police could do little in curbing rape attacks on women. Many questioned his argument – including political leaders, even the Home Minister of the country condemned that simplistic comment of the DGP. Thereafter, many television channels had at least one discussion on DGP's observations (as it gives an opportunity to mount a "TRP-lure programme"). Hardly anyone pointed in these discussions that television, perhaps, has some role in the increasing incidents of rape and rape attempts recently. It looked as if the DGP was scared of doing that fearing a rebuttal of news channels. Such a social behavior and increase in such a trend cannot be attributed to anyone factor. A combination of them, some being reinforcing ones, as in the case of TV, could be talked about.

The DGP, nevertheless, should be thanked. For, he has brought to public attention that there has been an increase in the country recently in the criminal behavior against women. Year wise data for the last couple of years released in 2012 and published prominently in some newspapers has not provoked a public introspection anywhere and at any level, as if that was not a concern. But, the DGP's comment on women's dressing has caused instant media coverage.

Atrocities against women in Andhra Pradesh			
	2009	**2010**	**2011 (11 months)**
Murders	728	677	737
Dowry deaths	140	149	165
Dowry killings	522	570	528
Dowry suicides	1171	1247	1306
Atrocities on women/rape cases	1147	1228	1291
Kidnaps	1171	1239	1161
Harassment of women	9528	9720	10018
Homicides	2075	2281	2639
Other crimes against women	21482	20187	22034
Drug abuse – general	NA	309	357
Atrocities against SC, ST	NA	2405	2415

Source : Eenadu, December 31, 201; government reports

An analysis of the data points out one other factor that might have contributed to the increased crime against women. Whether that was a coincidence or there is a correlation needs to be verified. There has been a spurt in the number of television channels and in the kind of competition between them for "TRP coverage" has been so obvious. The "TRP coverage" is to interest viewers with luring contents and compete in that respect. The number of news channels has multiplied during these years and their priority in coverage has been fashion, crime and violence involving, particularly, women. In fact, in his autobiography, Auto Shankar (currently in Pune Jail for 18 rape deaths by this auto-rickshaw driver) pointed that his fellow perpetuators got the idea of rape and technique of rape from one or other TV serial or news programme. The extent of coverage of crime in primetime news bulletins, for example, between 2005 and 2011 had remained the same, i.e., around ten percent. But, in the case of many regional channels, it is higher than national channels. But a difference is now more channels are doing the same.

Complaints and registered cases under Domestic Violence Act in Andhra Pradesh								
Year	Hyderabad		Vijayawada		Visakhapatnam		Guntur	
	Complaints	Registered	Complaints	Registered	Complaints	Registered	Complaints	Registered
2006	44	19	21	14	10	10	-	6
2007	350	191	446	123	47	45	180	144
2008	273	214	431	168	118	85	181	112
2009	277	239	445	168	153	119	165	112
2010	419	377	529	216	209	188	159	119
2011	398	370	430	155	176	147	207	169

Source: Eenadu, January 2, 2012

And yet there was not one discussion in the media on this aspect of possible link for increase in atrocities against women in the country and other deviant social behavior.

Rural Coverage

It wouldn't be an exaggeration to say that India lives in villages even now. [6]Almost two-thirds of its population lives in the rural areas. The rate of growth of consumption (of goods and services) in rural India has out faced the urban since 2009 according to NSS. Even then the coverage of rural happenings in the mainstream news media has been marginal or negligible. In fact, its coverage in the prime time national news channels' bulletins was hardly two per cent in the last five years. Moreover, it was almost uniform as if there was nothing much to report or reflect. There have been so many comments in the last few years on how farmers' suicides, for example, were not covered even at the height of this crisis on the agricultural front in several States. Sainath of *The Hindu* wrote extensively during 2008-10 about this neglect of rural areas by the news media. A feature film, *PeepliLive* (2010) has very well depicted the neglect, ignorance, unconcern and insensitivity of news channels towards the realities of rural India.

Unlike national news channels, many regional news channels have daily segments (of 30 minutes duration, five days a week) on agriculture and some of these programmes, like the Anna Data of ETV, have made a mark over the years. But such exceptions add up to only a few.

The Ministry of Rural Development spends well over Rs 500 crore annually for promoting rural schemes and also has a Directorate for IEC with a budget of over 75 crore for 2014-15. The state governments, too, spend as much for the same purpose. Yet, going by the rural coverage in media, it cannot be said that such efforts have made much difference to the news media's concerns and priorities. Since the news media spend hardly a quarter of their revenue for news gathering, the Ministry's spending has hardly made a difference in the way the channels cover rural areas. It would be interesting to know as to what kind of difference they have made in rural people's lives or in taking up rural development issues over these years of television and channel viewership proliferation.

Theoretically, with the penetration of television and telecom connectivity in rural areas, migration to urban areas was expected to slow down, because, in both respects, rural India has seen amazing growth and connectivity. TV reaches little over one-third of village families in 2015 (against 19 percent in 2001) and phone connectivity in rural has gone up to 65 percent in 2015 (against 4 percent in 2001). In 2015 rural subscribers had outpaced urban growth. As such connectivity of rural is no longer a constraint for news media's reach if they want to report. But, has rural to urban migration slowed down? On the contrary, the 2011 Census shows that more villagers migrated to cities during that period, and it was the highest in three decades. The process of urbanisation has also increased over the years. The increase in urbanisation in 2001 Census was a mere 2.1 points against 3.35 points in 2011 Census.

Rural India has been experiencing unprecedented changes in the last decade and more in so many respects. The number of rural-centric schemes has multiplied with huge allocations of money of state and central government. MGNREGS, Rural Health, sanitation, drinking water, road connectivity and spread of telecom to villages – all should have compelled news media to take on. And that would have increased media coverage of rural beyond scams and other negative instances. Rural coverage has improved particularly of regional news channels in the last couple of years both quantitatively and qualitatively but no where near the potential and the extent that could help expand the reach of news channels.

A secretary (2012) of the ministry of Rural Development concluded that news channels do not cover MGNREGS and such other BPL targeted programmes because channels do not consider these people as their target since they are not "TV households". He seems to have understood the phenomena correctly. But the question is what has been done to correct such myths. In the absence of any such initiatives, channels take to TRPs. TAM perpetuates its priority with markets.

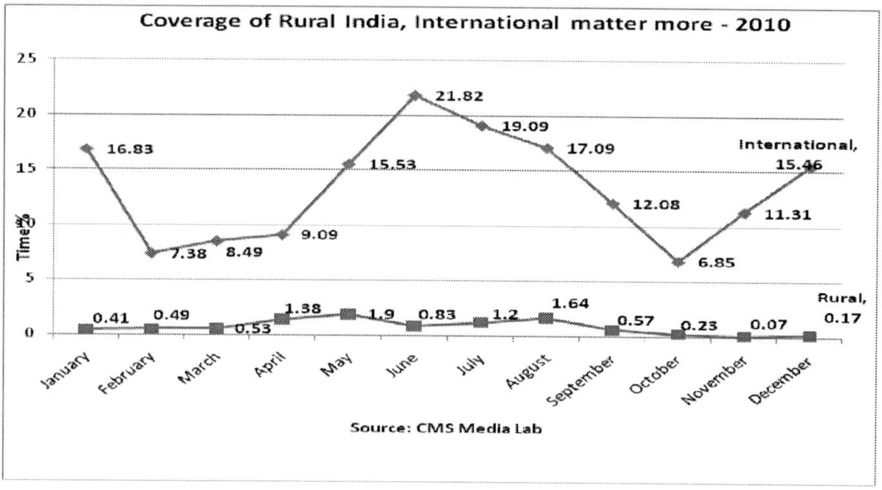

Social Development

Women and children centric social development issues remain chronic problems of the country, thereby hindering its holistic development. Even the states, which have made a mark in terms of economic development, are lagging behind on social development. It cannot be said that the states, which have displayed poor performance in the last decade, are "media disadvantaged" in their reach. They, too, experienced boom in news media and satellite television growth. There is no evidence to show that the states, which have a high media spread and growth, are also ahead on the social development front. In fact, the evidence could show otherwise.

The proliferation of satellite television channels since 2003 and that of news channels since 2008 has been remarkable in the country. This period between 2003 and 2008 was an opportunity for the news channels to take a "different course" in their content focus and pursuits. Yet, the time/space devoted to social development issues by news media during this period of high news media growth was low as if such issues have never been their concern. This is despite the fact that social development issues have the basic elements that TV channels look for to interest and attract viewers.

Even the news media coverage of women and their issues is no better. This is very surprising, because, as myself and P N Vasanti brought out in our research paper presented at the annual meet of the Press Council of India a couple of years ago (2007), the next wave of media growth (and expansion) in the country should come from women, and to realise that potential, news media should reflect and present issues concerning women more and in a far better way. But, there is no such evidence despite an increase in the extent of women engagement in media as reporters and anchors now.

At this point, it is also pertinent to ask as to what extent and in what way (adversely or advantageously) has the recent boom in media affected the women in India? It has certainly opened new vistas for employment, enhancement and empowerment of women and children. However, while the impact of media has been somewhat positive on economic aspects, there is no such evidence for the social aspects involving women. What difference has the boom in numbers made in terms of influence and impact? Do we have any evidence? For example, with regard to the RTI Act (2010), it is observed that women applicants and women related issues constitute hardly ten percent of all RTI applications in most states as if women are not even aware of this Act. The news media made no effort to raise this issue.

Reach of Media among female population

(Per cent rounded)

	National		Hindi Belt States	
	Urban	Rural		
Expose/ Reach	**Female**	**Female**	**Rural + Urban Female**	**Rural only Female**
Press (frequency in a week)	27	7	16	6
TV (frequency in a week)	74	35	27	15
Radio (frequency in a week)	26	25	26	24
Cinema (frequency in a week)	30	20	15	11

Source: IRS 2007

The growth rate of media reach among women was naturally expected to be more since 2003. Between 2003 and 2007, for example, it was higher among women than in the case of men – for all segments of television programmes, including news and current affairs.

Growth rate between 2003 and 2007 in the reach of channel		
		(percent)
	Male	**Female**
Any Publication	31.6	22.7
Any TV	14.7	19.0
Any TV and C&S	41.6	38.1
Any Radio	30.0	40.0
Television Channels of		
News & Current Affairs	29.5	44.7
Serials	30.7	41.1
Film	29.1	33.7

Source: IRS 2007

An Indian Express sister publication, [7]"SME World" (Oct 2008) confessed in its editorial that "in retrospect, we happen to realise that, unintentionally, the magazine has not given women entrepreneurs their due". The editorial further observed that "we are witnessing a scenario where a number of women entrepreneurs, who possess capabilities of influencing board room decisions, are finally making their presence felt on business horizon." It quoted a study by a research outfit claiming that "10 per cent of business start-ups were being launched by women entrepreneurs, thus, reiterating the fact that Indian women are willing to take on challenges of the competitive business world." Some television channels did make efforts to reach out to women. The viewership growth rate provides evidence of that. But, that has not been picked up by most channels. It is not that channels do not feature women prominently. But the concern here is what kind of coverage it has been and in what context and with what motivation their coverage has been. It is more TRP lead coverage than with a concern and interest to contribute or correct a range of basic issues of girls and women.

Market Views for Converge

One of the reasons for limited view of women in media is the perception about women in the context of "market". Consumerism gets its momentum more from women. Women are prime targets of consumerist campaigns all over the world. If media are cause and effect of consumerism; neither can be sustained without the active role of women. It is not in the interest of consumerism to have women outside the purview of mass media. In fact, it is the extent of women's involvement, which determines the growth momentum of both. Since the ultimate interest of advertising is to sustain and push consumerism further (consumerism and media), no wonder women-centric advertising has increased substantially in the last decade. More recent efforts of advertisers to tap the "potential markets" should give boost to the reach of mass media among women.

An intervening variable in this process, however, is the perception of advertisers about the identity of "decision makers". Women are generally viewed more as "home makers" rather than as decision makers. But, in the new "life style" phenomena sweeping across media, women too have emerged in so many different ways. With one million elected Panchayat representatives, several Self Help Group (SHG) activists in rural India and the presence of so many women in "white collar" jobs, the outlook of "media planners" should change, if not shift, towards encouraging better media coverage of women concerned issues not just in metros and not just about "life style" topics, but also about basic needs and social development issues concerning women. Another dimension of changing India is increasing girls' enrolment in schools and colleges. The media has a chance to gear up to these emerging opportunities. All this means tapping growth opportunity among women. But that is not equally evident in the priorities of the news media (in the news bulletins).

What has been the role of mass media? Media has the potential to positively contribute to these processes. Beyond creating "awareness", what has been its concern and role? Going by the visionaries, who propounded television for India, whether it was Indira Gandhi or Vikram Sarabhai, the intensity of gender and social development issues should have increased substantially. To what extent are some of the women and social development national tasks and concerns a priority for news media? And, equally important, what has been the approach towards contents covering various issues? Bits and pieces of field research on "impact of television" on social development issues do not indicate affirmative insights. But, there are no systematic research and analysis. What the government has been concerned about is to create awareness, not so much with outcomes. Triggering the processes towards achieving larger goals require a different treatment in the media, particularly television news. Merely adopting a 'more is merrier' approach is not enough for realising those aspirations.

Crime Against Women

Sexual harassment (molestation), dowry, child marriage, female foeticides and infanticides and domestic violence are the major crimes against women. Together, they indicate the quality of life in the country.

Is the gender bias in the country getting worse or improving? With so much media, particularly, television channels, one would expect it to get better – at least in the last decade, the period when India experienced channels and viewership boom. But 2011 Census results show contrary trends that should make all those channels concerned with content strategies to ponder over it.

The National Sample Survey data on sex ratio (of 0–6 years) suggests that gender bias is getting worse in the country. Of course, if we go by Census data, it has improved marginally from 962 in 1981 to 915 in 2011.

Sex Ratio

Year	Sex Ratio
1981	935
1991	922
2001	927
2011	914

Female foeticide is the highest among emerging middle class according to an analysis by Surjit Bella and Ravinder Kaul[8].

2011 Census has indicated the failure of laws against Sex Determination Tests (SDTs). "Social distortions" and "life styles" are attributed as responsible for the declining trend in child sex ratio, which dropped from 927 to 914 between 2001 and 2011.

In terms of increase in the number of channels and their impact, correlations are negative in the context of crime and violence (against women), too, and other deviant patterns related with social development (*National Crime Report 2015).* Rape incidents have increased the most among all cognizable crimes – by 13.4% since 1971. Commenting on this trend, the Times of India reported that this increase, undoubtedly, reflects increasing violence against women.

Age of Marriage 2011			
	Total	Rural	Urban
Male (<21 Years)	41.7	48.3	27.9
Female (<18Years)	30.2	33	24

Source: 2011 censure

In 2011 the percent of married women who acknowledged getting married before 18 years of age was one-third in the case of rural and one fourth in the case of urban. What difference the Govt. compares had made and in what way proliferation of television channels made difference in this regard?

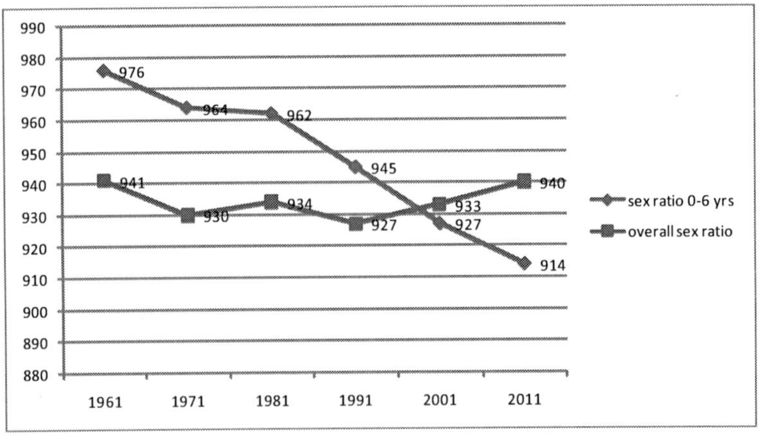

Figure 1: Alarming Trend (Females per 1000 males)

Source: Census

Health

Coverage of health services

As a basic need of most people, how much is the media concerned about health of people? What impact has it made on the health status of the poor and marginalised? What aspect of health matters more to the news media and whose interests are reflected more in their coverage? Take the case of epidemics. The number of people, who are affected by and are dying of diseases, such as Dengue, Malaria, Encephalitis, etc., has not come down. These could have been minimised with increased awareness and simple behavioural changes if the role of media had been more active in this regard. Dr K. P. Kushwaha, head of BRD Hospital,

Gorakhpur, which reported 470 children's death in Poorvanchal within three months in 2011, said that awareness would have brought down that number.[9] Gorakhpur has three local news channels. TV channels missed an opportunity to play a proactive role in this regard. They could have made a difference locally. He also said that drinking water purification practices could have been improved. The least that the local channels could have done was to increase awareness about the dos and the don'ts.

Pneumonia and diarrhea are known as killer diseases and responsible for death of six lakh children below 5 years annually. It is also known these diseases could be prevented with timely interventions. Similarly, it is known that breast feeding up to six months after the child is born could save children. And ORS rates continue to be below and 43 percent children suffering from diarrhea receive oral rehydration therapy. Experts have said that awareness on these and hygiene could save tiny tots from dying. (Pioneer, August 22, 2012 – quoting Dr Bhatnagar of AIIMS). News channels could make a difference by taking to such issues seriously.

An analysis of prime time news bulletins of news channels for three years (2007 – 2010) by CMS had indicated that "any health" related issue accounts for less than one per cent of prime time news bulletins against 4.4 per cent devoted to crime and another two per cent devoted to the coverage of news related to religions or religious personalities. What should also be of concern is that health coverage was constantly below one per cent in the last three years, except at one point in time when it was four per cent. That was during the Tsunami period. (Remember, an equivalent per cent of that coverage for Anna Hazare's fast in Delhi was 94 per cent).

Health related stories seldom have follow up coverage. More pertinently, mass media's pre-occupation is primarily with the curative aspects of health, not much about its preventive aspects. Prominent coverage is driven by one or other drug manufacturer or by the interests of the pharmaceutical industry. Even with regard to drugs, there is hardly any coverage. For example, spurious drugs including expired drugs being marketed rarely get any investigative or preventive coverage. The surveys carried out by the government, as well as the industry have brought out that as high as one-third or more per cent of popular drugs in the markets of Delhi and other metro cities are spurious. Yet, the news media has seldom done any proactive programmes to sensitise the public and minimise the scope and use of such drugs, except for isolated coverage as hard news like a police raid on a drug store or a death after drug use. Moreover, these are never followed up. In fact, there is more news media coverage of police raids for video piracy than for spurious drugs.

Awareness and sensitivity among people, timely information flows and prompt media coverage are expected to facilitate disease control. In fact, news media could help in a big way in preventing and also in fire fighting measures. As a result, for example, one could expect decline in deaths of children in hospitals over the years with increased availability of round the clock news channels. But what we see instead is significant increase.

[10]A national survey by a government agency brought out (2012) that much more than half of milk in use across the country is adulterated. Earlier too regional surveys have indicated that trend. But most news channels limited to their news bulletins for one time, a few channels had discussion programmes also. But a channel which did such coverage at length bothered more to discuss how adulteration takes place, with what, the extent of adulteration and what are different ways of adulteration take place as if people are being sensitised to take on to such practice or replicate rather than discuss ways of knowing about adulteration and measures of avoiding, coping with adulteration and whom the matter should be taken to.

The Case of MMR

With continued high Maternal Mortality Rate (MMR), its reduction has been one of India's priorities as a national concern for four decades. Several initiatives have been undertaken over these years and some are still continuing. There are both national schemes and State initiatives. Recent Census (2011) results too remind of this task. This issue involves people at grassroots, their lifestyle and changing habits and behavior patterns and elements that could interest channel viewers. But how much media coverage has this issue received in the last decade in particular? Hardly any, as if it would not interest the viewers.

It is not that the government did not do anything to sensitise the nation about the MMR issue. Not only budgets were specifically allocated for this issue, but special schemes and campaigns were also launched. But, not much of that got reflected in the media coverage; except announcements and inaugurations by Ministers. The issue has not become a national concern. None of the surveys, including the ones conducted by CMS during the decade, showed Reproductive and Child Health (RCH) or MMR as an issue of national concern. The study also indicated that the gatekeepers of news media think that issues involved in RCH/ MMR "do not interest" their viewers/readers nor do they help in encouraging the compulsions of "competitive coverage".

The declining sex ratio was covered and discussed in media may be a couple of times with focus on "missing girls" or "sex discrimination tests" or female foeticide, etc. But all this coverage by the national news channels did not add up to even 10 to 15 news items in isolation in a year. In fact, a majority of news items on health focused on one or other aspect of HIV/AIDS in 2008. Even the Millennium Development Goals (2002 - 2015) with focus on women's health, infant care, nutrition, etc. never mentioned media coverage as a factor for creating concern in the interest of a large section of people. One-third to half of news items dealing with women and health covered in news bulletins on various TV channels were related with HIV/AIDS.

But since the public is not as much a consumer of MMR related news items as that of HIV/AIDS, such issues do not get similar coverage. Also, channels cover HIV/AIDS relatively more either because there is "foreign" money involved or a "VIP angle" or it is a part of an "advertising agency" drive with a PR push. Such issues concern the channels only to the extent the above mentioned elements are there.

Health & Medicine Coverage		
Year	**N (%)**	**T (%)**
2004	0.4	0.40
2005	0.8	0.80
2006	2.2	1.70
2007	0.85	0.79
2008	1.13	1.01
2009	1.74	1.87
2010	1.09	1.19
2011	1.17	1.00
2012* (Jan to May)	0.98	0.87

Note: N: No. of Stories; T: Time; Figure are based on Prime Time (7-11 PM) Coverage of 6 National News Channels

Source : CMS Media Lab

So Much Coverage Does Not Mean Much!

The round the clock news channels cannot be blamed for everything going wrong around us these days. But when there is scope for 24x7 news channels to reduce the intensity of a calamity and even to prevent further deaths; certainly their role could be questioned. Even more so when the issue is something on which the channels have been reporting off and on. With so many rounds the clock news channel it is not too much to expect that they contribute to the reduction in the deaths of children in children hospitals. But the deaths seem to have increased recently for whatever reason.

The death of over 74 children, spread across a period of five months in 2011 just on the outskirts of Kolkata, is an instance to ponder about. In Hyderabad and Tirupathi, too, similar incidents were repeated more than once in 2011 and 2012.

Firstly, half a dozen local news channels have been operating in Kolkata, for example, for some time with certain competition between them. Secondly, relatively speaking, these Kolkata based channels are more grassroots oriented. In fact, in this specific context, channels have reported about the death of children in hospitals more than once in the previous one year. Thirdly, in this specific instance, the credit of reporting 30 deaths in October 2011 itself goes to these channels. They were prompt in reporting the deaths from day one; but, very clearly, such reporting could not alert or avert the recurrence of similar incidents in nearby hospitals. This is, perhaps, because their reports, especially, the structure of reports and their angle were more like that of reporting spot news rather than suggesting a way forward. Otherwise, on the 6th day, how can the channels talk about the use of acid as an antiseptic instead of real antiseptic agents during child birth as if confused about the core of the issue, i.e. the basic right of a child to survival, with India being a signatory to the UN Convention?

In this regard, its pertinent to question - If death was an *error,* then, how can that be repeated again and again? If it was *neglect,* then, it was evident that no one cared about these channels' news reports; and if it was *ignorance* (of nurse or others), even then, the channels missed an opportunity to share the real facts at the very outset and help avoid the death, although that is not the job of news channels. But that could be a concern for a news channel.

Moreover, the news channels reporting the deaths of children for six consecutive days in one month and for many more days in one year have not created any flutter or concern in the local civil society or seriousness among the concerned authorities. All that the relatives of those affected could do was to go berserk and ransack the hospital. This is how the reporting of such incidents by news channels often ends up.

This is not the first time that such incidents have happened in West Bengal and Andhra Pradesh. In 2002 and 2004, there were two major such instances and in 2011-12, in three different months, deaths took place in government hospitals. Here, one can ask, what is the use of having so many local news channels if they cannot contribute in preventing such instances? In Bengal, all news channels covered these incidents in every news bulletin on those days with actual footage from the hospital including bytes from the staff and others and also had brief discussions on the issue. Has all such reporting by news channels helped in preventing such incidents?

The fact is that the coverage could not help in preventing newborn deaths in government hospitals. For example, had the concerned authorities or local civil society taken these channels' news reports seriously in the initial days, would have, perhaps, led to some preventive measures. Or, had any of those a dozen channels gone beyond treating the incidents merely as routine 'breaking news' to "interest" the viewers, to enquire into these incidents and meet the hospitals' responsible functionaries, some actions could have been possible towards preventing further deaths in such situations in the government hospitals.

Yet another way of looking at those so many deaths in October 2011 is to ascertain as to what kind of learning the news channels derive through such incidents? Since, in Kolkata, such deaths at birth had happened in hospitals in earlier years too, channels were expected to be more sensitive towards this issue and also proactive in digging out earlier enquiries on child deaths in hospitals. That is where the "concern" of the channels is expected to dictate interest beyond reporting "an incident". Another aspect is specific special skills (apart from concern) that the news staff should have to prevent such deaths in the hospitals. (By specifying that relevant specialists were not there or a particular machine was not there, government doctors are running private hospitals, oxygen was not there, etc)

The reporting further makes us think of what is a beginning and end of a "news story" that news channels cover. How important stories in the news bulletins could be taken up for a discussion and what should be the scope and structure of such discussions. Otherwise, all this coverage would make little difference in the same way as so much coverage of poll campaigns by channels has made little difference to voter turnout!

On an average 60 children are dying a day in Andhra Pradesh. UNICEF reported (2012) that 22000 children died in one year (2010-11) in Andhra Pradesh. This report was given to the government a few months before the deaths in Tirupathi hit the headlines (on a day when no other TRP driven news was there for news media). This report analysed the reasons for the deaths and specified what need to be done to better the situation. But no news media had referred much after several deaths of children in a number of hospitals in the state (2012).Even in West Bengal media reports had not bothered to look for such reports of specialist agencies like UNICEF.[11]

In Niloufer Hospital Hyderabad alone, for example, 7011 children died between March 2011 and April 2012. But media coverage was limited to individual instances as if they are isolated happenings.

Why does so much coverage of such instances make so little impact? The news made no difference to in correcting the situation with measures by the government by the hospitals, etc. Even when all local news channels report the incidents.

The reasons for news on channels not making any difference could be several. One could be the way news is presented, i.e. its structure, scope and source. It could be such that the presentation is not credible enough. The death of newborn babies is presented as "another news item of the bulletin" without evincing a concern for such deaths and enquiry into systemic causes. I criticised such a similar perspective in my edit page column Kaleidoscope in Delaware County Daily Times (USA) in 1968 (I was, then, a Ph.D. student) for giving Pulitzer prize to a photographer for his photograph of a US soldier killing a Saigon citizen at a close range during the height of the Vietnam war. My argument, then, was that the cameraman was interested more in capturing a "beautiful picture" of the killing even when he could have attempted to stop such a killing of a civilian. These days, I see such situations quite often where the reporter is more interested in covering an incident controversially (for which he is paid) rather than with a possibility of preventing or minimising the calamity even when it is possible.

Another reason for news coverage not making difference could be the tendency to simplify such incidents or report it in a routine manner like any other news and politicise it by quickly incorporating bytes of party leaders to prolong the coverage. In fact, even in this case of newborn deaths, the Bengali news channels were divided in their perspective. Pro-Mamata channels presented the news in one way and the others did it differently. In the process, they diluted the seriousness of the issue.

Yet another reason could be an isolated view of such deaths, forgetting to link these to earlier happenings and the efforts made before. For example, similar baby deaths may have been happening in many other government hospitals in some other cities too for the same reason. There may have been several enquiries into such incidents earlier and elsewhere and Enquiry Committees may have presented reasons for similar child deaths in government hospitals. But the emphasis in media reporting is about appointment of yet another Enquiry Committee.

Resurgence

"Bihar is in the grip of yet another lethal outbreak of viral encephalitis, which has claimed the lives of 82 children in Magadha division so far." That was a four column front page banner news story in the Hindu one day after the nation celebrated children's day with fanfare on November 14, 2011. This was the second major bout of disease to strike the state of Bihar in the previous four months. In 2009 too, 46 children died of the same viral disease. But there were no cases of encephalitis in 2010 because of "massive immunisation drive". Thereafter as "there was no awareness programme or immunisation drive", encephalitis revived in 2011, according to Medical Directorate sources.[12]

It was during this period of 2009 – 2011 that Bihar too witnessed the doubling of local news channels (from two to six - not counting cable news). This is in addition to a dozen Hindi news channels that too are available for television households in Bihar. Yet, local channels have not taken to distinct priorities in their contents. Given the kind of uproar that encephalitis had caused, not once, but more than a couple of times in the previous two years and the number of children who died, local news channels had taken to "strategic programmes" (awareness + sensitising + action prompting). As if there was no concern for such a role and proactive programming. Nor was there any evidence of national Hindi news channels (from Delhi, Lucknow or Kolkata) doing something specific towards protecting 0 – 5 age children, particularly since it was realised that precautions could help curtail causalities from such epidemics. Also, there was no example of any other channel, entertainment or children, doing anything specifically about such bouts of epidemics taking heavy toll of children in many states of India.

Of course, the prime responsibility about such epidemics is that of Health Department and the medical fraternity. But, it is fairly well known that the health services are pre-occupied with curative efforts. In any case, they fall short of coping with bouts of such preventable diseases, and whatever campaigns they take up are more in reaction and in an ad hoc way. The news media generally view such happenings as a source of negative news or as another source of advertising revenue. In any case, one thing that comes out is that coverage by news channels of such epidemics, or deaths of children in the hospitals, made no difference in minimising the scope for death of infants or in speeding up redressal, season after season. This, however, does not mean that media coverage makes all the difference. No, but if news media pursue the matter with concern and systematically over time, it could make a difference. Its support adds to and expedites the process of mobilising doctors, civil societies and the bureaucrats. The point being made in this chapter from this example is how the news media misses such opportunities to make a difference locally.

[13]A report of Naandi Foundation released by the Prime Minister on January 10, 2012 had brought out that awareness among mothers about nutrition was very low. This was indicated in the report as one of the reasons for 42 per cent of school going children being malnourished for which the Prime Minister said that the nation should be ashamed of. By saying so, the Prime Minister reminded that various communication campaigns over the years have not lead to preventive measures to correct the anomalies. One of the reasons for continued deaths of babies in hospitals is this malnutrition of pregnant mothers and birth of underweight babies. State governments and the Union government have been carrying campaigns and media was reporting launch of such campaigns year after year.

News Channel Coverage of Tsunami (2004)

CNN and BBC news channels are viewed around the world as "standard" and benchmark by other channels for setting their own priorities. Generally, television channels are "copy cats" just like individuals tend to do, often, in real life situations. Local channels imitate the regional channels and these, in turn, imitate the "national" channels. All of them get influenced by global brands, such as BBC, CNN and the like.

BBC and CNN news coverage of Tsunami calamity in India in 2004 brings out the kind of priorities with which they operate. Despite Tsunami having all the dimensions that should interest any news channel, these two channels hardly covered it, as it affected the Indian coastline. CMS Media Lab study for WHO indicated that the coverage was low because India did not go for any foreign aid, and since the coverage of news was more "donor" or "aid" oriented (when it is not VIP oriented), India did not figure much in either BBC or CNN coverage, as did Sri Lanka or Indonesia. Also, because no foreign VIPs visited India in that context.

"Peddling myths by Western media as an opportunity to build and expand viewership in the competitive scenario was evident even in the coverage of Tsunami devastation." This is how CMS Media Lab summed up that coverage by CNN and BBC news channels.

Global media coverage of local calamities

A Pro-Active Media Enriches Parliamentary Democracy

Parliament and media are the two sides of the same coin of democracy. Free elections alone are not enough for sustaining democracy. A free-press is equally indispensable for the very relevance of the Parliamentary system. They are complimentary to each other. They sustain and mutually reinforce each other. If media is the Fourth-Estate, then, the Parliament is the third pillar of the (e) state. Unlike media's relations with the government, the relationship between Parliament and media should never be adverse. The legitimacy of democracy depends on independent media, its reach, how much concerned it is and how effectively it could mold and mobilise public opinion.

Recently, the Parliament and its functioning have received a new impetus both negatively and positively with the spread and proliferation of television channels in the country. In the process, awareness about democracy has deepened its roots in the country. In fact, the very perception of elected representatives and the very standing of Parliament have undergone qualitative changes, recently, with Lok Sabha and Rajya Sabha having separate TV channels. The electronic media taking to 'live' coverage and review of Parliament proceedings beyond the "question-hour" has added a new dimension. In fact, Lok Sabha TV has elevated itself with the help of its distinct discussion programmes, thereby, reminding the news channels of what they are missing!

There were occasions recently when critics felt that the television studios have become parallel forums or extensions of Parliament debates with frequent presence of MPs, Ministers and political party leaders debating before cameras; sometimes giving a feeling of pre-empting the following day's or week's debate in the Parliament.

Of late, [14]there has been a decline in the space devoted to Parliament coverage in the newspapers from about a page more than 25 years ago to about five per cent of their space in 2011 on the days when the Parliament is in session. This per cent, however, goes up marginally when the proceedings in the House are dramatic or have revelations or heated debates.

The All India Radio (AIR) has been broadcasting the highlights of Lok Sabha and Rajya Sabha deliberations separately for decades, although only for five minutes. Obviously, in such a short duration, it is not possible to give details and do justice to all the participants. Nevertheless, AIR makes special effort to refer to as many members' names, who participated in the discussion during the day. Because of its short duration, the details of the discussions are not given priority. AIR listeners' surveys indicated that listenership to Parliament reviews, including the weekly *Saptahik Sameeksha*, was never beyond two per cent. Long hours of live broadcasts of no-confidence debates in recent years, however, had more than 10 per cent listenership, particularly, in rural India. The low listenership could be because of a clash in the timings between these broadcasts and peak hour TV viewing.

A CMS Media Lab study (2010) of TV news channels' Parliament coverage reveals that it dealt more with Ministers' statements rather than discussions leading to or as a follow-up to such statements. And, the coverage outside the Parliament House was limited to one to one interview with Ministers and party leaders. The channels give far more coverage to walkouts, walk-ins, disruptions and the like than to the Question-Hour. Daily newspapers, on the other hand, give a better Question-Hour coverage, as appropriate to the State of their circulation.

In the 2011 monsoon session, for example, there was hardly any coverage of any of the economic issues. The coverage was mostly about Ayodhya, CBI, CAS, PAC, Kashmir-Kargil-George Fernandes. For two or three days, when the Parliament was in session, the news channels had no news to report in their main bulletins of the day. Channels have a tendency of being limited to certain "telegenic-faces" from political parties for bites and short-cut images as well as for studio discussions. Unlike newspapers, the television makes icons and sticks with them no matter what the occasion or even the issue is. That is how it has been "more of the same" despite proliferation of news media and current affair programmes and much expanded scope of deliberations in both Houses of the Parliament.

Media-Sensitised MPs

Instances of Parliament Members raising questions based on reports in news media, particularly, in the newspapers, have been on the increase recently. With increased competition between newspapers and TV news channels, on the one hand, and among newspapers and TV channels themselves, on the other, there is deliberate effort on the part of media to "sensitise" and even try to set the tone of deliberations. In fact, based on media coverage, many MPs decide their priorities for participation in the Parliament. Nevertheless, thanks to television coverage of Parliament, some of the Members, old and new, have molded themselves as serious and more responsible MPs and have distinguished themselves. In the process, members' preparatory efforts for active participation and their representations have significantly improved. This difference brought about by the news channels, recently, has to be acknowledged.

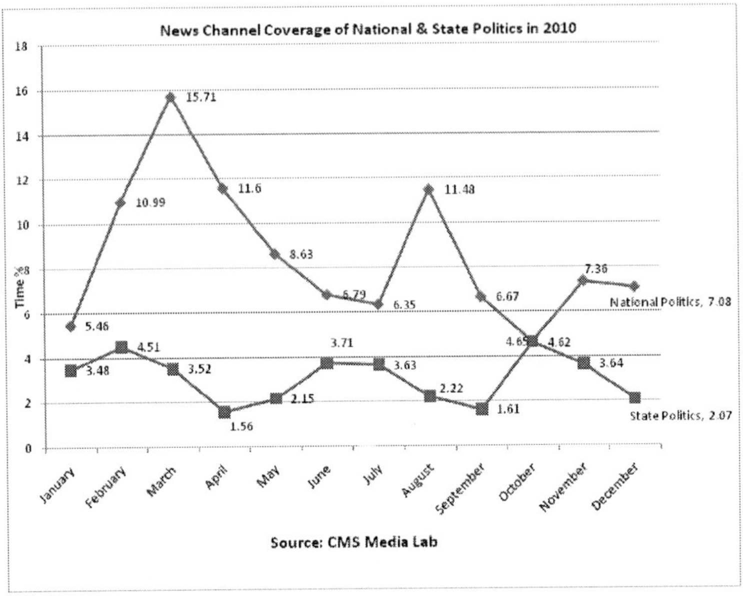

Media Orientation of Parliament

Proliferation of private TV news channels has added to "media orientation" of Parliament, its décor and deliberations. Members' dressing and speaking styles as well as references in the speeches have become specific (with names of places, instances, etc.) and more pointed. But, at the same time, media coverage, particularly, live coverage has led to more frequent House rule violations; and regulations have changed the very complexion of such coverage. Nevertheless, it could be said that the perceptions about MPs and the public standing of Parliament has become more transparent. But, in the process, it has also become a bit tarnished, as the footage of the (more frequent) untoward Parliament incidents are repeated in too many bulletins. The coverage of State Assemblies by television channels has further added to this phenomenon and some of the unfortunate events (in UP, Gujarat, J&K, Orissa, AP Assemblies) involving violent exchanges (including throwing chairs, micro phones, etc.) and live coverage of the same, remain fresh in the viewers' mind. Such incidents have created an adverse picture of the politicians in general and the Parliament in particular, to the extent of discouraging viewership of such coverage and spreading indiscriminate animosity against each other.

In a democracy, political parties and political leaders are its key players and harbingers. Confidence and credibility in them is indicative of robustness of the democracy itself. This is how media coverage of political parties and leaders, specifically in the Parliament, acquires significance. Some time ago, the noted editor and author Khushwant Singh also observed that media coverage of politics has become "at best a source of shock and amusement", as it is more like a "circus". Unfortunately, quite often, the live coverage of Parliament (as well as Assemblies) does give such an impression. Political leaders should be more concerned about this phenomenon and in this regard, the news media could help in taking a "more concerned" view of the Parliament and sensitise the larger constituency to bring to fore the tendencies associated with the functioning of the House that need to be decried.

Moulding leaders

When[15] NTR started political party in Andhra Pradesh there was no private 24x7 news channels in Telugu and yet in the next few years some 20,000 new leaders at grassroots have emerged. All that happened because of their activities closer to people, the issues they took up and the efforts they made towards implementing government / party schemes. In the last two decades, after NTR era, hardly a few new leaders have emerged from grassroots. Many observers in Andhra Pradesh contend that the boom in news channels coincides with a period of agitations of all kind. Telangana agitation and its penetration into educational campuses, being a continuing one. A new focus and new forces has emerged. All that because (TRP centric) of hype in the coverage of politics. Many persons have come to fore because of channels projecting them as if they are leaders.

As an analyst of public policies for over 30 years one change I notice is in the vocabulary and tactics of those who swept into politics along with the channel boom. This style and priorities are different from those who were in politics much before the era of news channels. Political aspirants find figuring in news media prominently by any means is a more assured way of penetrating into politics. For example the two Rajya Sabha members of two different parties were happy for becoming hero in their respective parties for a cockfight in the House and in the full glare of cameras (September 5, 2012). They were not known before for any speeches or interventions in the House. It suited the news channels, for channels got so much for so many hours of coverage without spending and making effort.

Participation Beyond Voting

Media and Parliament together nurture and sustain democracy and make it relevant to people and participatory beyond voting once in five years or so. In the process, media helps in strengthening the Parliamentary traditions, and in promoting and supporting responsible representative concerns of Members of Parliament. So, the television channels should have a far more serious and analytical approach in covering the Parliament than the present one. They could aim at creating more participatory and interactive programmes with the involvement of a larger public to enhance the scope of representative character of discussions in the two Houses of Parliament as well as in the State Legislative Assemblies. Media should encourage and uphold "good Parliamentarians". Respect in Parliament would, in turn, amount to respect in the very freedom of press. Hence, media should be concerned about any trend, which amount to disregarding or denigrating the Parliamentary tradition and democratic culture in the country.

Unlike more than a decade ago, when senior journalists used to cover Parliament proceedings, today, it is the turn of the juniors. In fact, Parliament reporting has become a training ground for 'cub' reporters, irrespective of their familiarity with House rules and regulations. This is also because TV cameras (and loudspeakers) are installed outside the Parliament hall, so that senior journalists could pick up "serious discussions" as and when it comes up in the House. Also, news agency copy is used more often for capturing the Parliament deliberations, because the news agency reporters stay in the press galleries throughout the day. And, there is a tendency of "sharing of copy" by journalists of different media establishments across the country. This also means "same reporting" by as many journalists.

The Committee system on which our Parliamentary practice depends is, more often, a media casualty, because the Committees attracts media attention only when there is a scandal or controversy or politicians are involved. Film actress Kareena Kapoor gets more media coverage on her dating than the Parliament proceedings on normal days or in the normal course, then speaker Somnath Chatterjee once commented. However, recent controversies like Lokpal Bill have brought Parliament Committees to Centre stage. But that is because of polarisation of political parties and reports of agencies like CAG.

Newspapers and channels, of late, increasingly carry "surveys" of all kinds on timely issues, as if they have representative relevance and character, when, in fact, they are "deceptive surveys" in more than one way and often mislead the very legislative process in the country. Let there be no doubt that such surveys are not substitutes to deliberations in the Parliament and Assemblies. At the most, they are a good beginning towards broadening the very scope of democracy. "We the people" and "Big Fight" like debates by TV channels, on the other hand, go a long way in bringing out the pros and cons of issues and supplementing Parliament deliberations.

In recent years, there were occasions, when media had to be reprimanded for its (mis)reporting of Parliament debates. The frequency of stopping live telecast in the middle of Question-Hour or the number of instances of "expunging" certain remarks of one or other Member by the Speaker has been on increase. Yet, there is hardly any occasion when media has gone against the House Advisory Committee guidelines for journalist representatives.

More recently, [16]The Speaker of Lok Sabha (as well as Assemblies), has more than once expressed anguish at the tendency of media politicising Parliament reporting and, even more, neglecting "pro-active" discussions in the House. And, many Members of Parliament, across political parties, keep blurting out their anger at the media for ignoring their participation in the House on substantial issues related to their respective constituency and of national relevance. On the other hand, some members are picked up by cameras, irrespective of their participation. Even the presiding officer of Rajya Sabha (Vice President) had quipped about such media preoccupation of trivialising Parliament reporting.

News media need to project credible accounts of Parliament deliberations, as they are serious and are often complex. Dumbing down of Parliament news as short-sound-bites and as fast-cut images will not do justice to understanding and appreciating the MPs' concerns and participation. In fact, going beyond the news bulletins, Parliament discussions need more background material and analysis. Based on various CMS studies, it could be said that Parliament debates deserve sensitive reporting and discussions without any subjectivity. This is despite the fact that about a quarter of news channels' bulletins are about party politics. Democracy not only needs journalism that restrains from hyping differences and divides in the country, but also gives a fair chance to pluralism in the debates and a lot more representative character in the coverage.

Media Coverage of Elections: More is Not Merrier!

Political parties, political leaders and elections have always received priority concern by the news media. If elections portray democracy-at-work, media has been at its best in upholding the democratic process. At the end of an election, if Election Commission is the real winner, media cannot be behind. Going by extensive coverage, media deserves praise for sustaining and steering the poll campaigns, reminding voters' issues and concerns, and bringing to fore the virtues of candidates and leaders in so many different ways interactively and analytically by way of field based discussions and animated studio debates. Never before were elections in India as transparent and live as in these polls. What more media could have done? And how differently could they have covered the poll process and party campaigns?

Nevertheless, since two Lok Sabha elections (2004 and 2009) were held after the media boom, particularly the news channels boom, it is time to ponder over it. Those, who are not so much interested in politics, perhaps, would say that television, more or less, has gone "berserk with polls". Some others would say that it was yet another festival time for channels. The media pre-occupation with politics is well known, but not to the extent it was at election time.

Overall, TV's role has been significant and as never before. In fact, some of the channels succeeded in bringing together contending leaders on an "American style-poll-debate" platform. Even in the case of daily newspapers, there has been a spurt. In the last couple of weeks of campaign, newspapers devoted as much as a quarter of their editorial space to election coverage. In the case of TV news channels, it was not less than one-third of news time.

Among the States that went to polls in 2003, an "incumbent" party won the elections only where exposure to TV was the highest in that State. For, TV is known more for "negative effects", particularly in the context of politics. This aspect of course has nothing to do with individual channels. It has more to do with the very character of television. Unlike newspapers and radio, TV lends more scope for negative reporting, amusement and emotions. This is how it holds on to its viewers.

More is Not Merrier!

No wonder why some channels' coverage was quite extensive to the extent of "trivialising", perhaps, because it was presumed that such coverage, otherwise, is "boring" or "too serious" to hold on to viewers' interest. That is how channels covered a lot of filmy personalities, TV serial characters and their "dummies" often with filmy dialogues and even puppets. Between animated "nautanki" type programmes and studio "jugalbandi" (with pollsters and studio experts), channels made extensive field reports. Repeat of visuals over and over within a day and in so many different ways amounted to "more of the same" and an impression of an "over load".

Poll coverage on AIR had always been limited in terms of the time devoted to it, but far more "informative" and "absolving", particularly its "bridge-programmes" linking capital cities. However, to the credit of TV channels, it must be said that their field coverage of campaigns had been much beyond the State capitals and urban centers. The earlier model of political party leaders reading out on AIR and Doordarshan as part of "poll broadcasts" for over two decades had neither made any difference to the scope of poll campaigns nor had those broadcasts ever attracted any listenership with increase in the number of contesting parties. They made no difference to political discourse. Based on the votes polled in the previous election, a total of eight to nine hours were devoted to poll coverage by AIR and DD stations in each State that went for election.

What difference has the media made in enlightening the voters; mobilising higher voter turnout; and making the campaign centered around issues of concern, rather than on caste, community and on individuals and emotions?

Voter Turnout

Since the boom in news channels, three Lok Sabha polls were held – 1999, 2004 and 2009. What has been the trend? Apart from extensive coverage of polls by news media during these years, the Election Commission too carried campaigns appealing voters to caste vote. Even efforts made by civil society groups locally have increased significantly during these polls at the national,. state and for the municipalities.

Voter turnout did increase marginally in the two Lok Sabha polls after 1991 – 92 from 55.9 to 62 percent in the 1998 poll. But there after that is when the proliferation of news media and competitive coverage become marked the voter turnout has decreased in 1999, 2004 and 2009 Lok Sabha polls. How come? Why so?

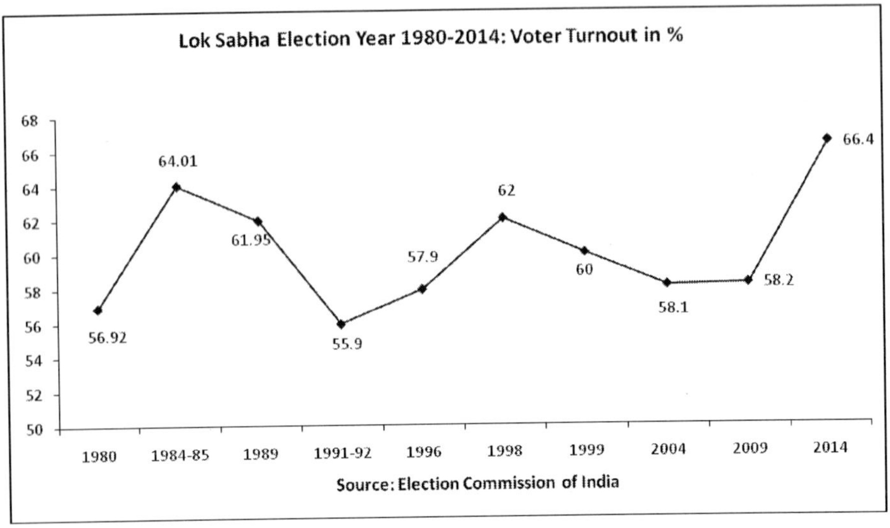

Generally it is assumed that voter turnout for State and Municipal elections would be better than for Lok Sabha. Delhi and Mumbai are relatively "high news media zones" and concentration of news media operations too is high in these two metro cities. And also obviously the presence of political leaders and intense party activities too is high. Civil society groups are also active in the electoral process in both these cities as in many other cities across India. Voters in Mumbai and Delhi are also relatively better educated.

An analysis of voter turnout trend for elections to Lok Sabha, Assembly and Municipal Corporation indicates that turnout has not increased in the last 3 to 5 elections.[17] The turnout in 2009 Lok Sabha poll in Delhi for example was not more than what it was for the Lok Sabha poll of 1996 and 1998. However, in the case of Municipal election for Delhi Municipal Corporation, the turnout in 2012 was higher than what it was in the 1997 Municipal elections. But it was the same as in 2002 Municipal election.

Over all, the voter turnout for Lok Sabha, Assembly or Municipal has not increased much beyond 60 percent. In Mumbai city and suburbs the turnout in the 2012 Municipal polls declined as compared to the 2004 Municipal elections, but increased as compared to 2009 Municipal elections. Even in Mumbai in neither election the turnout reached 55 percent.

Marginal increase more recently since 2014 by a couple of percentage points in voter turnout was more on account of updating of voter lists until last days of voting day and better management of Polls by the Election Commission. It Was not on account of Voter a activision as much as media coverage of polls.

Even if no direct relationship cold be in inferred or attributed between coverage of electoral campaigns by media and voter turnout, extensive media coverage should not dampen voter enthusiasm in the polls. There are of course other intervening factors, both external ones like note-for-vote and other lures or candidate characteristics and internal ones like reliability of voter lists and their updating by the Election Commission.

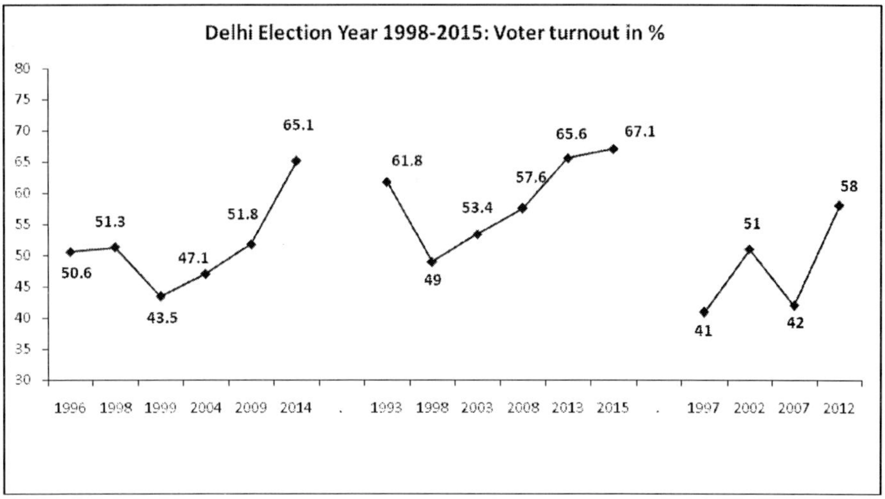

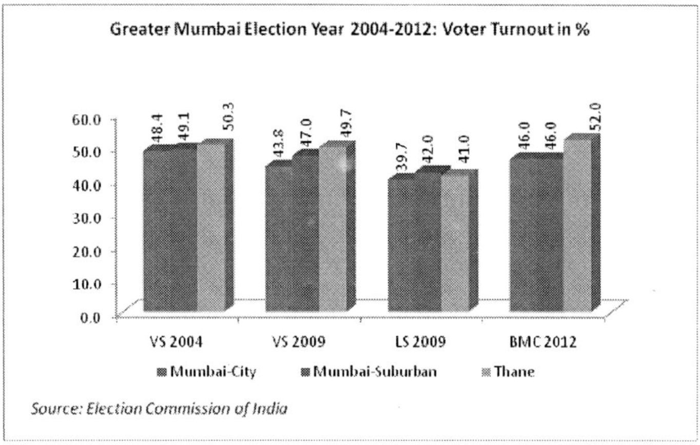

More Media, Less Voter Turnout!

The proliferation of newspapers and news channels and competitive compulsions arising out of it, is expected to increase the focus on substantial issues of the country, and reflect the concerns of people more. Has it? Moreover, did it have any impact on the increase in voter turnout in the elections held in the last 10 – 15 years? Voter-turnout had increased only marginally in Delhi, where media reach is relatively higher. But the turnout increased far more in Chhattisgarh, where media reaches hardly one-third of the voters. There is no evidence that media's poll hype has made much difference to voter turn-out in Delhi. In fact, compared to 1980s, when there was hardly any television coverage, voter turnout has lower. The joke shared in a post poll analysis by a NDTV comical (G*ustakhi Maaf)* was that BJP lost in Delhi because of extensive TV viewership and it won in the other three States because there was not much TV viewership! In fact, since 1998, voter turn-out increased more in MP, Rajasthan and Chhattisgarh than in Delhi. It means that the media rather facilitated the poll outcome, although differently. The double-edged potential of TV was too obvious in poll campaigns. So was the boomerang phenomenon! In Chhattisgarh, the Aakash Channel was supposed to have devoted itself to boost the chances of Ajit Jogi. In fact, whenever there was blatant "over use" of electronic media by an incumbent, that party never returned to power. This is only one example.

Obviously, democracy is not meant for merely voting. Has there been any change in those previous processes that amount to strengthening democracy itself? For example, what difference has the proliferation of poll surveys (and exit polls until 2011) undertaken by the news channels made? How much difference does the poll campaign coverage make in enlightening voters or in swaying voters? Pre-poll surveys and exit polls were undertaken by the news media as major part of their poll coverage. In fact, such surveys have become revenue–earners for TV channels). This is how pre-poll surveys and exit polls were hyped and stretched on and off with animated discussions. Against such a dilemma, great editors like Girilal Jain adopted poll surveys assuming that it meant ensuring more objective coverage.

Do Poll Surveys Make a Difference?

Over the years, CMS, based on its post-poll surveys, had maintained that media's coverage of pre-poll surveys do influence the poll process. Based on the insights inferred from conducting election studies for over 35 years, I wrote extensively that pre-poll surveys and even exit polls (when conducted prior to the completion of the poll process) do make a difference to the poll process. Realising this kind of scenario, as early as in 1987, I wrote on the Rights and Wrongs of pre-poll surveys in Media Monitor (defunct) of [18]India Today and suggested the need for Dos and Don'ts for poll–eve surveys being covered in the new media. I also advocated that media editors should be the first ones to understand the pros and cons of such surveys in a far better way.

With far more media reach today than it was two decades ago, such a concern has to be more. The implications, however, cannot be expected to be uniform. The Editors should be the first one to discriminate pre-poll surveys, which are part of party campaigns.

Academically speaking, media poll surveys are expected to improve the content and quality of an election campaign and the very process itself. This is something our media need to view more seriously and professionally by going beyond competitive and immediate commercial concerns. Going by the poll outcome since media boom in the country, it could be said that when it comes to credibility and campaigns "more is not merrier".

What Difference have the Surveys Made?

Despite proliferation of news media and their reach in recent years and efforts made by some of them to motivate voters to go out and cast their vote, what difference have they made on the voter turnout percentage? Curiously, voter turn-out has remained more or less at the same level in the last couple of decades. In fact, there is a further decline in some pockets where voters are exposed to news media relatively a lot more and more intensely, even in the 2004 and 2009 Lok Sabha polls. While prominently promoting pre-poll surveys in 2004, some channels maintained that their poll survey was "definitive" and that voters could see "the results of next months' election today". If the outcome of a poll is a "foregone conclusion", as news channels often tend to make out quoting poll surveys, where is the motivation for voters to go out and cast his or her vote? Frankly, this aspect did not occur to me until eminent editor Girilal Jain (of ToI) posed it to me 30 years ago. Is that the reason why voter turnout has not been increasing despite dramatic change in the demographics of voters, proliferation of news media and also in the number of poll surveys recently? To what extent do they empower voters with objective information and enrich our electoral process? Can one say that media hype of poll survey does not enthuse and enlighten voters to go out and vote? This aspect needs to be pondered over, as we are inundated with poll eve surveys these days.

Conflict Resolution Approach

Not mere conflict reporting, but conflict resolution and even conflict prevention or avoidance could be a concern of the news media. The journalists reporting war, both in the field and at the desk or studio, need to have different kind of concerns, sensitivities and skills. In [19]my book, *Controlled Mass Communication in Inter State Conflict*, I suggested in 1971 that mass media could be used as an indicator of the intensities in trust or tension in inter-state relations and as a possible source for inducing trust. My contention was that if the mass media of the countries engaged in inter-state conflicts present a two-sided version of the contentious issues on a reciprocal basis rather than their own version and a one-sided view, the process might help establish effective communication and promote trust between the two countries. Such a possibility is even more evident today with the spread of television. This book tried to put forth the view that attempts to resolve a conflict are more likely to be successful when the parties are conscious of and publicly acknowledge the other side's point of view in their communications. Despite so much research in US on the subject, an offensive and offending approach was evident in its news media. A new factor as a result of competing channels is that one or other channel (out of a dozen or two) might go hawkish or even provocative, thereby undoing all the restraint exercised by the other news media.

Going a step further, Tom Nusbaumer, editor of War and Peace, proposed the use of "peace journalism" approach in reporting conflicts a couple of years ago (Tom Nusbaumer, Covering Conflict, www.mediachannel.org/atissue/warpeace/front.shtml). For, there have been 19 wars and 17 flash points, which have erupted on the globe since 1999. Not all of them, however, received media attention. Media coverage of such happenings in a two-party (good vs. bad) or in a *tug-of-war* mode need to be questioned. Shared goals, common interests and interdependent approach in media reporting as a distinctive model in covering a conflict or war will go a long way instead of hyping the cause of conflict, suspicion and betrayal between the States and people involved. Exploring possible solutions and acknowledging each other's apprehensions have the potential of the much needed "healing touch". In any case, reportage should not end up being a tool "for war", as is the case with most American media since September 11 (2005) and in an unprecedented uniform way. There was hardly any persistent endeavor evident in media coverage towards finding solution to the crisis or even presenting alternate options before the nations for "War against Terrorism"

Over all, newspapers have been more concerned, considerate and foresighted in their coverage of Kargil conflict than the TV channels. However, during the height of Kargil clashes, the media coverage evoked war hysteria in the country, as if hawks dominated the media. Certain deception in TV coverage was too glaring – because of the extent of repeat, re-enacting and headlining, hour after hour. But, then, perhaps, it is more in the character of TV as a medium. Sheilaja Bajpai aptly wrote on Kargil TV coverage that it was "funerals, which brought everyone together" (Hindustan Times)

Also, media coverage of Kargil was as if there were only two viewpoints – one being that of the ruling BJP's. Anyone who raised issues on Kargil hardly got due shares in the coverage and, in fact, became a suspect. In that process, TV has, in a way, redefined "patriotism". There was hardly any dissent in any of the media during the seven–eight weeks, as if they were all echoing the same view point in endorsing the government's stand, as never before, in support of a war, as if they were all using the same "hand out". In fact, it was an "illusion of information over-load". Kargil was a one sided coverage – dogmatically one sided – by both the countries. It was only in the later part that Pakistan's point of view got some coverage. Someone could have easily said that the Kargil media hype was meant to cover the government's "lapses", and that the media poured more oil into the fire and it amounted to beating the drums of chauvinism – something that the channels do better (than short sighted politicians) in their country.

The first ever survey on exposure to electronic media in Kashmir Valley was done by me in 1974. That study established how viewership (and also listenership) of Pakistan's electronic media was more and credible and why and how. Later, in 1976, myself and the then Secretary of I&B Jamal Kidwai went there to reorganise Srinagar radio and TV kendras by inducting local creative talents and correct the imbalance in the coverage of India. But, soon thereafter, the imposition of Emergency demolished all that momentum.

News media as well as the government's initiatives have been after-a-crises responses. "Creative initiative" even in the case of individual channels has been temporary - more as hype and forgotten too soon thereafter. Nevertheless, conflicts have provided an opportunity to our channel people to showcase their initiatives irrespective of their seniority. But there is no institution building approach in television channels (because of temporal outlook) by incorporating learnings/experiences. That is also because channels operate on a breakneck speed (repeating things more). They hardly seem to engage in stock-taking for insights and considered initiatives.

Thanks to competitive compulsions in the media scene recently, the Indian news media have been relying on hyping phenomenon on occasions of even lesser consequence and of shorter duration. Kandahar, Kargil (1999) or Agra (2001), of course, falls in a different category. During the two months of Kargil War, India lost 519 troops. Kargil, perhaps, was the first armed conflict that gave the private Indian television channels an opportunity to cover war extensively, including from the front line.

Indian television's war coverage was as good or even better as that of any US news media. In fact, in the first few weeks, the Indian media made far more forthright and objective reporting and analysis on "America Strikes Back" or "War Against Terrorism" or the war against Taliban, without being part of any "imbedded arrangement'.

Twice before Kargil and once thereafter, I wrote that neither the Doordarshan realised its role nor did the Ministry come up with a communication strategy appropriate for the challenge in the Kashmir Valley. But, each successive Prime Minister since Indira Gandhi talked of a special package for electronic media in Kashmir Valley and announced budget amounting to crores of rupees. It was in 2011 as part of the 12th Plan proposal. *But see, on the other hand, what the private channels did. Writing "Has media hyped Kargil conflict?" in 1999,*[20]

I wrote in a Sahara Times column, "It is good that the Ministry of I&B has taken the initiative now with Rs 430 crore package. I wonder whether it will be sustained and the proposed ....'Kashmir Samachar' acquires credibility. But what is even more important than budgetary allocation or setting up transmitters is creative response with relevant programming and scheduling strategies. In this support, Kargil has a lesson - allow private media to operate freely instead of proliferating the inane" (Sahara Times). It was against this background that the CMS study finding (2005) is relevant. The finding showed that private television channels depicting life on both sides of the border made a dent and difference in the myths of the viewers in the valley.

Broadcast Editors Association (BEA) took "serious note" of threats given by the MNS Chief (Raj Thackaray) in Mumbai against Hindi news channels and described it as an "assault on the roots of democracy". In a statement BEA said that it does not believe in reacting to such aberrations with an element of vindictiveness -in the larger interest of public confidence in democratic system and rule of law. Raj Thackaray in turn threatened some channels for "misquoting" him. If news media would not have reported such aberrations, the way they did prominently with Raj Thackaray's "infiltrators" view, provocative action-reaction could have been avoided (September 2012).

TV editors of BEA did well by promptly calling on the government for action against Raj for the threat to TV channels and for providing protection to news channels. But they could have as well also advised their own fraternity not to report in the first instance such provocative statements by such aspiring "leaders". For it is news media's blowing up of such divisive statements which build such persons as leaders. The media does that "for its own" end which some call TRP reasons. That being the case, news media, particularly byte based news media, should be sure of their own priorities and also concerned of implications of what and how they report. It is blowing up of such statements that prompt such reactions and threats by political activists, criminal behavior in the case of some others – all to grab the headlines of news media. Blaming "publicity seekers" (like Raj) alone is of no use if "publicity givers" themselves are all out for such coverage for "their own reasons".

This reporting of Raj Thackaray (August 2012) is not an isolated instance. But a glaring example, one which also brings out that news media does not learn from past experiences. But this is a good example for how news media, particularly news channels, are good at bringing out latent conflicts and divides than in promoting solutions or way forward with a healing touch which potential too news media has. As Prime Minister Dr Manmohan Singh reminded addressing Kerala Union of Working Journalists (September 14, 2012), news media could play a prominent role in promoting communal harmony and inter-community dialogue. He was speaking in the context of recent tragic incidents in Assam and their reverberations in Mumbai and other cities. It is not that there are no examples. But they are exceptions and were mostly ad-hoc and not strategic.

Countering Corruption

Way back in July 2001, the Press Institute of India took the initiative of organising a discussion on "Countering corruption: the role of media". Ajit Bhattacharjee, the director, asked me to deliver the key note address. What I said then is presented here for its relevance today.

The Dilemma!

Insensitive to corruption! That is the impression one gets today considering the way corruption has spread and is prevalent, no matter which stream of public life one comes from. However, if on the other hand, one looks at the extent of corruption coverage in news media, day in and day out, one gets a different feeling. Does it imply that media reporting of corruption makes no difference (has no influence or impact) on civic consciousness? Certainly, something is missing in this present paradigm.

Collective Civic Action and Media's Pro-Active Initiatives

Apart from individual level experiences, recent field surveys at macro level have brought out the extent to which corruption has spread, not just at top and national levels, but also affecting common citizens in availing basic civic services. This is irrespective of people's educational or economic levels. No wonder, then, that the space devoted to corruption by daily newspapers is nearly three per cent against hardly one per cent two decades ago. There are, of course, instances (many more recently) of a media report leading to government action and even collective civic action, when it comes to exposing a fraud *swami* and the likes. But, there are hardly any examples of boycotting a corrupt politician.

The point is that the citizens are more often passive and collective civic action against the corrupt is rare until Anna Hazare's movement (2011-12). Even "media crusade" was missing and "collective media concern" towards rooting out corruption is limited. The media coverage is mostly about personalities, politicians and polls, not so much about systemic aspects, which sustain corruption.

Has corruption been part of our agenda at national or state level? Yes, it is more as rhetoric, an accusation or a failure. However, CMS poll eve surveys over the years have shown that, individually, voters are concerned about corruption and the corrupt. The percentage of such voters was invariably below 25 per cent – even in Tamil Nadu and Bihar at the height of revelations of local corruption. In fact, that was hardly 15 per cent in most states. Nevertheless, such a concern has not led to collective civic action or doing something about it on a sustained basis. And, even actual voting behavior was not so much influenced by the candidates' corruption record.

Concern Against Corruption: Proactive Initiatives Missing

One conclusion that could be drawn from media's corruption coverage is, what I call, the "mere reporting mode" rather than the "to mould" or "provocative or preventive coverage". Also, one does not find much media reporting of instances where a citizen or a community did something about rooting out corruption, so that more people could emulate the approach.

Are our laws standing in the way of media playing such a pro-active role?

Certain Contradictions

Then, of course, there is a glaring contradiction regarding the priorities and preoccupation with certain issues in media reporting or coverage. For, (as a young girl sang at a Mr. N. Vittal's meeting some years ago about the all pervasive nature of corruption), the kind of life styles being projected, perpetuated and hyped, particularly on television, sustains corruption (among the middle and lower middle class people and even more in the minds of young). Such coverage breeds greediness, the root cause of all corruption. That is what television promotes - consumerism, life styles and "self-centered" values.

What are we doing about such phenomena at the policy level and as concerned citizens? Unless we do something about the "breeding process", how can we expect to root out corruption?

The much debated "paid news" controversy deals with some deep rooted issues related with the news media concerns and compulsions. Conflict of interest is an underlying factor that does not allow the news media to unleash its potential. In this respect, government policies are as much responsible as is the corporatisation of media.

Preoccupation with Politicians and Corporates

What are our media's priorities? The instance of corruption involving a politician or a bureaucrat attracts media coverage more than corruption going on systematically and affecting many common people. The ones, which can be politicised, are hyped, but they are also forgotten very soon. The opportunity to bring to fore a deep rooted malice involving and concerning most common citizens is ignored for the sake of sensational angle in news converge. This is what the problem is all about.

[21]A recent CMS study brought out the fact as to how "middlemen menace" is causing havoc in perpetuating corruption in public services. When it comes to media, we now have a new functionary of middlemen– with potential for the mischief. Have we ever talked about those functionaries and their role? It is these people, who now orchestrate how a corrupt deed should appear in media. I am, obviously, referring to corporate "PR" and their new found role of lobbying. The less the concern in the news media about corruption, the more active role PR people will have in the media. Even civic society initiatives do not get a chance of media coverage, unless they operate through a PR. Corporate PR is causing havoc and, yet, we seem not to be bothered about what it all means.

This is yet another issue where I do not find much change over the years. If one were to analyse the origin, source and priorities of news, one gets the impression that media exists more for the government, politicians, bureaucrats and businessmen, not so much for communities or citizens; not to the extent they normally deserve. That is how some time ago I started describing this phenomenon by saying that our present mass media is, in fact, more like "marketing media". This situation, of course, is prevalent even more today than when I said based on content analysis studies. Now, newspapers hardly spend 20 per cent of their revenue for news collection against hardly 10 per cent in mid 1970s. The Hindu group is the only which spends much more.

Corporate Corruption

The country has been witnessing, recently, a series of financial frauds, bungling or/and manipulations affecting million of common people. During the same period, we have seen the proliferation of news media, including 24 hour channels and on-line news, and most operations (in the news rooms and financial markets) are computerised. Yet, how many instances are there of news media preventing or doing an "expose in-time", "if not before", so that millions of investors are not deprived of their life savings? Take, for instance, the US-64 crisis. Just a couple of days before the crises came to fore and the freeze that followed, who were the ones who sold the shares at Rs. 14? Did we hear anything about it? Was it difficult to report? As readers, viewers or investors and citizens, aren't we entitled to be more "enlightened" and "better informed" by media, so that particular corruption could have been prevented.

On the contrary, there are stories floating around as to how media people were "aware", but not "concerned enough" to put across the goings on in their columns. What were the media establishments themselves doing? Harish Khare of The Hindu (then) described this phenomenon as some kind of a "Jugalbandi". Is the "page three journalism" busy in building up busy bodies and the corporate manipulators?

How else could senior journalist Harish Khare write some years ago (The Hindu, 13 July, 2001) that "Economists and pink paper" editors, who are otherwise good at explaining the corporate sins of the pinstriped entrepreneurs, are doing their best to fudge the US-64 issue". He referred to how such misleading takes place deliberately. In fact, the "power and punditry" being attributed to columnists today is such that they could, perhaps, do a better job in exposing corporate corruption than Enquiry Commissions and Committees. But, they do so only if they wish and only when they are not part of a Jugalbandi!

Unleashing the Power of Television: Case of Anna's Crusade

The role played by news channels initially in promoting (marketing?) Anna Hazare as a second Gandhi (?); portraying his movement as a second freedom movement; and in mobilising support nationwide against corruption is a good example of what channels can achieve and how they could make a difference. The fast that Hazare undertook in April 2011 at Jantar Mantar, New Delhi and the second one from 16 August to 28 August 2011 at Ramlila grounds have sensitised people, cutting across divides and regional differences. This kind of simultaneous mobilisation in many parts of the country simultaneously was possible in such a short period because of television and the social media and a network of RTI activists on ground.

Apart from the fact that it was accumulated public anger against corruption in the context of a series of scandals that had come to light, it was the social media and television news channels, as if working in tandem, that were responsible for creating such an astounding effect. It was the power of an idea and the unleashing of the power of the media that worked. Facebook, SMS, websites, and Twitter have all contributed and helped in mobilising people.[22] Social media worked as appetisers. Two crore SMS messages had "prompted" 50,000 "missed calls" as an indication of solidarity for the Anna movement.

Never before has the media given such extensive coverage of a larger politic issue and cause. Even the national elections have not been covered with as much intensity. The TV channels covered it with ferocity, making special efforts to draw more people in support of the anti-graft movement.

The TRP is not a reliable indicator of TV viewership or for gauging its impact. Nevertheless, it gives an idea in a relative context. The following table gives us a comparative picture.

TRPs in various contexts	
Events	**TRP**
World Trade Centre attack (2001)	7.56%
Lok Sabha Election (2004)	10.22%
Mumbai floods (2005)	9.71%
Mumbai train blasts (2006)	11.78%
Jaipur, Ahmadabad, Bangalore blasts (2007)	10.72%
Mumbai terror attack (2008)	17.81%
AP CM YSR Reddy chopper crash (2009)	12.31%
Babri Masjid demolition case (2010) ??	11.54%
Anna Hazare campaign for Lok Pal (2011)	12.41%
	(Mint, 28 August 2011)

Events that had high TRPs in the last ten years (2001-2010) were all tragic accidents, except the Lok Sabha polls and the Anna Hazare movement. During the same period, the number of news channels increased in the country from five in 2001 to 141 in 2011.

Election coverage involves staggered, interactive and field coverage over weeks. It is supported by ground level activities (of party leaders and workers). There is a difference in the viewership. The coverage of Anna Hazare over a couple of weeks brought people out for a peaceful expression of their anguish against corruption, and to lend their support to the movement for the Lok Pal Bill and against corruption. This is in contrast to the accidents, whose coverage was limited to a day or two. News channels together with social media not only awakened citizens of the country, but made them participate and endorse the cause, and motivated them to take proactive initiatives, like pledging not to take or give bribe.

It is not that the news channels have not covered corruption before. In fact, an analysis of coverage in the last six years brings out that news channels had devoted hardly three to four per cent of their prime time to issue of corruption. But, between 2008 and 2010, the coverage of corruption stories aired during prime time news increased by six times. A series of scams unfolded and continued to be in public glare (thanks to the news media) for weeks and months. In the history of television news, this was perhaps the first time that news channels devoted their entire prime time for one (non-entertainment and not-political) story,—for six to seven days (out of the 13 days) of Anna's fast. It was a non-stop coverage. English and Hindi news channels devoted more than three-fourths of their transmission time to this event, starting with Jantar Mantar (April) and Ramlila grounds (August 16–29) to Hazare's fast. Some regional channels, too, devoted as much coverage to the agitation. The coverage showcased the agitations not only in Delhi (at difference places, like Tihar Jail, the PM's residence, India Gate, Parliament, JP Park, etc.), but also in about 65 cities across the country. The coverage was such that it brought together more people with flags and in different colours, attires, paintings, slogans, and even street plays.

The support given by channels to Anna was unprecedented, unusual and unnatural. The impact achieved could not be otherwise; nevertheless it brings out the power of TV. But, what is challenging is to achieve such a response in the normal course in the context of issues that concern the common man. The challenge for channels is to achieve a similar active response without such saturated and "coercive coverage" as a part of their normal programme schedule. The subject topic involved could be too deeply held behaviour.

The coverage of the Anna movement and the response achieved proves that TV can achieve such a feat even on non-glamorous issues that deal with social and political problems by going against the TRP formula. TRP implies that channels rely more on sex, crime, glamour, cinema and similar greed centered (rather than need based) contents and priorities.

What motivated news channels to support Anna in such an all out manner of for days together as never before and as seen nowhere else in the media world?

In the first instance, channels did not expect that Anna's call would receive such a massive response across the country. Once it did, they realised that it was their movement too to capture and take it on as "their own" and go all out. The fact that there was no "popular or well-known personality" overshadowing the movement and that Anna himself enabled channels to view it as their own "discovery" and also take the credit for the "good deed" led to the unprecedented coverage.

There were certain "dramatic" moments, too, and the crusade had all the elements of live, field and interactive coverage with colour, glitter, anti-establishment slogans/banners. Suspense and intrigue, too, was ensured. Suspense was built up as to when Anna would end the fast; what was happening on the government's side; are they agreeing or "yielding", etc.

The channels did not need to deploy much resource for that saturated coverage, which included OB vans and a couple of young (or cub) reporters (a training opportunity for them) and, of course, the familiar studio deliberations. It was only during the second phase (after the first week) that the channels could get one or two new faces for animated studio discussions. There was no research or any extensive preparation needed. It was truly a networked live national coverage– an opportunity for local identity and participation - the essential elements for building and sustaining viewership. Over 50 cities were covered at one point or other and there were dramatics, too. The agitators also prepared themselves as if they were playing to the glare of the cameras or the tune of channels (as some accused), which were "good enough for images and sound bytes".

Such coverage made economic sense too. Channels were not deprived of commercial revenue despite the coverage. In fact, the coverage was an "ad opportunity", too, in a similar way as cricket coverage. Some channels devoted one-third of their prime time news bulletins to commercials. One remarkable fact that stood out was that there was no violence – the TV crews and cameras being there 24/7 helped prevent any untoward incident and anti-social behavior that often happen in such massive congregations.

In this context, it is not merely the longevity of the coverage that is worth looking at, but also the kind of concern with which channels went about covering Anna's crusade – as if it was their own and as if they were making a big difference to the destiny of the nation. That 'concern' did the trick and made the anchors and reporters view it in a proactive manner. If only similar concern can be evoked for other issues, the channels could achieve in six years what the government could not do in 65 years.

Turning Point

The unprecedented way in which the news channels 'covered' Anna Hazare's crusade against corruption using the Lok Pal Bill as a contentious issue (they need one to take on), should be a turning point for channels to come out of certain myths or traps they were operating under. They now realise that they can unleash their power in support of contentious issues as well. Ample evidence is there for channels to come out on their own in a more proactive manner, even though some referred to that as a "disproportionate role" in projecting the Anna movement. The media may not have created the movement, but it was with their collaboration and support that the crusade could be magnified; and triggered a bandwagon effect.

Corruption, in general, is a common denominator with the educated urban youth at the forefront of the agitation. However, corruption in a specific context was hardly dealt with. More significantly, none of the elements of Anna Hazare's campaign did anything to threaten consumerism or undermine advertising (in fact PR and ad agencies rallied too) or clash with the interests of the channel bosses. On the contrary, some bosses, too, took proactive interest (having realised the power of the idea and Anna's arguments) by giving extensive coverage to the agitation. This argument here is more in the context of the power of media and not about the right and wrong aspects of their coverage of Anna. It is also a pointer towards the difference news media can make if it is concerned, takes interest and lends support deliberately to other social causes.

This chapter suggested alternate ways of distinguishing by taking to a different set of content concerns and priorities. No such discussion could be inclusive or comprehensive. An attempt is made to indicate how in specific contexts that pursuit could be. This refocusing of channels on core concerns of people is what I discuss as "needs based" content model.

P N Vasanti's column in Mint, May 31, 2012

A refreshing variation on TV

These issues have been overshadowed or even forgotten by our ratings-driven channels in their fight for eyeballs and amid conflicting interests ....It is a commendable risk taken by Shankar to break the current inertia in television programming

Fine Print | P.N. Vasanti: The unprecedented hype over Aamir Khan's Satyamev Jayate show and the response to it has once again reinforced the power of television in our lives.

The programme is now four episodes and one month old. The first episode touched an emotional chord with many viewers as it discussed the issue of female foeticide. The episodes since then have dealt with sexual abuse of children, dowry and medical malpractice.

The novelty effect and the controversy over Khan, one of Bollywood's biggest stars, bringing up these issues, appears to have waned a little. After the initial euphoria, especially online, attention across the print and electronic media is now slowly shifting to the issues that are being covered. For instance, the tweets on the last episode mostly feature Devi Shetty of Narayana Hrudayalaya and instances of medical negligence.

Clearly, the show is a milestone in Indian television, not just in terms of the production quality but also because of Khan's involvement, simultaneous broadcasts across nine channels in four languages, the show timing of 11am on Sunday instead of evening or weekend prime time, and the unprecedented Twitter trends.

Credit must also be given to Star India Pvt. Ltd chief executive officer (CEO) Uday Shankar for being far-sighted enough to throw his weight behind the show. This Jawaharlal Nehru University graduate and former journalist became CEO in October 2007, when Star was losing its initial popularity and struggling to compete with numerous emerging channels. Since then, he's been trying make the channel's tagline of Soch Nayi (new thinking) come true when it comes to content.

For instance, even the admittedly regressive soaps now have social issues intertwined in their storylines and enlightening the audience seems to be their new motto.

The role of television and its impact on our social mores, values and behaviour is well proven and also widely used in advertising. Very few have used this powerful medium to strategically influence issues that prevail in our society and matter to each one of us. Therefore, this novel attempt of bringing such issues to fore with good research back up, a high-profile celebrity and excellent production quality has been received well.

It's important to note that discussions on social issues similar to those picked up by Satyamev Jayate are not new on Indian television. Regional language channels and news channels have taken up various such issues in different formats, including soaps (remember Rajni, Jasoos Vijay, etc.), reality shows, talk shows, music videos, special campaigns, and of course, documentaries. National broadcaster Doordarshan and some local-language channels have undertaken commendable experiments that have sought to catalyse change in society and individual behaviour.

However, more recently, these issues have been overshadowed or even forgotten by our ratings-driven channels in their fight for eyeballs and amid conflicting interests. This is even more pronounced in the so-called national (read Delhi-based) English and Hindi channels. Even the news channels spend less than 5% of their prime time (7-11 pm) on social development issues as per the annual trend monitoring by CMS Media Lab.

Within this context, Satyamev Jayate is indeed a refreshing variation on our television screens. It is a commendable risk taken by Shankar to break the current inertia in television programming.

Understandably, Satyamev Jayate is not a ready-made resolution to the issues it is raising. It only claims to provide a platform from which people can derive inspiration and based on which they may be able to tailor their own solutions. But the larger question is whether this experiment of 13 episodes raising one crucial issue in each is a viable one. Do the huge resources invested in the production and marketing of this programme make it cost-effective or even viable for such experiments to be replicated? Or, will it go the way of other experiments—hugely popular while it lasts, but with no continuity or spillover?

Clearly, the issues raised need more than one episode for catalysing change in our behaviour. How will it be able to channelise the current interest on the issues raised, beyond generating donations through SMS and online action?

For going beyond traditional entertainment and bringing back crucial issues into the limelight, Shankar and Khan need to be complimented.

Satyamev Jayate certainly boosts the ongoing efforts of numerous activists, civil society and governments on the ground to meet these national challenges. The power of television is finally being put to use—productively.

P.N. Vasanti is director of New Delhi-based multidisciplinary research organisation Centre for Media Studies (CMS). She is a researcher and adviser on policy issues in broadcasting.

Link: http://www.livemint.com/2012/05/30224341/A-refreshing-variation-on-TV.html

Endnotes

1 The Hindu, October 2011

2 In a CMS round table meet on communicating environment in Jaipur on the eve of its Vatavaran film festival many journalists and activists shared their experiences. Harshvardhan,Who had worked with BBC and working with NDTV (at the time of this meet), made these observations.

3 Crime/Update, Crime in India 2015, National Crime Bureau Report, July 2016

4 Amaya Sen, 2005 The Argumentative Indian, London, Penguin

5 Social effects of mass media in India, by N Bhaskara Rao and G N S Raghavan, Gyan publications 1996.

6 As per 2011 census 68.8 percent population was rural. World Bank estimate in 2014 was 67.6 percent. Also see Times of India, 30 August 2012.

7 SME World is an Occasional publication of Indian Express devoted to small and medium size enterprises since 2008.

8 Financial Express, 5 November 2011

9 The Hindu, 29 October, 2011

10 Many news dailies of New Delhi reported in September 2012 about adulteration of milk which some news channels too picked up.

11 *Sakshi:* 22 August, 2012

12 The Hindu, 15 November, 2011

13 Nandi Foundation of Dr Reddy labs in Hyderabad is working charity for better health, education of poor.

14 Space devoted for Parliament coverage when it is in session. Lok Sabha Speaker Somanath Chetterje thanked CMS in a letter for bringing out how media coverage was on decline and how serious issues raised by many individual members was not being covered as against disturbing happenings in the house were being covered.

15 N T Ramarao had become Chief Minister in 1983 having won over whelming majority in a keenly contested assembly election in the combined state of Andhra Pradesh within nine months after he started an altogether new party and with no political background. During less than ten years (1983-94) of his leadership

and chief ministership, N T Rama Rao gave opportunity to altogether new faces mostly from down trodden communities from each of 23 districts. He abolished taluc system of administration to replace with over 1200 mandals to take the govt closer to people. In that process new persons including from women have come up at Village, Mandal, District and assembly and Lok Sabha levels. He even removed the entire cabinet of ministers to bring in new faces all this as never before in fifty years. The figure was arrived at by this writer based on his election studies In the state In the previous more than 25 years.

16 Successive speakers of Lok Sabha as well as other leaders had expressed disappointment and were critical of media priorities in covering parliament at the cost of more serious deliberations in the House and its Committees. They were observing so almost at the end of each session of parliament making no difference in the media coverage except that more recently they are a bit quantifying thanks. PRS Legislative Research, http://www.prsindia.org

17 Election Commission of India.

18 India Today had short lived publication, Media Monitor, (1987) devoted to coverage of developments In Media. It was discontinued too soon.

19 N. Bhaskara Rao, "Controlled Mass Communication", New Delhi, Chand Publication 1972.

20 Sahara Times www.rashtriyasahara.com

21 Middlemen menace is a practice that many citizens experience in availing some of the basic public services while some others pay an unofficial money for that. See CMS India Corruption studies 2005 and 2007 in particular.

22 In one of the interview at the end of India Against Corruption crusade from Ram Lila grounds in New Delhi, Kejariwal himself had gave out these figures, it was first time that "missed call" idea was used for a social campaign.

12

Repositioning and a Way Forward

If news channels pay sa̍me attention to the critical issues of concern for the country, local community and citizens as they do for consumers, markets, politics and investors, but with an intention to make a difference (rather than merely to add viewers), they would herald a new beginning. This has to be in the context of democratic traditions, developmental priorities and good governance concerns. Complexities in each case being what they are such coverage cannot be on an ad-hoc and short term basis. Rather, such coverage should be strategic, sustained and reinforcing with an intention to make a difference and influence people and communities. That is when channels would unleash their positive potential.

But for playing such a role, it is important that certain factors, features, phenomenon, trends, insights, myths, fallacies and short comings needs to be taken note. Some such suggestions are indicated here only as examples for consideration.

Paradigm Shift

The unleashing of potential is not possible without certain innovations and initiatives shifts in the paradigm of channel operations. What are these shifts? There cannot be fixed initiatives for such a shift in the paradigm for all channels. The suggested ones here cannot be exhaustive and inclusive. One is always on the look out to find more. Also, there is nothing like "the Best" for all times in creative crafts and endeavors. One is always trying to achieve the best and do better than before. That is why I have been saying that in creative media "better" could be better than "the best". It is an ongoing process and agonising too. That process to elevate or do better is what matters more. TV is a constantly evolving media because of technological innovations, creative ideas, changing societal values and competitive compulsions. Channels are constantly adapting to face emerging challenges and do more effectively.

If it is understood that creative endeavors are dynamic, the chase of channels is for "the better" in a relative context. The chase to achieve the best in that process is somewhat like chasing the *mirage* where "beating competition does not become the sole criteria". There could be other ways of innovation, excellence and making a difference. Competition of course is a "constant challenge".

A Process View

The process of unleashing or making a difference involves self imposed *dos* and *don'ts.* But, there cannot be dos for all situations or contexts. Similarly, there cannot be don'ts. But, it is possible that both dos and don'ts are needed in some situations to make a difference in the process of unleashing the potential of media. This is where the ingenuity of a writer or a producer matters or a channel operator comes to fore to make the difference.

In the 'process' context, one takes a long term view of things, not something taken in a hurry or through the "rock the boat" approach to remain on the top on a weekly basis. The pursuit of excellence in creative arts is more like a mirage. In that process, there could be cyclical happenings. Being "No.1" for a week may not mean much to be carried away as is often made out by the channels. The best is yet come. In trying to achieve the best one has to do better. That is an ongoing process, particularly in a creative filed. Television offers multiple opportunities to be creative- all the time.

Media are institutions with no specific terminal or deadlines or fixed tenures or durations for their operations. They exist individually with a mandate of their ongoing role as a part of the socio-political system. This is even more so in the case of news channels. Their outlook should not be temporal for a one time view of service. Of course, a channel could make a difference in some cases even with one news item or one programme or a series of efforts. Even deep rooted and structural changes of substantial nature are possible with a long term view and sustained ongoing efforts. Whereas the pursuit of channels hitherto reflects a temporal view, as if it is the current week that matters the most and, somehow, the channel should get rated high on viewership for that week and the next. This temporal view based on weekly performance of the channels (because TRP reports are either weekly or daily as in the case of the online *aMap*) adversely affects their orientation. No wonder why the News Broadcasting Standards Authority, headed by Justice J. S. Verma, (having no stakes in the management of channels) had proposed (August 2011) that TRP reports for news channels should be brought out on a monthly basis, instead of weekly as presently done. Interestingly, however, a majority of channels had opposed such a change (from weekly to monthly reporting). But, TAM the agency which produces TRP reports, maintained that it could change the periodicity only if channels that are the subscribers of its reports, make or agree for such a request. Since not all channels are members of the NBSA, its decision could not be expected to change the practices and priorities of channels. It was expected that the suggestion of Justice Verma should at least make channels to re-think. But, with channels' opposition, the idea itself has been forgotten (as of March 2012) or given up. Why? How come?

From a long term perspective, the endeavor to better the performance of a channel should be a continuing one. Over night or weekly yardsticks for viewership cannot be a criteria or guide for the standing of a channel. In a process, "the best" rated programme or channel at a given point of time does not necessarily reflect the optimum potential and such a short term view only helps in sustaining a channel with in a competitive scene, not in a and dynamic scenario.

To do better has to be a never ending chase. That is why I said that "better (for a week) is better than the best", and the "Best" is yet to come. Such a view implies prospects for long term and sustained endeavors. If a channel is "No. 1" or the "most viewed" in a week, what should it pursue further? What is the motivation for going beyond that level of performance and how should that endeavor be viewed, so that creative pursuits are constant and keep up with newer initiatives and improvements, particularly because creative talent sees no end and the more it is pursued the better it is likely to become (Like more water gets generated in a well each time water is taken out). This process is what I describe as unleashing the power of a channel. What helps this pursuit of unleashing is sensitivity to the surrounding environment and concern for larger and deep rooted socio-political issues rather than going mostly by the constrained opportunities offered by TRP compulsions. It's like doing what others are doing as if that is the benchmark. That is why it is better that the channels consider their endeavors as a 'process' rather than a short term or temporal activity.

Hence, in creative crafts and endeavors, nothing can be categorised as "the best". The best is yet to come; it's always being endeavored, it is constantly evolving from experiences, concerns, insights and by certain initiatives and experiments. This could also be because of changing social values, technological innovations and organisational dynamics. If television channels lose that sensitivity to longer opportunities and fall in the trap of becoming the best rated for the week, it could only become a rat race or a mirage to unleash their own potential.

Innovation and excellence come from insights and learning and that, in turn, should prompt experimentation. The electronic media has unique advantage to experiment with as many ideas and options or alternatives (including in reaching out as focused or target oriented, and yet remain as "mass media"). In fact, if television channels are not engaged in experimentation constantly involving various variables, they are bound to lose their edge and advantage and, ultimately, lose out in the competition itself.

This process of acquiring insights has to be based on reliable and multiple methodologies. There cannot be fixed or all time methods that suit all channels in the same way as is the case now with regard to the TRPs.

First and foremost, the channel managers and producers should, on their own, realise, remember and reiterate certain fundamentals. Sensitivity to these aspects is necessary for channels to unleash their full potential.

Contentious Arguments

Some contentious issues and the arguments that are being put up from time to time could be summed up as:

1. Has the agenda setting function for the country shifted from Assemblies and Parliament to media? Sometimes one gets that feeling. If so, what does it mean in the context of the role of media democracy and responsibilities of elected representatives? In such a situation, should the priorities of news media be left to "market forces" of the day or is there a need for certain moderation or restraints? In May 2011, two Supreme Court Judges have noted that in "such a situation" where things are otherwise driven by market forces as inherent in globalisation, liberalisation and privatisation (LPG), the need for a regulator is all the more felt.

2. Double edged character of media - This potential is known, but what is not so much realised is the fact that the negative potential of media drives faster, gains momentum and spreads faster. If such trends are not checked or/and moderated, as felt by the two Supreme Court Judges, the real potential of channels never gets a chance of having an impact beyond the markets. If so, who should be the moderating agency – the civil society or the government or the media itself or all of them together and individually?
3. Homogenising diversities - A fundamental objective of consumerism is to emerge, expand and entrench into a "mass market". It means narrowing or marginalising regional differences of all sorts. This plurality, which we often site as a unique strength, could be under threat as media tend to cater and promote consumerism by promoting a "mass market". More is not merrier for plurality and regional diversities, which is too evident with the kind of proliferation and boom in the cross media scenario. The other implication of this phenomenon is that "choice", as implied in proliferation and growth, becomes merely notional. Choice becomes narrow as media contents become "more often the same" with respect to their priorities, structure and content. To sustain that process, channels have to become bigger and bigger. This trend also implies emergence of monopolies across the media. That is how two competing groups, Zee TV and Star TV, surprised everyone in May 2011 by coming together (Zee+Star). Together, Zee and Star account for 40 per cent of TV viewers in the country and almost two-thirds of the revenues. Now, MSOs, who were fighting each other until recently, too have come together to increase their bargain power with broadcasters. Earlier, there were such "coming together" arrangements between The Hindu and The Deccan Chronicle; between The Hindu and NDTV; and between DNA and Dainik Bhaskar – all to maximise their market reach. Similarly, the Reliance Industry has taken significant hold on TV-18 (CNN-IBN and other channels) by aligning ETV channels with this group.
4. Mass markets -: This trend in media and among channels is attributed (in one to one discussions) to TRPs. TRPs tend to lure channels to "more of the same" and promote the trend to become a market phenomenon because that is the path for mass

markets. And, the notion of mass markets is based on "consumerism". Consumerism, in turn, is based on motivating people to buy, use, change irrespective of a need or essentiality (all that in such a way that one's own temporary comforts or advantages, even if at someone else's cost or discomfort, are sought). Thus, mass media, particularly, satellite based channels thrive more by supporting and sustaining consumerism, mass markets, sparking greed in individuals and temporal interests.

5. Is greed a driving force? Competition is good, particularly in creative fields. Yes, with increased competition between channels, the technical quality of their contents and range and quality of programmes should change for better. But, the speed of proliferation of channels and the intensity of competition between them in the last couple of years (2005–2011) was such that there is no evidence of commensurate increase in the concerns and relevance of channels to make a difference. In fact, quick proliferation and the compulsions of "survival" in terms of viability have made them to rely more on greed in individuals than on the "need" aspect of people.
6. Bolstering individual or personality dimension is more characteristic of media coverage than community or societal or value dimensions. This trend in concerns and coverage pampers "I" more than "We" and "Us", "yesterday" and "today" more than "tomorrow" and "day after" (greed). Consequently, the organised sectors, corporates and markets get reflected more than the unorganised sector and civil society. In the process, channels depend more on mediators like public relations, lobbies and advertising agencies. Most of what one sees in the contents of news media is at the instance of those elements.
7. Preferring conflicts - Perhaps unwittingly, media tend to divide or segment people or/and pamper and prompt conflicts between individuals and groups. This is even more so in the case of television channels (perhaps because of the nature of technology and the structure of business). Conflict resolution is not a concern or priority of media as much as conflicts. Conflicts of all kinds are not unusual phenomenon of all kinds anywhere. As the old ones get resolved, new ones arise (how do the old ones get resolved and the new ones crop up and are coped with? Media are a source for that process). The media role is important in

that process. Conflict resolution requires special efforts and even skills. Also, for the resolution of a conflict, media need to have first such an intention or inclination. The compulsions of the "model" being followed (as required for TRP) are such that they have the elements for sustaining conflicts. More often, channels appear to believe that in life, negative contents attract more viewers rather than the positives ones. There is a myth in this regard that is being perpetuated – that conflicts, negative contents and deviation in behavior attract more and get more viewership rating.

8. The basic human values associated with relationships between people and their association and linkage with environment matters much less for channels. But, the cause and effect dilemma haunts the media. The sensitivity and concern that a particular coverage may cause and lead to certain efforts, immediate or delayed, is secondary to media. For example, take the issue of channels reporting the "vote casting rate (price)" on the eve of polling in a keenly contested Assembly or Lok Sabha election. Such repeated reporting could have two different impacts on the people – it could either prevent people from taking that money or it could increase the expectations of voters for getting a higher price for their vote. In other words, such coverage creates demand and increases supply. Similarly, the reporting of climbing a water tank by an unemployed youth could alert authorities, but, at the same time, it could also prompt imitation by more youth as an easy way to get the attention. Showing a crime on TV, for example, a rape case, could be a cause or/and effect. Another example is the "abortion clinics". The more the media reports about such centers, the more such incidents happen. For preventing any such thing, the structure of reporting by channels has to be different than what it normally is and calls for different kind of skills.

9. The checks and balance approach - Fourth Estate notion has given news media a feeling of being much beyond the rights and privileges of individual citizen and justify even an arbitrary position and coverage. This, in turn, makes media to resist external or societal questioning, as and when media coverage causes or promotes deviant behavior; whereas a better course is respecting the "checks and balance" approach where everyone (all the Estates of the

State) in a society maintains limits on his/her own and at the instance of others. Equilibrium in such functioning is good for everyone to bring out the best in him/her for the society and people. Out of such sensitivity should arise the issue of accountability and responsibility.

How far can a precedent of yester years justify when the paradigm of media operations is no longer the same? Until a few years ago, even after independence, for example, neither profit nor mass market view were the sole criteria for media. Unfortunately, today they have become the primary concerns. Earlier, content priorities were decided by a professional editor; today it is the proprietor or the manager, who decides the direction. Earlier, independent trusts were operating media; today it is more corporate operated with other business and/or political interests. And expansion vertically and horizontally as fast as the business interests is part of that process. Against such shifts in the paradigm and compulsions, can we expect similar self restraint as before (or is self restraint alone good enough today)?

10. Transparency in operations, ownership and control aspects is far more significant in the case of news media; it's even more so in the case of news channels. Given the kind of ever changing scenario, which includes mergers, acquisitions, and in the interest of those, who are in control of media, it is important that there is transparency about those dynamics. If stocks of media companies or those having major share holding are traded in the market, and media reporting is meant to benefit those stocks, does it auger well for objectivity and balanced reporting?

    Why should media establishments be outside the purview of RTI Act? By bringing them under the Act, media could better their credibility. No channel ever tried to sensitise viewers as to its record on certain basic parameters, like conflict of interest aspects, independence, objectivity and fairness doctrine.

11. Spectacle, not simplicity - Spectacle fascinates channels and gets special attention. Television channels prefer to fascinate their viewers rather than provoking or motivating their sensitivities. Spectacle and glamour in presentation and often repeat and hype of contents is what television channels are known for. Often simple, but sincere happenings will not get as much priority in coverage as

the ones with glamour and spectacle. This is apart from the interest in crime, sex and other such luring elements.

12. Not the basic issues of people - A myth prevalent among TV channels is that basic issues of people involving pathetic experiences, life struggle and deprivations, do not interest viewers (as they do not like to see the same again); instead they prefer to see glamour and dreamy and deviant behaviors, like crime, sex, etc. Finding certain scope to present ideas or themes in an interesting (luring!) way is the crux of coverage for which the creativity, innovation and ingenuity of producers is needed. That is what could be the differentiator for a channel or programme from the other. For example, what is the basic premise of "reality shows" of channels? More often, such programmes belittle the sensibilities of people.

The channels should direct their strategies more towards maximising these features.

Correctives in the paradigm should not always come from channels or the government. It should come from the viewers themselves, although government policies and content elements do matter. But, they alone cannot yield the kind of changes or correctives that are needed from time to time for keeping the channels distinct.

Clutches of New Gatekeepers

The growth of Indian media in the years beyond 2000 has been described as unprecedented anywhere. But the growth opportunities are far more than what has been realised in the last decade.

a. The paradigm shift that has come during the last decade appears irreversible currently, as that trend is global and has the backing of global investors, marketers and corporates. More often, it is facilitated by the governments. But the opportunity to change has to be explored to excel in the increasingly competitive media scenario. Hence, media consumers need to be more active and discriminative.

b. News media need to get "out of the clutches" of the "new gatekeepers" by coming up with a new strategy for contents. If this new model has to be a win-win one, then, it has to take up the needs approach where contents not only interest people, but also are in the interest of people.

c. (If market has to be the indirect regulator), then, users, citizens and civil society groups have to be active, articulate and even argumentative and, for sure, discriminative.

d. The research, today, is more focused on monitoring and is often misleading and caters to competitive interests. There is a need for independent, transparent and longitudinal research on trends and effects, not merely indicative or surrogate type for preference or liking.

e. In fact, education is the best bet for introducing correctives and standards in media. Such skills, capabilities and concerns need to be built into the educational system. Otherwise, more "copy cat" skills would be acquired at the prime age.

The movers and shakers of media including news media are the same "new gatekeepers" across the globe. For example, the phenomenon of "paid news", as noticed a few years ago in India, is now being talked about even in China. Shanghai correspondent of New York Times[1] described at length on April 2012 how "cash buys Press, TV coverage", although the Chinese regulations too ban paid promotions without labeling them as such. He described that such a practice of "masquerading as news" is so wide spread that many news media have rate cards listing the "news-for-sale prices". However it was not clear from this article how much this practice of "paid news" is present in the context of "getting to positions of power" in China as in the case of India.

Is Impact on Society a Concern?

It is too well known that circulation of newspapers is increasing and that was more due to the fact that in recent years, the TV channels have proliferated as never before. But is there any evidence to assume that influence and impact of media on society has also increased or is increasing? Of course, in the case of markets, there is such evidence.

Society is much more than markets; it is inclusive of all sections of people, all institutions including family, culture and customs. Society is concerned more about long term relationships and implications to living conditions of people, deep rooted social concerns, including phenomena like corruption, for example. Media has been covering corruption for long and that coverage has gone up significantly in the last couple of years (even before Anna Hazare's movement). But is there any evidence that such increased media coverage has contributed in curbing corruption?

The news media of the country, of course, deserve credit for exposing many big scams involving corruption in the government and political leaders in the more recent years. They are also pursuing such happenings vigorously facilitated by the RTI Act.

The growth of media has been phenomenal. Despite the boom, the overall reach of media, in relation to the total population, has expanded only marginally in the last decade – (going by NRS, IRS), perhaps because contents and content priorities of news media are of not much consequence to one-third or more people, who are outside the reach of all mass media. Today, the contents of media cater more to the markets, not society. Has this phenomena been seriously looked into? Not so much. The CMS Media Lab, over the decade, has revealed that despite proliferation and boom in numbers, there is no change in the content priorities of news media. But there are signals in 2011 and 2012 from some individual channels that are trying to come out of such a content model.

We know that television in particular has double edged character in terms of effects. But what is not so much studied is that the negative effects of TV drive and spread faster, irreversibly and immediately. Such a trend has been indicated by media research.

Those who are concerned about society want some restrains and responsibility on the part of the broadcasters in particular. Those who are concerned about markets do not want it, as that would imply regulation. They are not in favor of any restrains on the contents of news media. The reasons are obvious. The ones interested in the markets are organised and are also skilled to use media to sway public opinion and even bully the powers as and when required. The former, the ones concerned about the society and about future, speak in general, in isolation and often in conflicting voices.

That is how criteria and yardsticks are promoted to decide the policies on such concerns and priorities. That is how TRP has come into being and has become the currency of the industry. It caters to the market demands, not so much the interests of society. It is not just a question of sample size of TRPs, it is the very concept, its objectivity, the methodology followed and the way TRPs are used (or misused) as benchmarks to prioritise contents. In this process, what is doled out is what interests viewers momentarily or as surrogate for "what is in the interests of people and society". And as drivers of that process, there are "new gatekeepers" - all self appointed champions of markets. They guard the interests of markets even at the cost of the foundations of society and the credibility of media as the Fourth Estate. In this process, the overall credibility and potential of media to make a difference positively has declined, but the solace is that it has declined the world over, not just in India, and across all other wings of public life. The malice is deeper.

But newspapers should thank news channels. Because of the "appetiser effect" of news bulletins of channels, newspapers have revived their credibility and are reinventing their markets and their relevance. They are now repositioning to sustain themselves.

What is Differentiating?

What difference does the coverage by a news channel make on its own and in what respect and in what direction that difference is evident?

Is the power of media same in the context of social change and social development – as in the case of consumerism, brands and markets or politics and entertainment? This is a question often raised in academic circles and by concerned civil society groups. A certain view gaining ground in this context is that, if at all, the influence of media is not the same. But it is not about television per se, as it is more related to contents strategies and content priorities of channels.

It is not merely a general belief, but research over the years has indicated that the mass media influences are less when the change involved is attitudinal and value or behavior based. "Awareness" alone being the concern of media in such situations will not be good enough to "motivate" or "influence" people. Awareness could only be an essential first step, but it does not assure or ensure the more critical next steps involving behavioural changes. Mass media's influence is limited mostly to such a role, unless it is preceded or/and accompanied by other efforts at interpersonal or group level or in conjunction with other social media. That was one of the reasons for the top down media news flow model and that is why channels' concerns remained limited and "constrained". To do more, further and beyond this model, channels need to adopt an "engagement model" with an intention to bring change or influence by way of structure of coverage or in the very scope of coverage.

Sensitivities of News Media

Quite often one hears that media lacks sensitivity to societal issues, which are related to societal values and concerns, such as equity and social justice. For some critics, it is a fashion to criticise media on that count and this criticism has been there for long. Such criticism of media however, has increased and spread further since the recent proliferation following the privatisation, liberalisation and corporatisation of media. The root cause for larger insensitivity to such issues could be traced back to the educational system and economic compulsions. But, this phenomenon could also be described as a chicken and egg syndrome. At the same time, certain special role of mass media in that process could be reiterated. This role could be actualised by way of promoting or perpetuating those concerns, values and priorities. It requires the media to play a proactive role by not limiting itself to a "reflective role". Such a role requires venturing beyond the "reporting view" of a journalist.

In this context, observations of two distinguished scholars are relevant to recall. Nobel laureate Amartya Sen's frequent observations could be said to be at the bottom of the current dilemma, including the criticism that the media is facing. These are: one-dimensional way of looking at people; clash of civilisations leading to confusion on the very identities of people, which, in turn, has led to a tendency to partition people into color, creed, majority, minority, rich and poor. Writing in The Hindu recently, Amartya Sen specified two "barriers" to quality in the Indian news media, which are laxity in professionalism in achieving accuracy and the bias in the choice of what news to cover and what to ignore, and the way this bias relates particularly to class divisions in India. This bias in coverage may not be unpleasant, but it "contributes quite heavily to political apathy"[2]

[3]Another noted scholar Noam Chomsky, talking in the context of his favorite themes of exploitation, deception and media, contends that concern for human rights, sensitivities to minorities, gender and ecological issues is what brings balance in developmental endeavors, social justice and sustaining human values. When in December 1948, the United Nations General Assembly adopted and proclaimed Universal declaration of Human Rights, the mass media was not so wide spread. Otherwise, mass media would have been specifically included as part of that declaration. In such a situation, the model of news media in particular would have been altogether different than what we ended up having now.

Once a television channel gets liberated from a fixed content model based on TRPs in chalking out its destinies, the chances to distinguish it will improve and a more inclusive framework would be possible. The insights of Amartya Sen and Noam Chomsky offer scope for such a framework for repositioning of channels. One may as well find other such holistic insights.

A. Equilibrium Between Channels

An analysis of monthly viewership shares of English news channels for 32 months (2009, 2010 and 2011) brings out a relative trend in viewership rating. The three English news channels, which project themselves as national, account (according to TRP) for more than 70 per cent of share in English news channels viewership. But, what is interesting, is that during these 32 months (up to August 2011), the trend between the three was almost constant. There was marginal difference in the trend in a few months, but that was insignificant to indicate a major initiative or shift by any of the three channels. It was perhaps because there was no strategic or deliberate change in the contents/programmes of these three English news channels during the period.

A similar analysis of four Hindi news channels which account for about 55 percent of Hindi viewership (as per TRP) for 32 months do not reveal significant differentiation in the positioning strategy of the news channels. But it reveals that the variation in the case of Hindi News Channels was marginal and much less than English news channels, perhaps, because the number of Hindi news channels competing with each other is much more than in the case of English News channels.

It's important to note here that viewership trend being so consistent and also uniform (over 32 months) where is the competition or are the channels trying to reach equilibrium? Where are the "push and pull" (of competition) factors that differentiate contents? Impact on viewership or changes in viewership patterns between channels will be evident only if there are major, deliberate initiatives with regard to content topics, format, participation, etc. The chase for eyeballs does not seem to prompt experimentation or initiatives in content or schedule strategies. What other insight could be drawn from this analysis.

Between 2001 and 2008, inflation in media (ad) rates was less than three per cent in real terms (according to R. K. Swamy's Media Directions) including television. What does this stagnation mean? More likely, this could mean no thrust towards spending more for variety in contents, their quality and relevance, etc. This was also because of stagnation (or leveling off) in viewership. The ad tariff and ad revenue inflow, too, has remained, more or less, the same or it has seen only marginal change. This is also the case with regard to News channels and reminds the scope for a break through.

It was against this background that NDTV English is seen as trying to come out of TRP grip and take to some "social development" campaigns and promote them extensively. NDTV is trying (experimenting) with a variety of contents, peeping out of the TRP model. This is perhaps because this channel has either slipped in its ratings or, more importantly, it does not bother to become the Number One Channel (as per TRPs). That is how it has taken to collaborative/sponsored(?) programmes mostly on hitherto neglected issues of social development that are amenable for extensive promotion, while earning revenue too in that process. (This analysis was made before NDTV filed its suit against TAM's principles in New York court in August 2012).

Some news channels try to distinguish by "shouting" more than the other channels, as if they have taken "*bhang*"; they either go on and on the same point/discussion for too long or repeat the same visual again and again, or present news with the anchor standing instead of sitting at desk.

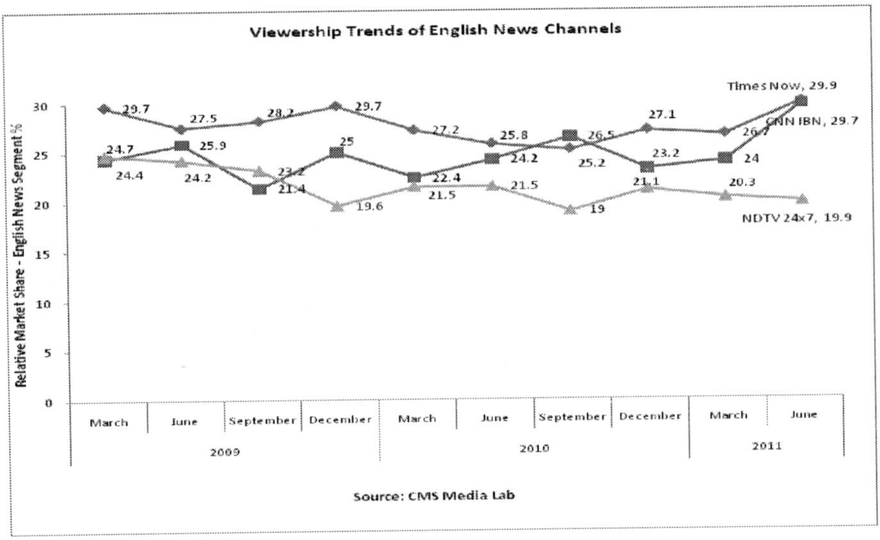

B. Do Channels Have a "Self Belief"?

What has been the focus of News Channels? The focus on contents indicates or reflects the concerns and priorities of a channel. How do they perceive and position themselves with regard to such a focus? How do they claim or describe that? For some, it may be only a marketing strategy. A quick analysis of two dozen news channels (in Hindi and English in October, 2011) of their claims as indicated in the tagline at the bottom of their name logo, brings out that the outlook of news channels is not so much about impact or difference they try to make. Their positioning is more in the context of a "race" with other channels rather than a vision (only one channel - Doordarshan News claims a vision). The claim is more for being "the best", "speed", reflecting "lifestyle", "experience" and "truth". More channels claim "speed" in giving "news" as their focus. The way some news channels have adopted their tagline is similar to how consumer brands have positioned themselves.

Some news channels have adopted a slogan or *shlokam,* like *"Tamso Ma Jyotirgamaya"* (take us from darkness to light), more as a decoration rather than something which is reflective of their content focus or objective.

What is in a name? Some channels like Zee News, India TV, Live India have changed their "tag lines" in the last two or three years just like consumer brands. For example, India TV changed from "*Badalte Bharat ki Tasveer*" to "*Aap ki Awaaz*". Someone else changed from "*Shreshtha*" to "*Sarva Shreshtha*".

News channels should have a self belief related to the what, how and why aspects – only then, they can distinguish in a scenario of multiplicity of news channels and the competitive compulsions between them.

I remember when the discussion came up in Shastri Bhavan in 1974, it was the first Director General of Doordarshan (P V Krishnamurthy), who chose the *"Satyam Shivam Sundaram*" tagline, which was displayed prominently as Doordarshan's "pursuit", but over the years, that was downgraded and slowly reduced and even removed and replaced as if indicative of change that DD had gone through. Today, it is "vision of India" for DD News. Krishnamurthy argued that he wanted Doordarshan to reflect good and bad aspects of life as well as beauty, knowledge and grace, etc.

Most of these news channels advertise in their own channels as well as in the print media as to how they are the "first" in reporting one or other "news", or/and how they have made a difference in correcting a mistake in the public domain on the basis of a report in their channel (although that news flashed in all news media at the same time). Such a claim does not indicate the channel's "role" or "mission" or its viewer orientation. But it does reflect a self belief or anxiety to promote the channel with "claims" in the same way as consumer brands do.

To what extent and how consistently and seriously channels endeavor to achieve a self proclaimed mission? "*Spoorte*" (inspiration) is what another channel claims. On the other hand, for example, TV-9 (Telugu) claims (Merugaina Samajam) "For a Better Society" as its tag line; it repeatedly campaigns against caste, dowry, corruption, etc. with slogans, and also some promotional spots on those themes. Also, the chief of that channel talks against such social barriers whenever he talks in the pubic and tries to justify the tagline. The orientation of the tagline is more with the receiving end. In fact, some other news channels in Telugu, which came after TV-9, too have such claim as their tag line (like "public good every second", "with you to support you"). One news channels has "on your side" as its tagline, but it doles out more of the same as any other news channel, indicating nothing of that sort in the contents as claimed in the tag line.

C. The Idea of 24x7 News

A critical appraisal of round the clock (24X7) news channels gives the impression that they have reached a plateau in their viewership. The concept of "round the clock news" is neither adding to the growth of viewership nor to any significant expansion of channels individually or together. News channels realise this trend. "News content" in a news channel now (2012) comprises [4]hardly one-fifth of time against twice the duration earlier at the outset. With multiplicity of news channels in the same language/region, the compulsions of competition are such that they require constant experimentation and innovation. Going by TRPs, news channels have started prominently including cinema, crime, cooking, yoga, spiritual/religion, vastu, sports, tourism, adventure, etc. Some news channels have taken to topics like health, skill development, youth, agriculture, etc. But there is no evidence to confirm that all those add on programmes have increased the viewership. At the most, such a mix of programmes had enabled channels to hold on or retain viewership in a relative context. After the first two or three years of 24x7 news channels, the time actually devoted for news of the day or week has come down from 15 hours (out of 24) to 10 hours a day and now to much less time (even after including repeats (most news channels repeat programmes between mid night and 5 a.m.).

It was, perhaps, because of lack of concern and priority for impact; it was just to figure prominently in TRPs. The per cent of "passive viewers", more often, is much higher than active viewers. The extent of repeat and the nature of repeat by 24-hour news channels often inhibit serious or active viewing. And then crowding the screen with too many points to read or/and see.

"Breaking News" and later "First on" or "Exclusive" and, more recently, "What is Making News" and the like measures may be of interest for a short period at the most. Such "gimmicks" (of competition) do not help distinguish a channel even for the "speed" in giving information. Viewers prefer speed along with definitiveness or specific-ness and "contextual relevance" of such information. There is the possibility of one or other such breaks and scrolls going wrong fully or partly, which means eroding the very credibility of news bulletins. Most news channels must have experienced such situations more than once. Such scrolls may be relevant during days of crisis and calamity. This is how CMS field surveys in Andhra Pradesh in the last couple of years, during the period of proliferation of news channels in Telugu, had indicated the beginning of certain repulsiveness or irritation for round the clock news channels. The preference, instead, is for a channel with a couple of comprehensive news bulletins a day.

D. The Idea of Prime Time

What is prime time? How was this prime time demarcated? Why was it needed? In general parlance, prime time in the context of television viewership is the time when maximum number of viewers are likely or expected to view (or pooled to view) with some regularity. Why should this idea of prime time be constant and apply in the same way for all types of channels particularly for news channels? And for all days? Why it should be alike for all regions of the country?

Prime time idea has come into use and has become a benchmark in the "industry" as a spin of TRPs. This has gained ground to "assure" and cater to the interests of advertisers. That is what it is meant for and used for.

The idea is more a part of urban life styles, not so much to rural and certain occupations or vocations. This could be a reason for why viewership has not expanded or gained among certain sections. For example, for women, the 6–11 pm prime time is not as convenient as the 2–4 p.m. But, then, women were not so much a concern at the time when the prime time idea was floated.

[5]Unless the idea is better understood, the potential of channels cannot be explored in a better way. For example, it could be argued that one reason why despite proliferation of channels, their reach has not expanded commensurately last decade is because their focus is limited to a "primetime". By focusing on 7 to 11 pm as primetime, channels are already limiting themselves to one-sixth of their potential (6/24); instead of 24x7, they are focusing on 4x7. This idea was designed keeping in view more of those in the "organised sector", urban conveniences and those whom advertisers prefer to reach, and those whose lifestyle is more or less similar, stable and somewhat fixed. The ones whose time schedules are flexible, doubtful and are from unorganised sectors, cannot be "lured" in the same way with (targeted?) programmes? Sometimes, those may not be even aimed at by channels. Anna Hazare's fast at Ramlila ground was covered by news channels for 13 days and all through as live. Has that changed the viewership pattern or fluctuated significantly between prime time and non-prime time? Consider the instances of floods in Mumbai or the terrorist attack on Mumbai – was there any significant difference in viewership at various time points of those days.

Prime time is more a marketing idea to build loyalty for a channel. For that, it focuses on a time chunk with two or three programmes. A general marketing strategy is to maximise viewership on a few rather than across programmes/time segments. The prime time idea is part of such a strategy. Should every channel follow that pattern is the next question. Is this helping expand the overall reach of news channels? This is yet another idea to cater more to the advantage of advertisers.

While convenience of time matters, the regularity in viewership is the direct result of functionality of programmes. Viewership depends more on relevance and, of course, interest that a programme serves and also the lure angle that it might involve. As such, channels should focus on making every programme/every time slot a "prime time, which is not limited to two or three hours of a day, but which is forever and at all the places.

Has there been any experiment to redefine this "prime time" concept? It has to be done by individual channels. This idea of prime time could be reviewed as a part of "disruptive programming" that news channels could consider repositioning themselves.

The Practice of Fixed Point Chart

In the present world of instant communication, live coverage and competitive compulsions, old ideas of operating channels limit their scope, particularly, in the case of round the clock news channels. One such outlived idea is the 'Fixed Point Chart"(FPC) where programme schedules were prefixed by cycles. When this idea became a practice, the technology, competition and news media scenario was different. The cycle at one time was year long, later, it was 13 weeks long. Programmes were organised or restricted by those pre-fixed time slots or schedules. This idea limits the programme initiatives and, more importantly, the potential to differentiate a channel. Equally important, fixed time slots do not allow justice for the complex topics of discussion to be comprehended at viewer end. With better technologies in hand, it should be possible to reduce the duration of fixed point chart for a week if it cannot be scrapped altogether. That should also be possible with the kind of programme promotion options now available within the channel and on other media/new media/social media. These days, the frequency of "disruption" of FPC is more than a decade old, when a news channel either had to replace pre-scheduled programme altogether or change the time schedules. Technology is no longer an inhibiting factor.

Because of this FPC practice, complex subjects too are being tried to compete within 26 or 27 minutes (30 minutes schedules). There are, of course, exceptions when some news channels go beyond such limits as in the case of the coverage of Anna Hazare, floods, terrorist activities, etc. Just think how a complex subject like press freedom could be discussed in 27 minutes by a panel of four experts and a talkative anchor.

Fixed Point Chart idea belongs to the radio era when one had to plan early enough to mobilise personnel (engineers, announcers, producers, artists, etc) and where studio facilities were limited. That was how it was in the earlier years of DD. Today, with changed scenario and competitive scene such a compulsion is not there. Also, there is "out sourcing" of programmes and programme promotion. It is time that the News channels get themselves liberated from this "Fixed Point" idea.

They need to be dynamic enough and geared up to give live as well as networked programmes anytime keeping viewer end compulsions. However, to convince, there could be a "programme schedule" for the week. What is a compulsion is a programme promotion. For this, channels should come up with new ways of going about, as they do during the times of Lok Sabha or Assembly elections and emergency situations.

New News Channels Taking to Old Models

Most often, news channels come into being by taking to or going by TRP framework or taking the advice of a consultant to whom TRP is the ultimate guiding factor and who has given the same advice to other clients, i.e., channels, too. As a result, the new ones are filtering away an opportunity and becoming the "also ran" types despite initial enthusiasm to be different. But the case of launch of Rajya Sabha channel (December 2011) explains the height of the phenomenon of taking to a beaten track, despite there being no compulsion to go by TRPs. They may be doing so in anticipation of support from advertising agencies, though they have a role model in the Lok Sabha channel that has achieved serious viewership by taking to a distinct content model.

Rajya Sabha channel started to telecast a month before the Winter Session of 2011 with three hour daily broadcasts. It is good that it included news bulletins in its package unlike the Lok Sabha channel. But the distinction ends there. The news bulletins of Rajya Sabha channel did not give any signal for something new or a different content model.

Some 300 more news channels could be expected to become operational across the country once their applications get cleared in the coming months/year. It means that as many new news channels will be added as there are already. Is it going to be more of the same? How else are they going to be different? How many of the existing will get merged or change their status? How many new channels will come up with distinct content models?

Fixed point of chart is an outdated concept particularly for news channels. This is an inhibiting practice from taking initiatives and for differentiating contents. Yet, the Rajya Sabha channel had taken to Fixed Point Chart from the very outset. This channel also provides good example of how channels, which start without a positioning strategy in a competitive scenario, end up nowhere. Here, it is worth pondering over if the Rajya Sabha channel would end up as yet another "news channel" like NDTV or Aaj Tak or is it like Lok Sabha channel with distinct content strategy and also a positioning strategy as a public service channel?

How can the Rajya Sabha channel expect to take up complex and contentious issue for discussion in 30 minutes with one ad break and five participants in all? Think of it - what will be use of that discussion if the topic is as complex or confused as "Should electronic media come under purview of Press Council of India", as if the discussion is in terms of "Yes" and "No" bytes.

Yet another aspect that matters for making viewers comprehend better and become wiser in that process is that participants in such contentious discussions should indicate at the outset their "conflict of interest" if any, as anchor introduction generally do not indicate that perspective or the possible angle of the participants.

A newly started (November 2011) news channel like Rajya Sabha channel, could introduce such practices instead of mimicking the practices of older channels. If news channels also become copycats, it is nothing but flittering away of an opportunity to make channels potential forums for good governance and functional democracy.

Whereas, on the other hand, the HMTV in Telugu (2010) started departing from the existing TRP driven model by taking to "interactive and open house" format based programmes on contentious issues, which most other channels were avoiding, like dividing the State of Andhra Pradesh by forming a separate Telangana State. This channel first went out with open public hearing discussions across the State, covering both sides of the divide with "disa-dasa" (new directions) This "open to anyone" format was never before tried by any news channel for catching a truly public expression on a burning issue of the day. Secondly, it was a live telecast with no scope to edit and curb or curtail a speaker from making the point. Thirdly, most importantly, the duration is not a fixed 30 minutes or one or two hours; but the discussion lasts as long as there are speakers and everyone, who wants to speak, gets a chance. Some of these live telecasts went on for four to six hours at a stretch. Fourthly, the chief (MD) of the channel himself moderated and anchored the programme and demonstrated his commitment for a serious debate by giving an opportunity to as many people and to different viewpoints.

That is how this channel, despite of being known in some quarters as a pro-separatist, became a relatively popular channel in both the sides of State and won the CMS Academy news channel award as well as other awards. Even on the TRP count, it achieved the fourth place out of 14 Telugu news channels in Andhra Pradesh – all in a matter of less than a year of its launch.

Yet another recent example of a channel that adopted a more inclusive approach, as against the TRP based, is that of a Tamil news channel called Puthlya Thalaimurai Tamil News Channel (July 2011). In a matter of six months, this news channel excelled the market leader (Sun News TV) in the already crowded news media scenario. In fact, this news channel continues to improve its rating even going by TRPs (Its market share in viewership had gone up from 25 per cent in December 2011 to 29 per cent in January 2012). How did it distinguish itself? First, it advertised and positioned itself as an independent news forum with focus on "issues and concerns of people" (rather than that of political parties/leaders). Its unique point was its intent to give unbiased news coverage and giving contents with focus on basic needs of people of the State. That is how it expects to achieve break-even in less than two years (against industry's benchmark of three years!). This news channels could perhaps achieve this feat because the promoter was from education business and with academic background, which hardly any other serious news channel could claim. Yet another feature of this Tamil news channel is that its staff is governed by a publicly stated code of conduct and it ensures that there is no conflict of interest.

Another news channel (NTV – Telugu), when it started (2007), it took up surveys as its differentiator – surveys on politics, personalities and performance of government and then in the context of elections to State Assembly. That did help the launch of the channel and the Surveys helped repeat a special programme more than a couple of times.

Disruptive Programming

Contents of the television channels, today, are based on certain misleading notions and formula adopted mostly on the basis of surrogate viewership yardsticks and as a reaction or in response to competitive compulsions. This practice, in many ways, has limited, restrained and constrained creative caliber and the genius of channels. This is also true in the case of news channels. This is not only with regards to the subject of contents, but also their scope, structure, schedule, formats and even participative aspects. Tinkering with marginal changes will not do anything for distinguishing news channels. All practices require a relook, a review and redesign. That is not possible without systematically "disrupting" the present priorities, practices, schedules and systems of deciding the contents, programming patterns, etc. What is needed as an interim measure, before the channel starts distinguishing itself, is "disruptive programming'. This involves doing differently with respect to time schedules, formats, subjects, participation, and even studio design, dress codes, and durations of various programmes (could be shorter or longer than at present), tagline, etc. A recent Gemini News channel's attempt to present Telugu news bulletins from outside studio, from a market or street corner is one such example (whether it has made a difference has to be talked by the channel).

Disruptive programming calls for more creative initiatives, quickness in execution and mounting programmes spontaneously from within the channel. The duration of such a period could be six to 12 months during which period it should go for strategic research to facilitate and lead on to a new programming phase without losing viewers in the process.

Disruptive programming should lead to distinguish the channel from its competitors. Innovative initiatives have to be far more daring (full of risks!) and executed confidently, backed by promotion strategy. The ingenuity of channel operators (producers) should be evident.

A good example for a channel to start disruptive move could be by way of redefining the very idea and practice of "prime time". The way the screen is used with bottom lines like "breaking news" could be done in another way. Changing tagline or/and converting it into practice in programming and program schedules is another type of disruptive programming.

Transformable Programmes

Elements that sustain human sensitivities, like the five elements of nature that sustain environment - Bhumi, Agni, Gali, Aakasam, Neeru and the nine "soft corners" of people (anger, luster, greed, jealousy, pity, love etc.) are used to interest and lure people to programmes of television channels, including news channels.

Based on field research over the years, it is suggested that a "needs based programming " is more likely to work better and give better results in terms of viewership, impact and positioning of a channel in the long run. The needs based strategy for a news channel consists of more "entertainment-education-informative-empowerment" based contents (More specifically, this could be soft areas where television hitherto made hardly any difference). This broadly means programmes that empower viewers, activate them as citizens, discerning consumers, sensitise parents, etc. and build capacities to resolve conflicts locally. To make such a difference, one has to have a strategy and sustained efforts. In this process, there cannot be fixed formula or dos and don'ts that will work in every situation and for every channel. Things have to be dynamic with contents that have potential to lead and elevate viewers and people to higher levels of life styles, civic life, productive role, human relationships, etc.

Interesting, But not in the Interest

This dilemma is more obvious in the case of TV channels than in the case of print media. What induces or motivates people to watch a channel more than other? Obviously it is the interest that the content arises in the viewers.

Making a viewer interested to look at the screen, even if it is the same content that is being shown again and again, does not necessarily mean that it is also "in the interest" of the viewer in the immediate context or otherwise. In fact, it happens in exceptional cases when a channel shows something that is "interesting" to look at and is also "in the interest" of the viewers, particularly to more viewers if not to as many viewers; and if not immediately, then at least, in the long run. Such content could be described as a "win-win offer". It is interesting to see that the TV could also be "luring" people to look at it. The viewers may get lured because of the relevance of the content or because of one or other susceptibility of individuals. Such elements of susceptibility or temptations include, sex, violence, crime, glamour, greed, love, anger, valor, etc. The difference between the two positions – greed based and need based - could be subtle and often, it may not even get noticed.

To the extent viewers are discriminative of what to see, they are likely to view something that is considered of some interest by them. Since viewership or looking at of a screen is what matters for getting TRP and since getting TRP is a compulsion, channels tend to focus more on that only. Anything else, "in the interest" of viewers matters only after making people to look at the screen.

To produce something in the interest of viewers requires more efforts, some concern, some resources and, may be, a technique in the presentation. Whereas producing content merely "to interest" the viewers may not necessarily require all those efforts. To produce something that will attract viewers would be relatively easier, much quicker and may not need as much resources. But over time, such contents may not be of consequence and may cause alienation or passivism of some viewers.

Emotions like greed lures or attracts people across various sections and prompts interest in watching such contents much faster than in the case of needs based contents, which are "in the interest" of the viewers.

The latter requires more often a strategy, planning and some kind of pre and post research and involve learning, resources, and it may also involve team work. On the other hand, greed based contents could be produced with limited efforts and resources. More important, a differentiation between the two requires some concern, sensitivity to situations and discriminative skills in people. Needs based approach has the chance of having more positive elements to make a difference than the contents that lure viewers.

Quick or, even better, instant gratification by way of any of those temptations is the strategy adopted by television channels more often and in general. Greed oriented programmes get repeated more often than need based ones. This is also a consideration for the viability aspect of channels. A classical argument is - if a channel cannot lure or attract or interest people to view it, how would the need based contents or the ones which are in the interest of people get a chance to be seen and making a difference?

The Indian civilisation has a tradition of communicating "what is in the interest of people" through folk tales, epics, and all kinds of vocal culture and creative arts in an interesting and enthusing way. This model is described as the "entertainment – education" approach. Field research shows special sway towards such an approach. In fact, the leads for this approach have come from field research, not so much from TRPs. Such an entertainment – education approach requires relatively more field research and more infinity in every aspect.

An analysis of the channels' contents in general including news channels brings out that there was not much effort to offer entertainment – education based programmes. Whatever programmes were available, they were more an exception; not as part of a strategy to make a difference and impact or as a reach out effort. The TRP outlook and approach is based on maximising viewership -primarily and solely - as if the impact is bound to be there, sooner or later, with "more the merrier" logic.

With proliferation of channels and keen competition among them, one cannot imagine contents and programme schedules without planning, strategy, research and innovation. Here, it is suggested that the need based approach to contents with entertainment-education strategy is more likely to distinguish the channel in a positive context. Needs orientation comes from concerns and that should become the driving force.

Entertainment-education model for contents of channels has better chance to persuade people towards one or other behavioral changes. Greed based contents generally generate more interest among more people than the need based contents. Need based contents are in the interest of people, whereas greed based contents may not be necessarily in the interest of people.

Pre-Emptive Initiatives

As the criticism of the content priorities of channels increased a few years ago (2007–2008), there was pressure on the government to do something against channels by creating some kind of a *Laxmanrekha*. To counter these pressures, owners of big media came up with pre-emptive initiatives by launching pressure groups, starting with Indian Broadcasters Foundation (IBF), then, the News Broadcasters Association (NBA), Broadcast Editors Association (BEA) of India and a host of other groups as frontal agencies. At present, they even have a hold on the Editors' Guild of India (with senior editors of newspapers getting isolated), which was until then headed by and under the control of newspapers. Some of these bodies, in turn, formed similar groups, like the News Broadcasting Standard Authority (NBSA, 2010) and Broadcasting Content Complaints Council (BCCC) and roped in some credible names, like Justice J. S. Verma (retired as Supreme Court Chief Justice) and Justice A. P. Shah (retired as Delhi High Court Chief Justice) to head them as "self – regulatory" initiatives. These agencies put together do not represent even half of channels in the country. For example, the ones dominating or behind these organisations are the same four or five big news media. Irrespective of all that, the idea of self regulation is good and should be welcomed by all means and it should be seen that self regulation efforts succeed by making a difference both by way of preventive and promotional measures. Although one or two initiatives already taken by NBSA justify their initiative, but is that good enough to make the difference?

The way these frontal organisations are opposing any independent views should be pondered about. The gang up of "investors" is so obvious, giving the impression that all stakeholders are with them, when the conflict of interest is so obvious. "Investors" trying to dominate the priorities is nothing new in the market driven economies. But, in creative fields, like mass media, investors' interests alone should not dictate the policies, priorities, and contents of channels. Such initiatives should not be aimed at consolidating the control of a few media outfits and letting the big becoming bigger; thereby paving the path for monopoly, including cross media monopoly. This is even more so in fields like news media, which have long term implications and also to national goals. Eminent people like Justice Verma and Justice A. B. Shah, Kiran Karnik and the like personalities associated with NBSA or IBF should ensure that a balance is achieved in the media concerns. Transparency in media operations could be the trick to narrow down the polarisation between the investors and stakeholders. A big channel trying to become bigger is not bad, but becoming so without making a difference is deplorable. The outcome should be a win-win opportunity.

Endnotes

1 Reproduced in Business Standard, 5 April 2012.

2 The Hindu, 7 January, 2012. http://www.thehindu.com/opinion/op-ed/article2781128.ece

3 Noam Chomsky is an internationally acclaimed thought leader over fifty years. Of his many books two are relevant more directly "Manufacturing Consent", 1988 and Determining Democracy, 1991. His quotes are available for a clique.

4 Hardly one fifth of telecast time of 24 hour news channels is actually devoted to hard news. The rest is a mix of repeat of visuals and bulletins are accounted it would be much less than four hours news in a day's telecast. ...see "why do TV News bulletins have to be always cluttered"? CMS Media lab 2010.

5 News channels considered for more than a decade 7 to 11 pm as "prime time" with focus on those hours to showcase their coverage. Thus they positioned their telecasts for those who watch at that time see "regaining viewers trust is the real issue" in Business Standard, 6 August 2007. "prime time is getting less important" L V Krishnan, Business Standard, 11 April 2008. Broadcast industry has reached a plateau. "Uday Shankar" Exchange4Media, 16 February, 2015.

13

Correctives & Initiatives

If news channels pay special attention on critical issues of concern to people, they could not only a make a difference in the lives of people but also establish themselves beyond the kind of growth levels they have experienced so far. Presentation of those issues or themes of interest could, however, be made in an interesting way by using creative talents, elements and strategies. These issues could cut across democratic traditions, development process and good governance mechanisms. Such intention and effort of channels should be aimed at making a difference; such an interest cannot be ad hoc or a one time effort. Such efforts have to be strategic and sustained. The outcome of such efforts should be measured on a long term basis, not limited to a weekly or monthly perspective. What are the measures, initiatives, correctives, repositioning and reviewing required for the operations of the channel? A few are discussed in this chapter as examples, some reiterated again.

Not as Fundamentals, but as Desirables!

Television could be a far more creative medium than most media. It offers the scope for showcasing creative genius. The elements and features that could be manipulated to advantage effect and for making a difference could be many. But, there cannot be fixed or rigid principles or fundamentals to guide that pursuit. There could be several options, some desirable and some undesirable, in a given context. It is the ingenuity of producers to decide what could be the right mix or combination at any point. It all also depends on the context, time point, situation, audience, resources, competitive scene, etc. One also needs to be aware of and concerned about unintended effects of any such creative feature, even in the case of a news channel. All such aspects or features need to be remembered and be optimised. Appropriateness of these aspects in the context of a channel or a programme is what makes one aware, sensitive and concerned about. That is why some such aspects are summed up here. These cannot be all inclusive or in any order. These are only indicative to help distinguish a news channel – from being bad to good and from being good to great, and thereafter, sustaining such a position.

A news programme could be described as a "bulletin", not a "show". Seriousness, updating, timeliness, compilation of all that is happening around us is what and how a "bulletin" is viewed. A "show" is something that is "enacted" or "created", therefore, if a news programme is referred to as a "show' it looks as if the news is acted upon or animated and is a repeated activity. As such, news bulletin and news discussions should be positioned seriously. Only then, the contents of news bulletin could be viewed more attentively than when viewed as a "show", where the news is "presented" laced with shouting, tinkering, and some dramatics. News and serious discussions and other such current affair programmes also should not be viewed as a "show".

Experimentation

Mass media thrive on experimentations. Improvements and distinctiveness of a channel comes from learnings and constant experimentation. For gaining insights from experimentation, reliable methodologies are needed and these too need to be evolved, as there cannot be fixed methodologies for all such occasions and for all types of experimentations. Channels are bound to lose out if they are not engaged in experimentation based innovations and initiatives. Innovative ideas come from experimentation, and competitiveness flourishes from such learnings. Only then, the channels can distinguish themselves from others in a multiple channels scenario.

In the Interest or Only to Interest!

The best bet for a channel is to offer what is in the interest of people in an interesting or appealing way. The first step for a channel to be successful is to distinguish and differentiate itself from the rest in one respect or the other. Only when viewership and impact are constant concerns of a channel, it could distinguish itself. The impact potential should be the motivation for viewership. Recognising the subtle difference between these two is critical for that process. Exploring and expediting that convergence is what distinguishes a channel. This clarity and sensitivity is essential for a channel to sustain itself.

The Dilemma of Hyping Between Greed and Need

The content model of television, including news channels, hitherto, has been one of prompting and showcasing greed in people more as if that is a sure way of luring people to view a channel or a programme. This should not be a factor for slowing down in the expansion of viewership and for channels not making much of a difference for larger good. The current content model is based on chasing the viewers, who are "consumers" in the market, because that is what advertisers look for, and they are the ones, who help the viability of a channel. The more "consumers" become the concern, the more their greed becomes the rallying point. In the process, it is forgotten that people as citizens have needs that too need to be catered to. That, in fact, could be a more durable way of sustaining viewership. A differentiation between greed and aspiration should be obvious in channels' contents/programmes.

Competition Should not be to do More of the Same!

The competition should increase competence to do better and different and to do it differently and more relevantly. The positioning strategy should help distinguish one channel from the other channels present in the same market. The general tendency among news channels are that "more is merrier", that is, repeat of footage, a theme, an incident, a byte, etc. Doing that, obviously, is easier and less expensive. Repeats help in reminding an issue, but credibility and effectiveness may not come from such repeats. In the process, a criterion of "news" is how often a byte could be replayed and repeated. Sometimes, to fill the space or to stretch a short story long, footage is repeated using various techniques, like slow motion, freeze frame, etc. This tendency of news channels gives the impression that channels are doing "more of the same" and "all channels are the same". Restrain is needed in using footage again and again in the same bulletin and in many bulletins during the day. To explain a news story better, replay will, of course, help, but that should be used with restraint and sensitivity.

Reporting with Sensitivity of Impact

At one time, the news media used to be a source of solace for the disadvantaged - by voicing their interests. Today, the trend, with proliferation of news media and competitive culture, is to provoke or promote more divides and differences in people. That was what Justice M. Katju said on November 1, 2011. How else can one explain the anguish of a retired senior Judge of Supreme Court when he says so, while holding a responsible position (Chairman of Press Council of India)? A healing approach in reporting requires some understanding of the socio–economic conflicts and sensitivity about the impact of such news reports. The news channels should know the nature of impact of their programmes, so that they are not only able to avoid programmes promoting conflicts and divides, but also help prevent it. Adopting a conflict resolution approach in reporting and presentation requires special sensitivity, and skills.

Fourth Estate Concern

Fourth Estate concerns, positioning and pursuit in programmes are critical for a news media, particularly for a news channel. That concept implies larger interests and societal concerns, going beyond immediate business interests. Luring viewers without any concern about implications of contents at the viewing end is the anti-thesis of the Fourth Estate notion. It is in expectation of such a service that news media are provided special privileges, going beyond what an individual citizen is entitled to. News channels need to remind themselves of that expectation. This is not linked or on the extent of investments into the particular media.

Effects of a Programme Cannot be Undone

What has already gone on air or has been broadcasted by a news channel cannot be taken back or undone or pre-empted. Consequences of a broadcast spread widely and simultaneously; they can be addressed and diffused, if at all, only *after* the broadcast. Even that is not possible always, and the consequences of a (re)broadcast could not be pre-determined. News channels need to remember and be concerned about this potential of a news broadcast. Precautions, if possible, should be taken to neutralise adverse effects on any section of viewers. But once some such effects happen inadvertently, a news channel should not hesitate to regret and see how the situation could be corrected.

Consumerism, not at the Expense of Viewers

Globally, mass media including news media are influenced by consumerism and markets. One cannot get away from these interests altogether. What is desirable of a channel is to be sensitive towards supporting such interest in case of any section of viewers and moderate it as an outlet for citizens and the community. Wherever conflict of interest is too obvious, it should be better stated beforehand for transparency.

Transparency is the Essence of Credibility!

A news channel without transparency about its ownership or shareholding and owning responsibility for its operations cannot expect the same credibility as the one about which much information is available in public domain. And, without credibility, a news media cannot be expected to expand and distinguish itself from the rest of news sources. Some news channels in India are under the threat of being blamed for one or other "deal" or "relationship". One does not know which channel gets exposed, when and with what kind of accusation and revelations involving conflict of interest. A channel could also be accused of the kind of priorities it gives in its news coverage. "Conflict of interest" in that process is an important factor for threatening its credibility. Channels should evolve their own ways and measures, so that they are not under the threat of being exposed even by a rival competitor (as is being witnessed in Andhra Pradesh, where news channels are accusing each other for their motivations or political affiliations).

Futures Orientation, not Temporal View

Television is a highly investment and infrastructure based media. It is also a team operated media. As such, it cannot take a temporal view of its priorities. In its operations, contents and distribution, a channel has to have long term concerns and objectives. Such future orientation of a channel should be evident in its contents. A news channel cannot ignore long term interests for short term gains of a week that TRP promotes or even of a year.

Proactive Approach

News channels should consider taking up, directly or indirectly, certain functional programmes as a part of supporting public service programmes – on an ongoing basis. This could be issues like bonded labor, child labour, sanitation, disease prevention, education of poor children, enthusing handicapped, etc. Traditionally, news media undertook such "crusades". Even now, many channels have one or other programme of this nature with some periodicity. The important factor is the seriousness as evident from format, content and structure of the message. They should provoke viewers to think about or/and do something about it. All that the channel could do is to systematically pick up such themes, network with civil society groups and have follow up programmes with an intention to make a difference in one respect or other among one section or other of people.

Punditry View and Pre-Emptive Programmes!

Because of the pivotal role that the news channels could play in modulating (not necessarily manufacturing) public opinion and setting public agenda, the guest participants in news channel discussions often develop "punditry outlook" – they give the impression to know everything and what they say is the way it is - as news channels tend to limit participation (the same experts every time in news channels' studio discussions and on different topics) to a few such experts. Often, it is the convenience of the channel that determines who these participants are rather than their actual expertise or appropriateness for the topic in context. In this process, news channels reflect or present a limited perspective, knowingly and unknowingly. Channels need to be aware of such a possibility and should make special effort to widen the participation. Yet another possibility in this process, unnoticed mostly, is the pre-emptive potential of such discussions. For example, while analysing the chances of a candidate or a party in an election, the channels tend to, unintentionally, give the "impression" to the voters that going out and casting their votes is not going to make a difference to the poll outcome.

Engaging Viewers

Channels across the country have been repeatedly asking viewers to come up with their complaints, if any, regarding the contents and present the same to the Content Standards Authority. This has been a good practice and it is more than a year old now. But, to what extent the viewers have been submitting their complaints to this authority and on what aspects of contents are not known. Such feedback should have strengthened channel's relations with viewers as well as improve the quality and relevance of its programmes. Channels should broadcast such a feed back as often as possible. Channels should come up with more such ways of engaging viewers (instead of going for induced or prompted awards and the like). Channel should also rope in the civil society agencies to promote "talk back" culture and should even go out to welcome "complaints" or suggestions from viewers. In fact, there could be a periodic interactive programme based on such feedback.

Feedback Should be the Sounding Board

Given the kind of complexity and also potential of contents/programmes, no channel could avail of and explore the opportunities without the support of research and feedback from within and outside. Feedback from the receiving end and the processes involved with some periodicity is even more essential for a broadcast channel. Such feedback has to be structured, analysed and availed as per the strategies and creative plans of the channel. Based on the feedback received or/and inferred from research, the channel should build a bank of ideas, insights and reminders. This is apart from whatever syndicated data is available from outside. There should also be some built in mechanisms to envision the future course from time to time. This could be done by a team within the channel itself or by an ombudsman type arrangement. They should be engaged in constant critical introspection. Such inputs should go into differentiating the channel from their competitors in such a way that the channel distinguishes itself with its contents. Ideas for experimentation by the channel have to come from research and feedback. Television offers ample opportunities for experimentation and experiments. One or other experiment on new ideas and aspects of production, scheduling, formats, etc. should always be there within the channel.

Unintended Viewers

Television channels, particularly news channels, will have unintended reach, immediately or after some delay, by way of word of mouth or even social media. Some may not have seen a news bulletin, but the "news" or a vision of it will be in circulation. That possibility should be kept in view in content strategies, programme schedules and structure. Growth and expansion of a channel and also its viability, ultimately, depends on such a potential. Channels should also be sensitive to the fact that they are likely to be watched anytime by a mix of viewers and that includes children and women, educated and illiterate, and well informed and the least informed. There are others, who may be watching a news bulletin or a programme later, after it is telecast. With technical facilities for recording and reviewing telecasts within the television set or in the set top box becoming easily accessible, the size of such "later viewers" is bound to increase in the coming years. Consequently, channels should keep such people, too, in view, particularly, because such viewers are "active viewers", who help in expanding and consolidating the channel.

Tagline or Life Line!

Most news channels have a tagline along with their name logo and the same is promoted very often every day and also in their advertisements outside. Channels try to indicate their concern or priority through this tagline and also try to distinguish themselves from other channels. An analysis of the taglines of some news channels brings out the fact that most of them are not sure or do not have clarity about the role or position strategy as to how they would like to differentiate from other channels. Obviously, a channel should be sure of what it proposes or intends to pursue and it should be proud of that, otherwise, what is the purpose of having a tagline (or changing it). The tagline should reflect the channel's resolve to distinguish or differentiate itself from the rest of the channels in terms of intentions or and impact.

Cluttered Screens

CMS studies have indicated that one reason why the viewers' comprehension levels — even that of regular viewers — of news channels' content/programmes is not adequate and has not improved, is because of the clutter on the screen. Even while the news bulletins have serious news on, the screens are cluttered with unrelated matters. In spite of this phenomenon being pointed out, it has not been considered by the channel operators. The news channels are too greedy to dole out as much as possible simultaneously. It gives an impression as if they want to send out all information for the weekly rating. The "breaking news" and "news flash" and the like need to be selective, and then the way that is repeated. Otherwise, they could erode the very credibility of such news channels. This practice deserves a re-look with different priorities and methodology.

The competition in providing news is based on the presumption that "more is merrier". Because of that notion, while presenting news, there is a tendency to crowd and overload the screen with too many things to see, read and hear – all simultaneously. This is affects the comprehension levels at the viewing end. This could be one reason why news bulletin contents are not adding to the viewers' knowledge. They tend to hype the perceptions more. The more the screen is "over loaded", the more the contents get "washed out". Therefore, a screen should be used sparingly for maximising focus.

Taking Advantage of Technologies

Television channels enjoy certain special advantages (and some disadvantages too) of technological maneuverability. Technologies enable a news channel to use certain "special effects" with unique potential to impact or influence larger public as well as specific sections of people. Live coverage from the field as well as from studio, simultaneously, offer opportunities for channels to reach out with special effects. For example, showing live footage of rallies from different cities against corruption, simultaneously, or even in sequence, gives special advantage. Taking advantage of this technique, some news channels interviewed Anna Hazare alone in his village in Maharashtra, showing, simultaneously, in the background the footage of his fast at Ramlila Grounds in New Delhi several weeks earlier with massive crowds, giving the "impression" that Anna was "doing it again" (and, in fact, one channel had that as the caption on the screen, October 3, 2011) without indicating anywhere that the visual being shown was old and obtained from a "file" or "library". One sees such (misleading) examples too often in the news channels.

Technology offers new opportunities to television channels, and helps them enhance their skills, presentation and also interest viewers. A number of techniques, like morphing, mixing, freezing, replay, simulating, slow motion, shadow, circle, split screen, etc. add to technological maneuverability. Sometimes, it is used even more in the news channels than fiction cinema. That is good. But, when it comes to television news presentation, perhaps, one needs to be more sensitive and discriminative in using such techniques as a part of news bulletin. The more such techniques are used and the more often for presenting news, the less credibility they may end up with, as it becomes difficult to know what is real (news) and what is not (tinkered technologically or manipulated). Not all news bulletin viewers have the skill needed to comprehend such news presentations. However, in special instance like rail/air accidents, calamities, etc., such techniques will add depth, understanding, etc. of the news and should be welcomed. In news "shows" such techniques could be used liberally, but not so much in news "bulletins".

Do not Ignore the Basics of Human Values

Channels should, as a strategy, stand up for the cherished universal human values of society. Unless a channel makes special effort, it cannot be unique in reflecting those human emotions or behaviors and values in a positive way. For example, what kinds of impression will the news channels' crime based features with criminal looking anchors, give and, what are they promoting? Is that deliberate? Is that attracting more viewers?

In the Name of "Reality"

Over the last couple of years, there has been proliferation of "reality shows" on television channels across the country. A quick reaction to the content analysis of these programmes would be that these channels have perhaps emptied or exhausted their creative genius and are in "wild goose chase" for filling time. The other impression is that they are looking for programmes that give training opportunities on handling camera and the like. And, the worse problem is that channels are not able to either recognise the real issues or concerns of majority of people in the field or those in wilderness, who need help.

The other impression from the news channels' "reality shows" is that even now, they could not get rid of the myth that "real issues do not attract viewership" or people do not like to see the grassroots' hard realities, as they watch television to "enjoy" or entertain themselves.

The real "reality" programmes (not "shows") that some news channels have taken up also provide good examples. The best example that I am familiar with for the last couple of years is "*Naveena*" (TV-9), which is mostly based on women's issues, examples of women's real problems, achievements, role models, etc. This is also a good example for more than one reason. It is an important example of how to make programmes "in the interest" of people "interestingly" and with all seriousness. The other aspect is the way the theme is chosen and the way a solution approach is retained. This programme, Naveena (weekly), has been going on for five years now. This is also an example of how to promote viewership for the programme. "Fake sting" operations based reality shows have even eroded the credibility of some channels' programmes.

In the wake of "reality" programmes, there are examples of 'fake news", too, which are based on "fake events", "fake stings" and "fake surveys". The surveys, sometimes, could be done without the channel knowing about the intricacies involved or their reliability aspect. But, the responsibility of verification is that of the channel; it is their credibility. One fake survey or one "fake sting" operation in a year or two is bad enough to damage the channel's credibility.

There is also "fake analysis" based ratings advertised by channels for their own viewership or for comparison themselves with other channels. Given the nature of proliferation of all kinds of channels and the competition between them, there could be "fake ratings" too. News channels should be cautions. Already, some viewers consider TRPs as "fake" – not based on reality or/and deliberately misleading or manipulated with an intention to mislead people or to serve the interests of someone else in a "hidden" way.

However, not all channels' reality shows can be viewed in the same way. Some or a few of them are good and innovative for incorporating a punchy way of communicating a message or activating citizens, for example, the one on urinating on road side or spitting at public places.

Disruptive to EE model (Entertainment – Education)

The 'Color' channel (Viacom) came into being with a bang using "disruptive approach" to contents. Since then, it has become a role model for many regional language channels; not merely for entertainment channels, but for news channels as well. It is now described as an "entertainment – education" channel. This model has been adopted by some regional language channels. Many channels, which were groping in search of an alternative approach, picked up the new model of taking up burning social issues (child marriage, son preference, dowry, etc.) using entertainment framework or format. Two other success factors required for this model are high production quality and reliable ongoing research back up.

Entertainment – Education Model

Entertainment – education is an old and traditional concept ingrained in Indian culture. In fact, that is how some of our epics and folk tales remain popular to date. Some channels, even recently, have demonstrated how well they could convey a public message effectively and also popularly through an "entertainment" format or context. This could be done even by way of having an entertainer or an actor as an anchor, and by making a difference in the lives of, at least, some of the viewers and even non-viewers. One Telugu news channel took up one such programme (*Naveena*) and the popularity that it achieved through it led to most of the other news channels taking up similar programmes. There are many such examples in other languages too. But, that is once a week (for 30 minutes) programme. Still, the impact that such programmes make has never been documented and showcased.

Emerging or Unfolding News

News channels tend to take the risk to be the first or ahead of other channels, and even the first to "break" –an emerging or evolving or unfolding story. One wrong report in such bulletins is remembered far more than ten others when the channel was right. This includes election "forecasts", number of deaths in calamities, etc. Therefore, care and caution is more important for credibility. Attributing such stories to some functionary in the related field is better than not giving a source for unfolding such stories. Active channels do keep a list of "resource people' for consultation on a range of issues on a short notice or while reporting the unfolding of happenings.

Linkage with Interpersonal Networks

So many research studies done over the decades and across the continents have brought out that when mass media work in tandem with interpersonal networks, the effect would be far more. Now social media, which are part of the communication networks, add and expedite the effect and diffusion process of what appears on a channel or in a news bulletin. The success of Anna Hazare's crusade recently (2011) is a good example showing the potential of news channels. Some news channels have set good example of such viewers' end linkage on an ongoing basis. This is one effective way for a channel to make a difference and distinguish itself.

Multiplier Effect

The best bet for a programme is - what kind of "multiplier-effect" it would have? What would be talked about the programme after it has been viewed positively or negatively (could be either way), and by how many people? This could also be described as the diffusion effect of a broadcast. The process (speed, steps involved, positive or negative, etc.) is more pertinent for multiplier effect. There are so many ways of achieving and ensuring post-multiplier-effect. These have to be locale and context specific. Not all contents of a channel can be expected to have such a potential. Selectivity and focused approach based on qualitative research helps to identify multiplier factors. The concern or look out for such potential of a programme has to be all the time.

Set New Conventions

There is so much scope for channels, particularly, news channels to set new conventions in presenting news programmes and bulletins more often, instead of doing it in the same way as others. It should be done in such a way that programmes help in enhancing the credibility of the channel and, also in distinguishing the channel from the rest. There is so much scope to come up with new conventions while presenting "surveys". For example, if participants in discussion programmes on contentious issues declare their "conflict of interest" at the beginning of the discussion – it will go a long way.

Children Specific Approach

News channels should increase the extent of coverage of children specific contents by design in the news bulletins and otherwise. For example, there are so many legislations involving children of various age groups. In this context, it's worth exploring what is the extent of their implementation and effect? If news channels could take up basic issues of the country, nutrition level of new born and the like, as they did by taking up cooking, yoga, fitness and Ayurveda programmes, they could accomplish a lot more.

In the ultimate analysis what should distinguish a news channel are its concerns, commitment, strategies, and research based innovations and experiments. It is better that the viability of the channel emerges out of such pursuits of its own, not necessarily from syndicated TRP based feedback and yardsticks.

Programme Promotion

It's agreed that even news channels need to promote their contents within the channel and even outside in print media, as done by some channels frequently. Promotion should be done on a weekly basis by reminding the viewers about the timings and even the themes of channels' 'feature' programmes. Channels should also promote interactivity by having a weekly programme, such as "answers to questions or interacting with viewers or talking to viewers" – where the channel's news chief, he or she, interacts with the viewers. This programme could even have some viewers discussing the pros and cons of the contents.

Is it a Bulletin or a "Show"?

Some months ago, I had to telephone a "TV personality" after watching the way he presented a news bulletin, to ask whether he had to "act while presenting" the news. I did that as he and his other colleagues too keep saying "show" while presenting news bulletins, at the beginning, before break and at the end of the bulletin.

Most news channels, irrespective of language and duration, describe their news "bulletins" as news "shows". For example, CNN-IBN describes its news programmes as the "Best News Show". Its "News readers" continue to describe their programmes, like the "show continues". "Show" is something generally associated with "entertainment" programmes and implies repetition of the same. "Bulletin" is a listing (of news) with time or periodicity and implies "informing" and some updating of information. Seriousness, updating and compilation are involved in a bulletin. The tendency among those news channel managers is to "position" themselves more as in an entertainment context than in an informing context. It is perhaps more appropriate to say that in radio, news is 'read"; in TV news is "presented"; and when it is more about switching from one item or story to another in a news bulletin of a TV channel, it could be "anchoring".

In neither case news could be described as "news show"; instead, one could say that it's a "bulletin'. It is important to recognise the difference, however subtle it may be, between these descriptions. While "read" is more neutral, "presented" takes an active view and "bulletin" reflects relatively a more independent view. Even veterans in news reporting and editing (in newspapers) apparently get confused once they are in television. Taking cue from English news channels, many regional news channels too describe their news bulletins as "news shows".

They could, on the other hand, call The Great Tamasha (of NDTV) as a "show" because it is news based acted/tinkered show. News should not be viewed (or promoted) as part of "show business" or "entertainment shows". The Great Indian Tamasha (of NDTV) and the "Week That Was Not" of Cyrus Broacha a (CNN-IBN) too are "news shows". Many regional news channels have taken to such news shows. Such humor based news "shows" have added to the critical way of analysing the news of the week.

Discussion Programmes

An analysis of discussion programmes on news channels on contentious issues or controversial topics of the week does not indicate making a difference at viewers' end or to the size of viewership. This is perhaps because the duration of such discussions (number of participants, format and how the topic and various aspects involved are covered) are not helping much in enthusing or activating people. May be such practices are not conducive to viewer enlightenment.

Firstly, these programmes are most often mounted, without presenting specific contextual analysis, on the background of the topic. Some years ago, for example, ETV-2's *Pratidwani* discussion programme used to start with a quantitative summing up of the problem under discussion before opening up the discussion to the participants. Also, at the end, the programme concludes with a "the way forward" like statement by the moderator. After the increase in the number of channels and competition that is no longer the case.

Most of these programmes are of 30 minutes duration with one or two commercial breaks and one minute scheduled for opening and closing montage, thereby leaving 27 or 28 minutes for actual discussion. Some Telugu news channels, as a way to distinguish them, have off and on extended the discussion beyond 30 minutes as a way of showing the seriousness of the discussion. In fact, one new channel, HMTV, went out of studio for open discussions – some of them went for two to four hours – giving an opportunity for as many local citizens to speak up. Some, very rarely, do such serious discussions without a commercial break.

The format of most of these discussions is studio based; participants mostly sit face to face or side by side with a moderator or anchor positioned a bit apart. NDTV started a format where the anchor stands in front of a podium when it is an audience included programme. Sometimes, some participants from among the audience get a chance to chip in. There are three to six participants in these discussions apart from an anchor or moderator. Assuming that the discussion goes meticulously, there would not be more than two or three rounds of talk with each one getting one or two minutes in each round. It means that any participant, or even all of them put together, will not be able to do justice to the topic even when they seriously try to stick to the core of the issue, which happens not more than half of the time. On other instances, one or other participant goes beyond the core issue and goes into general or related or personalised discussions at length irrespective of how strict the anchor is. This happened to me many times. At the end, the viewers, who had viewed the programme, could only tell about who participated or who spoke, not about what the participants had actually argued or said. They, nevertheless, are likely to watch again next day or next week because that has become a way to keep engaged next day in gossip or social networks.

Discussion or Debate!

A debate is more specific with participants taking a "for or against" stand on a poser and each gets a chance by turn. A discussion programme also debates a topic, but the difference is that the discussion is based on an open stand. But, in the case of a debate, viewers can make out that someone is for or against a question being elaborated; it's not so in a discussion programme. The Times Now news channel had taken to such debates (in 2012) on contentious issues without realising the limitations of 30 minutes discussion programmes.

News channels have two streams as flagships – news bulletins and discussions on current affairs. The personality or positioning of the channel has to be more on account of these flagship contents. All news channels have one or other current affairs programme either as a discussion or debate or as an interview or review based.

If there are too many topics in too short time for discussion – what can be expected? It is time that the news channels re-look and reposition these issue specific discussion programmes so that they could make a difference and enrich the viewers, thereby changing the positioning of the channel.

Moderator or Anchor?

An "Anchor" moderates a discussion programme on a channel by introducing the participants and by posing the questions and asking a particular participant to speak or intervene, keeping the focus on the topic. An anchor could be a functionary of the channel. In most cases, these anchors started as "news readers" or continue to do so in most channels. A moderator could also be an outsider familiar with the topic in context. He or she is one among the other participants and steers the discussion starting with his or her own position or analysis.

A panel discussion with an outside expert as moderator or anchor sometimes determines the seriousness of that particular discussion. Election time discussions in channels will have both an anchor (of the channel) and a moderator (an outside specialist). But the duration of such programmes is more than 30 minutes.

An anchor is not expected to show off his/her knowledge and take as much time as the other panel members could. He or she is supposed to bring out relevant aspects of the topic from each of the guest. A moderator, on the other hand, if he or she is an expert of standing could be expected to share his/her perspective for a balanced and comprehensive coverage.

While contents of news bulletins could be "more or less the same" between news channels, the formats of the current affairs programmes could be different from one channel to another with respect to their subject content, format and participation. In fact, these current affairs programmes, eventually, differentiate one news channel from another and give it a distinct identity and positioning among viewers.

As a strategy, the discussion programmes of some channels generate heat in discussions and even allow contentious arguments and accusations, and the participants (some guests) are invited more for such reputation than for their wisdom or a unique point of view on the topic in context.

The suggestions referred are only as indicative. And not inclusive! Channels themselves could come up with more of specific and indigenous interventions and correctives provided they look into with earnestness and determination.

Index

U

V

W

■■■